JOHN HUNT

HOPSCOTCHING TO HELL
SLEEPWALKING TO HEAVEN

AND 101 OTHER BIBLICAL INSIGHTS FOR THE MODERN WORLD

HOPSCOTCHING
TO HELL
SLEEPWALKING
TO HEAVEN

AND 101 OTHER BIBLICAL INSIGHTS
FOR THE MODERN WORLD

JOHN HUNT

Unless otherwise indicated, Scripture references are from the updated *New American Standard Bible,* copyright © 1960, 1962, 1963, 1968, 1971, 1973, 1975, 1977, 1995 by The Lockman Foundation, A Corporation Not for Profit, La Habra, CA.

Scripture quotations marked NIV are from *The Holy Bible: New International Version,* copyright © 1973, 1978, 1984 by International Bible Society.

Scripture quotations marked Amp are from *The Amplified Bible,* Expanded Edition, copyright © 1987 by The Zondervan Corporation and The Lockman Foundation.

Scripture quotations marked KJV are from the King James Version.

Printed in the United States of America

10 9 8 7 6 5 4 3

eBook Designed by Acepub

To my countless brothers and sisters from numerous denominations who have attended my Bible study classes over these many years.
And to Kevin McGuire, who has selflessly supported me in many ways and through many Christian outreaches. We have been through thousands of spiritual battles together, and his loyalty and selflessness know no bounds. Thank you, Kevin!

Acknowledgments

There are many people I would like to give a special acknowledgement to for their involvement in this book's publication.

I would like to thank my sister-in-law, Dalene Chandler, for typing most of this manuscript in her free time.

Lori Cripe and her daughter-in-law, Rachel Cripe, along with Robert DiPalma were responsible for the book's final edit—I extend my gratitude for their dedication and for the wonderful job they did.

To my son, Caleb, my daughter, Rachel, and my daughter-in-law, Christina, I am very thankful for their assistance in typing and in publishing this book as well (especially to Caleb for all of his efforts in making this book a reality).

Additionally, I am truly grateful to Jessica Lyons for her beautiful cover design and for going well above and beyond in her work.

I would also like to thank my spiritual brothers, Ben Gonzales for all of his encouragement, and Jim Carnine, for proofreading many of my chapters.

And most importantly, I'd like to say a special thank you to my loving wife Gail for all of her help and encouragement on this book (including coordinating with others to publish it without my knowledge at first); and additionally, for all of her support in my teaching and writing over the years, and for opening up our home for weekly Bible studies throughout our entire marriage.

Their assistance has been invaluable; and if there is one Scripture I would like to quote to them for their generous work, it is Hebrews 6:10:

> For God is not unjust so as to forget your work and the love which you have shown toward His name, in having ministered and in still ministering to the saints.

A Note on Quotations

All Scripture quotations are from the New American Standard Bible unless otherwise indicated. The following abbreviations are used for other versions:

      KJV   The King James Version

      Amp   The Amplified Bible

      NIV   The New International Version

All italics within quotations were added by the author.

CONTENTS

Preface

When I began writing these thoughts, I had absolutely no intention of publishing a book. I had previously written several other manuscripts—none of which were ever published, receiving one rejection letter after another from different publishers around the country. Ultimately, after my last book was rejected multiple times, I came to the conclusion that God was not calling me to write, and I just needed to focus on my real passion—teaching the Bible.

In a sense, however, this book was born out of a brutal beating I underwent in my spirit; and although I had no intention of sharing this experience, someone very close to me insisted I do so. Therefore, I will do my best to explain this battle, but I must do so in purely spiritual terms because this experience did not happen to me physically.

It transpired one day four years ago when I was simply running the race God has set before us, as described in Hebrews 12. Persevering in this spiritual marathon, I was merely putting one foot in front of the other and trying to keep my focus on Jesus Christ, the same way I have been doing for nearly 40 years. Suddenly, it felt like I was totally hit from a blind side—as if Satan had come out of nowhere and began viciously attacking me, thrusting me to the ground. In my spirit I felt like he had pinned me down with his enormous weight. I frantically tried to reach for my sword—my Bible—but I felt as if he had kicked it out of my reach. He was threatening to get into my head and totally destroy me, shrieking that he was going to twist my mind and drive me to do such horrible things that would completely demolish my Christian testimony and totally ruin my life. I could clearly envision his diabolical tongue trying to penetrate my forehead and poison my brain with all of his infernal malice and demands.

It seemed like all I could do was desperately pray and use my prayers as a two-edged dagger to repeatedly thrust into his side. He finally released me from his powerful grip days later; and as he stood over me, he wiped the red-hot pus from his punctured side and thrust it at my head. I instinctively protected my face with my battered shield of faith, and then he left me groaning in pain. Truthfully, in my spirit I felt totally overwhelmed and beaten into the ground.

Picking up my sword, I slowly and painfully got back up on my feet. I began hobbling back into this race God has set before me, and I struggled to get back my stride.

I realize all of this sounds extremely melodramatic and ridiculously overdramatized; however, the experience was so real and powerful to me that my hands trembled and the hair on the back of my neck felt like it was standing up. I felt so distressed and uneasy that a horribly unnerving feeling lingered with me for over two weeks.

Right after this incident I went to Tennessee to visit my brother, Tom, before heading for New York to visit some of the rest of my family. While in Tennessee I woke up early one morning and went downstairs in my brother's house to brew a cup of coffee. I was the only one awake, and I began reading a devotional by Billy Graham. After about five minutes, I set aside the book and picked up a tablet of paper and a pen and began to write.

I don't know what compelled me to begin writing, but the words started to flow out of me like water onto the paper. Word after word, sentence after sentence, and page after page began to pour from my spirit. Before I realized it, I was avidly writing again.

I kept thinking to myself, *What am I doing on this road? I've been down it several times before, and each time it's just led to a dead end with an iron door, welded and bolted shut, overgrown with thistles and thorns.* So I asked myself, *How did I get here? Did I not notice a fork in the path somewhere?* I also realized I hadn't sought the Lord in prayer about this. I had sworn off writing years ago because I thought God made it clear to me through my failures that I am not a writer. *So, what am I doing on this road?*

Yet deep within my spirit I sensed God's voice whispering, *"Run! Run, John; now is your time—RUN!"* As my thoughts continued to pour onto the yellow tablet before me, I kept wondering if God was truly talking to me, or if all of this was simply my imagination. I came to the conclusion that I really didn't know whether or not God was telling me to write again, but I decided I could not afford to take the chance of not heeding the prompting of His Spirit. I think it would be far better to stand before Him and apologize for misunderstanding Him than need to apologize for ignoring Him. Therefore, I continued to pour my thoughts onto the blank pages in front of me.

Jesus said, "Behold, I have put before you an open door which no one can shut because you have a little power, and have kept My word, and have not denied My name" (Revelation 3:8). Therefore, if this door is barred and shut like the previous doors, I must conclude that I misheard Him and that this effort has merely been a waste of His time and mine. But the spiritual battle I experienced just before writing this book may be an indication that this time may be different.

Over 30 years ago I submitted my first book for publication. That same day I felt a powerful urging of the Holy Spirit to open my Bible and read the very first passage of Scripture that caught my attention. I do not believe this is the proper method for reading God's Word (and I do not recall doing this before or since); however, when I randomly flipped open my Bible, the first verse that caught my eye was Isaiah 41:20:

> That they may see and recognize, and consider and gain insight as well, that the hand of the Lord has done this, and the Holy One of Israel has created it.

At the time, I felt strongly that God was speaking to me through this verse, regarding the manuscript I had just sent off that morning. That was many years and a number of failures ago. Nevertheless, I have never forgotten God's clear voice in that verse of Scripture. God pledges that if people would seriously listen to His words in Scripture, they will gain *insight*, wisdom and understanding (see Proverbs 1:1-7).

Insight is the ability to see and to understand clearly the inner nature of things and to see below the surface of superficial thinking and shallow reasoning. Biblical insights are almost like gazing into deep pools of water and discovering amazing life forms in a whole new world.

This is a book of scriptural insights, intended to help others see spiritual things in a much clearer way. It is prayerfully meant to encourage others to dig, search, and explore for themselves the wonders of an entirely different dimension. It is the spiritual dimension of the endless world of insights the Bible contains for all of humanity—not just for a chosen few.

How often do we hear, "The Bible is full of contradictions," or "The moral standards set forth in the Word of God cease to be relevant and realistic in our enlightened and permissive society"? The mantras of disbelief are endless, and the objections to seriously studying and believing the Bible are numerous. Without question, people both inside and outside the church casually or antagonistically dismiss the pages of the Holy Scriptures without ever giving them honest study or serious reflection.

However, here is my challenge to the believer and the nonbeliever alike: Read any portion of the Bible with an objective approach, and see how many insights to life and applications to living you can discover. I can assure any earnest seeker of truth that the insights in the Bible are without number because God's Word is without measure. It is infinite because God is infinite, and He has made His Word equal with Himself (see John 1). As one great theologian put it, "Ignorance of the Scriptures is ignorance of Christ." And if I might add to this statement, to neglect the Word of God is to be poverty-stricken when it comes to meaningful and lasting insights to life and discernment for living.

The Training of Maggots and Disciplining of Worms

"Semper Fi!" This Latin phrase is well known throughout the world by Marines and ex-Marines alike. It simply means "always faithful." It denotes a bond and a fellowship between brothers (and sisters) who have gone through a common experience in both their training and their ordeals. Their harsh discipline and tough level of instruction have powerfully taught them to always remain faithful to their country, to each other, and to their corps.

I personally went through the Marine Corps during the height of the Vietnam War in the late 1960s. Our training was very intense and, at times, even brutal. The Marine Corps had a unique way of taking young men from all over the country, from all walks of life, and breaking them down physically, mentally, and emotionally before they would build them up into the "lean, mean, fighting machines" they were seeking.

Two of the often-used phrases by drill instructors when yelling at new recruits were "You maggot!" and "You worm!" Of course, they used many other terms of endearment that won't be repeated here for the sake of decency and discreetness; however, you get the picture. The voice, the language, and the countenance of the drill instructor (D.I.) were meant to strike fear into the hearts of cocksure adolescents and fashion them into disciplined men.

It wasn't until I returned home from Vietnam that I became a Christian, and it was then that I began to read the Bible and discovered a man who I thought for sure must have been the very first Marine Corps D.I. His name was Bildad, and he was one of Job's three friends who began to attack Job's integrity and truthfulness when he said,

> How then can a man be just with God? Or how can he be clean who is born of woman? If even the moon has no brightness and the stars are not pure in His sight, how much less man, that maggot, and the son of man, that worm! (Job 25:4-6)

Well, Bildad was certainly in Job's face as he tried to break him down with his harsh language, implying Job was nothing more than a maggot or a worm. But in the end, it was Job who proved to be the stronger and better man in the eyes of God.

Job's painful experiences were God's difficult training ground and the Lord's challenging boot camp. God is still in the business today of looking for "a few good men" who can endure His painful drills and can undergo His trying instruction.

However, His school of discipline can often be exhausting and sometimes brutal. He knows how to break His new recruits and purge them from their arrogance and self-indulgent urges. He knows how to push a man and to press a woman until they surrender completely to His ways and until they are marching to the drumbeat of His perfect will. As the author of Hebrews put it,

> You have not yet resisted to the point of shedding blood in your striving against sin; and you have forgotten the exhortation which is addressed to you as sons, "My son, do not regard lightly the discipline of the Lord, nor faint when you are reproved by Him; for those whom the Lord loves He disciplines, and He scourges every son whom He receives." It is for discipline that you endure; God deals with you as with sons; for what son is there whom His father does not discipline? But if you are without discipline, of which all have become partakers, then you are illegitimate children and not sons.
>
> Furthermore, we had earthly fathers to discipline us, and we respected them; shall we not much rather be subject to the Father of spirits, and live? For they disciplined us for a short time as seemed best to them, but He disciplines us for our good, so that we may share His holiness. All discipline for the moment seems not to be joyful, but sorrowful; yet to those who have been trained by it, afterwards it yields the peaceful fruit of righteousness. Therefore, strengthen the hands that are weak and the knees that are feeble, and make straight paths for your feet, so that the limb which is lame may not be put out of joint, but rather be healed. (Hebrews

12:4-13)

Even Jesus Christ Himself had to undergo the humiliation of discipline and feeling like a worm, for David prophesied about Him when he wrote, "I am a worm and not a man, a reproach of men and despised by the people" (Psalm 22:6). But he (being a type of Christ) was actually writing a prophetic, Messianic verse to be fulfilled in Jesus. In the training of Israel, God said,

> Do not fear, you worm Jacob, you men of Israel; I will help you. ... Your Redeemer is the Holy One of Israel. Behold I have made you a new, sharp threshing sledge with double edges; you will thresh the mountains and pulverize them, and you will make the hills like chaff. You will winnow them, and the wind will carry them away, and the storm will scatter them; but you will rejoice in the Lord, you will glory in the Holy One of Israel. (Isaiah 41:14-16)

God's discipline prepares us for war, and once we are equipped with His spiritual armor, we are sure to gain the victory in whatever battles He sends our way, if only we remain "always faithful" (see Ephesians 6:10-17).

So the next time God's training school has made you feel like you have been reduced to little more than a maggot and have been diminished to little more than a worm, remember—it is because He is still in the business of looking for "a few good men" and women.

Which Came First, the Chicken or the Egg?

"Which came first, the chicken or the egg?" This is one of those questions that has baffled some people and has disinterested most everybody else. Who really cares which came first? Simple deductive reasoning might suggest the chicken came first and that the egg developed around it in the same way a placenta forms around a fertilized human embryo. Regardless, here is a question truly worth considering: "What came first, the light or the light bearers?" This is an extremely important question because whatever conclusion we make will suggest either that God is a liar or that science is greatly mistaken.

The theory of evolution hypothesizes our universe is some 13 billion or more years old. This suggested age of our cosmos has been deduced from simple mathematics: Light travels at 186,000 miles per second; in one year that light will travel about 6 trillion miles (a lightyear). Well, the farthest known stars in the heavens are some 13 billion light-years from earth. Hence our universe is at least 13 billion years old because that is how long it would take for the light at the edge of our known universe to reach us; i.e., for us to visualize those outermost stars.

Sounds logical enough, doesn't it? Looks like convincing science, right? Who can argue with such arithmetic? Well, God refutes man's "logical" conclusion regarding the age of the earth. Genesis 1:3-5 says,

> Then God said, "Let there be light," and there was light. God saw that the light was good; and God separated the light from the darkness. God called the light day, and the darkness He called night. And there was evening and there was morning, one day.

Notice God said He created light on the first day of creation and then separated the light from the darkness, calling light day and darkness, night. Then, three days later,

God made the two great lights, the greater light to govern the day, and the lesser light to govern the night; He made the stars also. God placed them in the expanse of the heavens to give light on the earth, and to govern the day and the night, and to separate the light from the darkness; and God saw that it was good. There was evening and there was morning, a fourth day. (Genesis 1:16-19)

Did you catch that? It wasn't until the fourth day that God created the sun, the moon, and the stars. He took the already-divided light beams, so to speak, which He created on the first day, and essentially attached them to the newly created light bearers (the sun, moon, and stars).

Of course this defies all human logic, because a natural man does not accept the things of the Spirit of God, for they are foolishness to him; and he cannot understand them because they are spiritually appraised. But he who is spiritual appraises all things, yet he himself is appraised by no one. For who has known the mind of the Lord, that he will instruct Him? (1 Corinthians 2:14-16)

If people say they believe God created the universe, then why would they use human reasoning to say God could not have created it in the way He said He did? Even if one considers the big bang theory, who's to say God speaking matter into existence wouldn't constitute such an explosion? Contrary to the theory, however, it wouldn't take several billion years.

The truth of the matter is God does not need 13 billion years to give us the light of the stars because He is not limited by time or space. He was the One who created the space-time continuum and, therefore, is outside the confines of time and the boundaries of space. In short, time and space are His creation, not His limitations.

Unfortunately, anyone today who espouses a young earth (say, 6,000 years) and the literal interpretation of Genesis tends to be ridiculed without mercy. They are vilified by academia and scorned by the mainstream media and, sad to say, even by some churches. However, the Bible says,

Let God be found true, though every man be found a liar, as

it is written, "that You may be justified in Your words, and prevail when You are judged." (Romans 3:4)

Even those who claim to believe in the God of the Bible often feel compelled to disagree with or explain away the scriptural account of creation recorded in the book of Genesis, for fear of looking foolish in the eyes of "science." But in the end (when they stand before this God of Creation), they will see clearly that He is a God without limitations and says exactly what He means and means exactly what He says.

Whether the chicken came first or the egg, it really doesn't matter, but whether the light came first or the light bearers, matters very much. Personally, I am betting everything that the light came first because God said it did. Where have you placed your bet?

God Does Not Have Alzheimer's

To say God is long-suffering and merciful is truly an understatement. He provides rain for both the righteous and the unrighteous, and He patiently endures the endless blasphemies and ongoing ungratefulness of mankind (see Matthew 5:45). This in no way suggests He is indifferent to the sins of man, nor that He forgets man's wicked deeds. On the contrary, God does not have Alzheimer's, nor is He absentminded.

When the Lord brought the sons of Israel up out of the land of Egypt and into the land of Canaan, He told them in the 25th chapter of Leviticus that every seven years they were to observe what God called the sabbatical year. The Lord instructed that every seventh year they were not to sow, reap, or harvest, but they were to let the ground rest, trusting Him to provide for them until the harvest season of the eighth year. Well, for the next 490 years while the Hebrew people were in the Promised Land, they simply ignored God's statute and refused to let their farmland rest.

Eventually, their disobedience and rebellion against God reached the point of no return, wherefore, the Lord declared He was going to use the Babylonians to destroy them and carry them off into captivity. God determined they would be in exile for 70 years because in the 490 years they were in the Promised Land, they should have observed 70 sabbatical years (see Leviticus 25; 2 Chronicles 36:21; Jeremiah 25). Now because of their noncompliance, God Himself was going to let the land rest accordingly.

In other words, for centuries it seemed that God did not care and was indifferent to their disobedience in regards to keeping the sabbatical year. His patience, mercy, and long-suffering were misinterpreted by the people to mean that God would not judge them for their rebellious acts. On the contrary, He remembered each and every sabbatical year they refused to obey His command.

Similarly, God could hold every single wrongdoing against us, but He chose instead to place all our sins onto His Son, the perfect sacrifice. We all deserve to be eternally separated from a holy God, and if God were fair, He'd send us all to hell. In His infinite mercy, however, He provides a way (the Way) to be able to spend eternity with Him. Consider the words of the Lord through

His prophet Ezekiel:

> "Do I have any pleasure in the death of the wicked," declares the Lord God, "rather than that he should turn from his ways and live? [...] For I have no pleasure in the death of anyone who dies," declares the Lord God. "Therefore, repent and live." (Ezekiel 18:23, 32)

God desires to forgive and forget, but if men do not repent of their sins, then He will never forget. He further proclaimed to Ezekiel,

> When I say to the righteous he will surely live, and he so trusts in his righteousness that he commits iniquity, none of his righteous deeds will be remembered; but in that same iniquity of his which he has committed he will die. But when I say to the wicked, "You will surely die," and he turns from his sin and practices justice and righteousness, if a wicked man restores a pledge, pays back what he has taken by robbery, walks by the statutes which ensure life without committing iniquity, he shall surely live; he shall not die. None of his sins that he has committed will be remembered against him. He has practiced justice and righteousness; He shall surely live. (Ezekiel 33:13-16)

The only way God is going to forget our sins is if we turn from them and begin to live righteously before Him. None of our past sins will be brought up on judgment day if we only repent of them. God longs to forget; in fact, He delights in forgetting, but He does not have Alzheimer's. He will severely judge us as nations and as individuals if we do not heed His merciful calls to remember Him and to obey Him.

Bad to the Bone

Throughout the last century, a number of prominent authors and intellectuals have insisted that man is "basically good," and the reason why so many people behave badly is simply because they have been denied a certain standard of living or they lack a specific level of education. These writers and social engineers believe man's environment is primarily what shapes his character, and therefore if his circumstances could be changed for the better, his behavior would naturally improve with his surrounding conditions. It is not just the humanists and progressive thinkers who feel this way; it is actually the overwhelming majority of mankind that believes this to be true as well.

You don't believe me? Well, here is my challenge to you: go down to any shopping mall, sports arena, or college campus and ask each person you meet this one question, "Do you think you are basically a good person?" This question can even be asked in almost every jail and prison in the country, and the responses are likely to be the same. The truth is, we would be very hard pressed to find anyone with the good grace and intellectual honesty to say, "No, I am not a basically good person. Actually, I am a monster of iniquity that is bad to the bone, and the only difference between me and others is simply a matter of degrees in regards to wickedness."

Such a response is likely to be seriously challenged, if not hotly disputed. Anyone who would say this about himself (or herself) is very likely going to be viewed as someone who has some serious self-image issues. However, what this person believes about himself and others actually agrees with what God has said concerning the basic character of all men. For example, it is the God of the universe who declared,

> Both Jews and Greeks are all under sin; as it is written: "There is none righteous, not even one; there is none who understands, there is none who seeks for God; all have turned aside, together they have become useless; there is none who does good, there is not even one." "Their throat is an open grave, with their tongues they keep deceiving."

"The poison of asps is under their lips"; "whose mouth is full of cursing and bitterness"; "their feet are swift to shed blood, destruction and misery are in their paths, and the path of peace they have not known." "There is no fear of God before their eyes." (Romans 3:9-18)

This is quite an indictment against the entire human race, and as if this were not insulting enough, God also said through His prophet Isaiah, "All our righteousness … is like filthy rags" in His sight (Isaiah 64:6, Amp). Consequently, to assume all men are basically good and can improve with prosperity and learning is truly naïve and downright foolish. In fact, some of the biggest rip-off artists, infamous scoundrels, notorious criminals, and mass murderers in human history have been incredibly wealthy and educated with tremendous resources at their fingertips and were not suffering with issues of low self-esteem.

From peasants to popes, the wretchedness of man can be seen. The truth is, even the most staunch believer in man's "basic goodness" would panic if he/she accidentally misplaced his/her wallet or credit cards. Why? Because deep down inside, they know men are not basically good and that given half an opportunity, many people would steal them blind (regardless of their social status).

Nevertheless, some very positive news in the midst of man's terribly fallen condition is that the Bible makes a definite distinction between "righteousness" and "goodness." It was Jesus who once told a very "good" man that only God is good; Christ even went so far as to say that all men are basically "evil" (Luke 18:18-19; Matthew 7:11). Though no one is good enough to meet God's holy standards, we can indeed be considered righteous enough through faith in His Son.

The word "righteous" or "righteousness" is mentioned almost 600 times in Scripture and, again, is something God imparts to men through faith. The apostle Paul wrote,

> If Abraham was justified by works, he has something to boast about, but not before God. For what does the Scripture say? "Abraham believed God, and it was credited to him as righteousness." Now to the one who works, his wage is not credited as a favor, but as what is due. But to the one who does not work, but believes in Him who justifies the

ungodly, his faith is credited as righteousness, just as David also speaks of the blessing on the man to whom God credits righteousness apart from works: "Blessed are those whose lawless deeds have been forgiven, and whose sins have been covered. Blessed is the man whose sin the Lord will not take into account." (Romans 4:2-8)

No man can be made "good" by his own merits in God's sight because there is no good in men. By his very nature, man is selfish, self-centered, egotistical, proud, lustful, greedy, and envious. In short, he is bad to the bone, and no amount of money or education can make him good or improve his fallen condition. When a man sincerely believes God, though, God then imparts to him a saving righteousness of faith, which is none other than the righteousness of Jesus Christ Himself.

It takes the grace of God to see our wretchedness and our need for a righteousness that is not our own. It takes the grace of God to realize no "good person" is going to enter heaven, because only God is good. "Basically good people" are bad to the bone, and truly righteous people are transformed to the bone. They have died to their old natures and have risen with a new life in God's Son.

The Steam of Self-Esteem

How many people today would say their lives seem like falling leaves that the seasons have torn off and condemned? Feeling hopeless and without purpose, many young people commit suicide, get hooked on drugs, drop out of school, end up in prison, join gangs, or do any number of self-destructive things. Their numbers are legion.

Many psychologists and psychiatrists today will tell us that people's lives often manifest dysfunctional behavior or lonely depression due to low self-esteem or negative thinking. When it comes to encouraging people to improve their self-image and overcome their insecurities, a plethora of books, seminars, and positive-thinking advocates abound. Usually their underlying mantra is getting people to look within themselves and see that they are good and that they are important and destined for greatness; all they need to do is to look in the mirror and see how unique and significant they are.

Well, personally, I think that kind of approach to improving one's self-esteem is very much like putting the cart before the horse. Such methods amount to little more than shallow sensitivity and sloppy sentimentality because they are constantly encouraging us to look for good within us in order to feel better about ourselves.

Contrarily, here is how my own self-esteem was infinitely improved. Are you ready for this? Oddly enough, it was the day I realized "there is no good in me"! I am a monster of iniquity, and there is not one sin against God or crime against humanity that I am not fully capable of committing. That's right! I said, and I fully believe, that there is no good in me. However, I do not suffer from low self-esteem, not in the least. Do you know why? Because the night I accepted Jesus Christ into my heart, I told Him in my own clumsy way that I honestly did not know how to be good or how to improve myself in His eyes. But I told Him that I wanted Him anyway, if He would have me. That night He touched me, and I woke up as a new man.

I realized for the first time that I possessed incredible worth and tremendous value. I could see this so clearly because I understood that God made me in His image and likeness, which gave me unbelievable importance. Ultimately, when I comprehended how He lovingly died for me, my existence suddenly had infinite worth and value. It was the apostle Paul who said that in himself (in his flesh, in his fallen nature), there was no good (Romans 7:18). He said to Timothy,

> It is a trustworthy statement, deserving full acceptance, that Christ Jesus came into the world to save sinners, among whom I am foremost of all. (1 Timothy 1:15)

Paul believed without a doubt that he was a sinful wretch who was lost and on his way to an eternal hell and separation from God forever. Nevertheless, Paul in no way suffered from "low self-esteem." He realized that his eternal value was all tied up in a Creator who is total goodness and perfection. Consequently, the secret of improving one's self-esteem is not to look inward, but outward. Trying to improve your self-image without God is like trying to pull yourself up by your own bootstraps, which is impossible.

Sure, people can say their self-importance has improved without God, but that's the problem—it's "self-importance" rather than "God importance." Because men and women are created in the image and likeness of God, anything that leaves God out of the mix will prove meaningless in the end (Genesis 1:26-27). Regardless of how terribly one's self-image has been destroyed, their true beauty and infinite worth can be seen in the reflection of the image and likeness of One who is utterly perfect and astonishingly beautiful, both inside and out.

Isaiah the prophet said that in the eyes of God, even a man's righteousness is nothing but "filthy rags," let alone his unrighteousness (Isaiah 64:6). The bottom line is that man has no righteousness in and of himself, and therefore all of his attempts at improving his self-esteem are pointless apart from the God who created him. John the Baptist said of Christ, "He must increase, but I must decrease," and Jesus said, "Apart from Me you can do nothing" (John 3:30; 15:5).

Christ is the steam in self-esteem that propels a purpose-driven life, and He is the wind beneath our wings, enabling us to soar to unimaginable heights. All of man's efforts at improving one's self-regard are simply the buoyancy of hot air, not the boiling steam necessary to drive the engine of genuine self-esteem. It all starts, though, with the understanding that there is no good in us, and ends with the conviction that we have eternal value in a Creator who has made us for everlasting greatness and has fashioned us for eternal glory and majesty.

Pigs With the Flu

In recent times, the world was dealing with a pandemic called the Swine Flu—a virus that mutated from pigs and managed to sicken and kill countless men and women around the globe. The cure for this spreading disease was limited at best, and quarantine appeared to be the most effective way of slowing its deadly march.

However, a different kind of Swine Flu has been around for thousands of years and has been the root cause of all the world's sickness, difficulties, and death. It originated with a couple of two-legged pigs. Pigs do not possess the capacity to appreciate what is truly valuable, nor do they have the good sense to be sincerely grateful for their master's provisions and care.

The cold, naked truth is that man did not evolve from screaming monkeys, but he has most certainly devolved into ungrateful pigs. Lest this sound too insulting and offensive, we would do well to recall it was the loving Son of God Himself who referred to some men as being pigs. Jesus warned his followers not to "throw [their] pearls before swine, or they will trample them under their feet…" (Matthew 7:6).

This fatal pig's virus spawned in the heart of mankind's first parents. Adam and Eve had every good thing imaginable: They had a blissfully happy and fulfilled marriage. They never had to worry about finances, sickness, old age, deadlines or death. They had a wonderfully enriching relationship with God and with each other as they walked continuously with Him in the cool of each setting sun. Every day was an adventure in romance and an exciting experience in a rewarding occupation. Their hearts' desire was complete at every turn and with every step. They lacked absolutely nothing emotionally or physically within a stimulating environment.

Yet in spite of their every blessing and advantage, Satan easily managed to stir within them a spirit of discontentment. It is truly amazing how quickly he enabled the happiest human beings in history to disbelieve God and to covet the only thing they were prohibited from having. With just one simple question, one brief statement, the devil utterly ruined a perfect world and, in an instant, the Swine Flu was born.

Conceived in the womb of ingratitude, it emerged between the legs of disbelief and covetousness. This lethal virus opened Pandora's box of death and suffering and unleashed an overwhelming fold of sorrows and difficulties. Man's discontentment unlocked the very gates of hell itself, opening wide the jaws of eternal death and devouring billions of unrepentant souls.

Man's incredibly unbelievable fall has now produced a very profound question: If two perfect human beings living in a perfect world with perfect harmony could be persuaded to disbelieve God, then what possible chance do pitifully imperfect human beings living in a terribly imperfect world have when it comes to believing God and being thankful for his provisions? Our only hope of fulfillment and chance of happiness lie within a "learned secret." The apostle Paul explains,

> I have learned to be content in whatever circumstances I am. I know how to get along with humble means, and I also know how to live in prosperity; in any and every circumstance I have learned the secret of being filled and going hungry, both of having abundance and suffering need. I can do all things through Him who strengthens me. (Philippians 4:11-13)

Until we learn how to be truly grateful for the blessings we enjoy in life, we will never be satisfied, regardless of how many advantages we may enjoy.

Thankfulness is the only antidote for this pig's disease of discontentment. Had Adam and Eve truly appreciated their myriad of blessings, the world would not be in the condition we see today. Ingratitude lies at the bottom of discontentment. It is a sense of entitlement that blackens men's hearts and blinds men's eyes to God's goodness and to their own good fortune in life. A man's thankless attitude spawns almost every form of wickedness and rebellion; an unthankful heart becomes a highway to hell,

> For since the creation of the world His invisible attributes, His eternal power and divine nature, have been clearly seen, being understood through what has been made, so that they are without excuse. For even though they knew God, they did not honor Him as God or give thanks, but they became futile in their speculations, and their foolish heart was

darkened. Professing to be wise, they became fools ... and just as they did not see fit to acknowledge God any longer, God gave them over to a depraved mind, to do those things which are not proper, being filled with all unrighteousness, wickedness, greed, evil; full of envy, murder, strife, deceit, malice; they are gossips, slanderers, haters of God, insolent, arrogant, boastful, inventors of evil, disobedient to parents, without understanding, untrustworthy, unloving, unmerciful; and although they know the ordinance of God, that those who practice such things are worthy of death, they not only do the same, but also give hearty approval to those who practice them. (Romans 1:20-22, 28-32)

When men refuse to give God thanks, their minds become depraved and their reasoning becomes absurd. When our lives become weighed down with discontentment, praising God is our only hope. Gratefulness is the only remedy for a swine's contagious sickness of ingratitude. The world is filled with pigs with the flu, but this swine's disease consumes one's soul rather than one's body, and no one is immune to its deadly effects. Only the continuous inoculation of thanksgiving and the constant injection of gratitude can protect us from this spiritual swine flu.

Life Below

It is truly astounding how many life forms flourish below the surface of the earth and thrive beneath the top of the world's waterways. These microscopic organisms far outnumber the hosts of living beings dwelling aboveground.

The Bible speaks often of something not ordinarily seen on the surface, yet which has the unique power to determine a person's eternal destiny: it is referred to as the "root." A root is the hidden life of a plant or tree, which is absolutely essential for its survival. If the roots of a tree are deep and widespread enough, there is a good chance the tree will grow again, even if it is reduced to merely a stump. However, if a cedar has a shallow or poor root system, there is a very definite possibility the slightest storm could topple it or parasites could destroy it.

Roots are rarely noticed, but their necessity cannot be overemphasized. The Bible speaks of roots dozens of times and stresses the important role they play for good and evil, for sickness and health, and for the destination of heaven or hell.

God warned His people through Moses if they engaged in any idolatrous practices, they would become "a root bearing poisonous fruit and wormwood" (Deuteronomy 29:18). In the fifth chapter of Isaiah, God gives seven different "woes" to the wicked:

> Woe to those who add house to house and join field to field.
> ... Woe to those ... who pursue strong drink. ... Woe to
> those who drag iniquity with the cords of falsehood. ... Woe
> to those who call evil good, and good evil; who substitute
> darkness for light and light for darkness; who substitute
> bitter for sweet and sweet for bitter! Woe to those who are
> wise in their own eyes and clever in their own sight! Woe to
> those who are heroes in drinking wine and ... [woe to those]
> who justify the wicked for a bribe. (Isaiah 5:8, 11, 18, 20-23)

Of these types of people, God said, "their root will become like rot and their blossom blow away as dust," and when God pronounced judgment upon the Philistines, He said, "From the serpent's root a viper will come out, and its fruit will be a flying serpent" (Isaiah 5:24; 14:29). It was the author of Hebrews who said, "See to it … that no root of bitterness springing up causes trouble, and by it many be defiled" (Hebrews 12:15). When John the Baptist condemned the religious hypocrites of his day, he said, "The axe is already laid at the root of the trees; therefore every tree that does not bear good fruit is cut down and thrown into the fire" (Matthew 3:10).

On the other hand, Solomon said, "the root of the righteous will not be moved" and "the root of the righteous yields fruit" (Proverbs 12:3, 12). It was Jesus who implied that roots were all-important in the type of fruit a tree produced. He said people would be known by their fruit, and a good tree could not bear bad fruit and a bad tree could not bear good fruit (see Matthew 7:15-20).

Lastly, when Christ gave His famous parable concerning the sower and the seed, He said,

> The one on whom seed was sown on the rocky places, this is the man who hears the word and immediately receives it with joy; yet he has no firm root in himself but is only temporary, and when affliction or persecution arises because of the word, immediately he falls away. (Matthew 13:20-21)

What Jesus was powerfully saying here is that many people can experience an emotional high when it comes to their faith in Him, but if they have little or no hidden life with Him, they are sure to fall away; their faith will dissolve when it is tested, due to the scarcity of "root."

A firm root in Christ can only be developed and cultivated in the dark, where no one else can witness it. Continuous prayer (when no one is around) is what truly strengthens and matures a person's commitment to Jesus, and regular reading of God's Word (when no one sees) is what enlarges and invigorates one's devotion to God. Jesus instructed, "I am the vine, you are the branches. … apart from Me you can do nothing" (John 15:5). Without a deep and hidden root system in Christ, our lives are sure to be fruitless at best, and poisonous at worst.

Remember what is most important for the health and survival of plants—its hidden life, what we don't see. Likewise, our spiritual life thriving below the surface is most important in our relationship with God. What moves and breathes in the darkness with God is sure to guarantee growth and produce righteous fruit in the sight of all.

Misery Has Two Daughters

Many despicable things exist in this world, but few can match the ugliness of misery's two daughters: poverty and malnutrition. With each passing day, the wretchedness of famine and the repulsiveness of destitution spread like an out-of-control wildfire throughout the globe.

According to Bread for the World (a Washington, D.C., faith-based organization), nearly a billion people in the world today are chronically hungry; nearly 16,000 children starve to death each day, as famine increases exponentially and scarcity disperses like cancer[1] Even the wealthiest countries are seeing more of their populations experiencing poverty and hunger, and of course, the never-ending mantra chanted by the world leaders is to throw more money at every social problem. From rock stars to movie stars and from hardcore atheists to the deeply religious, the drumbeat for financial aid grows louder with each new decade.

We are constantly led to believe that money, money and more money is what will turn back the invasion of these two ugly sisters and put their mother, Misery, on the run. However, governments throughout the world are flat broke and swimming in red ink. Countries are bankrupt and nations are collapsing under the weight of financial debt. Nevertheless, they continue to produce money out of thin air and constantly throw it around like confetti—hoping beyond hope, that money will be the magic bullet to eliminate virtually all of man's problems.

The naked truth is that no amount of tax increases or number of "stimulus packages" is going to solve anything. Celebrities can continue to beat their humanistic drums for more aid, and world leaders can do their nonstop rain dance for greater revenue, but there is only one thing that can put this miserable woman and her cursed daughters in retreat: obedience to God. Only obedience to God can rout these dreadful witches and their deadly spells. The Creator of all mankind explained this to His people Israel:

> There will be no poor among you, since the Lord will surely
> bless you in the land which the Lord your God is giving you

as an inheritance to possess, if only you listen obediently to the voice of the Lord your God, to observe carefully all this commandment which I am commanding you today. For the Lord your God will bless you as He has promised you, and you will lend to many nations, but you will not borrow; and you will rule over many nations, but they will not rule over you. (Deuteronomy 15:4-6)

Man's foolish solutions for every social ill and global predicament are absolutely useless in the face of what God has declared. Man's shortsighted answers to poverty and his nearsighted responses to malnutrition only exacerbate his troubles because he always deals with the symptoms and never with the root causes. This is as foolish as trying to mop up a flooded floor without first turning off the faucet, the source of the water.

Until men realize sin and rebellion against a holy and righteous God are what flood the world with famine and inundate the globe with destitution, their attempts to eliminate world hunger and eradicate global poverty are utterly in vain. As long as the human race insists upon solving its problems apart from obeying God, man's poverty, hunger, and troubles will continue to escalate to no end.

Newscasts reporting the plight of the hungry and articles heralding the ills of poverty fail to address the root causes to these problems. No amount of money can put an end to this ugly woman and her two horrid daughters. Though they sneer and mock at every attempt of man to slay them, they wither and suffocate in the presence of a nation that truly obeys God.

Let's Hear It for the Criminally Insane

It truly is a mystery how some of the most notorious criminals, serial killers, and mass murderers in history have managed to develop and cultivate a following of lovesick admirers and zealous devotees. From Charles Manson or Richard Ramirez (the Night Stalker) to Hitler or Mao Ze-dong, people have turned these killers into gods, worshipping them with blind devotion.

A number of condemned prisoners have actually received marriage proposals from women who have never even met them; yet these ladies are so mesmerized by their wicked deeds and hypnotic looks that they long to be with them. Some of these vicious killers have even been allowed to marry their fanatical admirers behind prison walls.

To most people, however, such profound attraction toward cold-blooded murderers is totally demented and idiotic. Why isn't this the case for everyone? The answers are undoubtedly complex and far-reaching. Each person who admires a hardened criminal may have totally different reasons and motivations from everyone else who does so, but there is one thing every admirer of the criminally insane has in common: a resentment toward God and His moral laws, consciously or unconsciously. These delirious fans may very well be educated and successful, law abiding and generous, and perhaps even religious, but spiritually, they are blinded and devoid of heavenly wisdom.

People who voted for Hitler, supported Stalin, and/or deified Mao were utterly lacking in godly understanding and spiritual enlightenment. They were easily fooled by their hero's words and their champion's charisma. Their spiritual blindness prevented them from seeing these monsters of iniquity for what they really were—criminally insane, cold-blooded killers.

Now here is the rub, the harsh truth, bound to offend the masses with its political incorrectness: If we support or vote for politicians who do not uphold the laws of God, then there is little or no difference between us and a person who is infatuated with someone on death row. Why? Because a condemned criminal is a lawbreaker and a political leader who tramples the moral standards of God under his feet is also a lawbreaker. Unfortunately, the biggest lawbreaker in all of recorded history is about to appear to a world primed and waiting for just such a rebel.

The Bible refers to him as "the man of lawlessness," "the son of destruction," and "the beast." He will come upon the world scene with all the power, signs, and false wonders of Satan himself. He will deceive and delude everyone who loves breaking God's laws because they refuse to believe and obey the truth of God's Word (see 2 Thessalonians 2:1-12).

The apostle John prophesied,

> All who dwell on the earth will worship him, everyone whose name has not been written from the foundation of the world in the book of life of the Lamb who has been slain. (Revelation 13:8)

In other words, this "man of lawlessness," this monster of iniquity will have the biggest following of lovesick admirers the world has ever seen. Not just hundreds, thousands, or millions, but by the *billions*, people will be mesmerized by this man who will defiantly trample the laws of God under his feet, as if to shout, "Let's hear it for the criminally insane!"

The world's infatuation with this coming "man of lawlessness" will be no less demented than the scandalous devotion of a woman who wants to be wed to a murderous criminal or to a man who insanely defies the God of heaven with his lawlessness.

What Do You Fear Most?

Fear is everywhere; you don't have to look far to find it. Infants fear loud noises and falling, little children fear spankings and the bogeyman, young people fear rejection and pregnancy, college kids fear failure and joblessness, the middle-agers fear financial losses and growing old, and the aged fear loneliness and dying. The things people fear are endless. Fears can be real or imaginary, but one thing is certain: Fear is everywhere!

What do you fear the most? Since the answer will obviously vary from person to person and from situation to situation, the real question ought to be: What *should* I fear the most?

Well, the Bible has an enormous amount to say about fear, and it very often tells us *not* to fear. There is only one thing that God says all men are to fear and to fear greatly, and that is Him. He commands us to fear Him because to fear Him means to obey Him. The Scriptures tell us, "The fear of the Lord is the beginning of wisdom" (Psalm 111:10; Proverbs 9:10). To fear God is to be awestruck by His holiness—not dumbfounded by His power. God is not so concerned that we realize He is actually Almighty (although I'm sure it pleases Him whenever we appreciate one of His sunsets or are astounded by His stellar galaxies); rather, that we comprehend His total righteousness.

If we enter a store and feel tempted to take something without paying for it, but then say to ourselves, *I could easily get away with this theft, but God would not overlook my act of dishonesty*, then that is "fear of the Lord." It is the beginning of true enlightenment and the start of genuine understanding.

It was Jesus Christ, the Son of God, who warned us to "fear Him who is able to destroy both soul and body in hell" (Matthew 10:28). He also gave us these warnings:

> I say to you, My friends, do not be afraid of those who kill the body and after that have no more that they can do. But I will warn you whom to fear: Fear the One who, after He has killed, has authority to cast into hell; yes I tell you, fear Him! (Luke 12:4-5)

> If your hand causes you to stumble, cut it off; it is better for you to enter life crippled, than, having your two hands, to go into hell, into the unquenchable fire …. If your foot causes you to stumble, cut it off; it is better for you to enter life lame, than having your two feet, to be cast into hell. … If your eye causes you to stumble, throw it out; it is better for you to enter the kingdom of God with one eye, than having two eyes to be cast into hell, where their worm does not die, and the fire is not quenched. (Mark 9:43-48)

In the book of Daniel we read of two different decrees given by two different kings. The first was given by King Nebuchadnezzar after having three men thrown into a fiery furnace for refusing to bow down to an idol. God protected these three men within the flames, and Nebuchadnezzar was so astonished that he issued a decree declaring that anyone who says a negative thing against the God of heaven would be "torn limb from limb and their houses reduced to a rubbish heap" (Daniel 3:29). A subsequent king, Darius, issued the other decree, proclaiming men everywhere were "to fear and tremble before the God of Daniel" after being forced to have Daniel thrown into a lion's den and then Daniel miraculously lived to tell about it (6:26).

Which decree was really better, Nebuchadnezzar's or Darius'? If we seriously analyze both proclamations, we discover Darius' decree was actually a much more powerful and insightful edict. Nebuchadnezzar commanded that no one dare say a negative thing against God; therefore, people everywhere and throughout all time could be deceived into thinking if they just refrained from cursing the God of heaven, they would be approved by Him. Whereas, Darius insisted everyone "fear and tremble" before the God of Daniel; his decree was the beginning of wisdom because it meant that men recognize their accountability toward God and, therefore, must act accordingly.

The apostle John tells us "perfect love casts out fear" (1 John 4:18). In short, John was saying, "The more we fear and obey God, the less we have to fear Him." Fear brings us to God and love makes us cling to Him. Once we truly love God, our obedience does away with any fear of Him. Therefore, our love has truly been perfected through fear.

What are we most afraid of? Our answer will most certainly reveal a great deal about us.

Hopscotching to Hell

Let's face it, hopscotching is a game for children, not for adults. The apostle Paul says, "When I was a child, I used to speak like a child, think like a child, reason like a child; when I became a man, I did away with childish things" (1 Corinthians 13:11). Jesus also referred to the religious hopscotchers of His day as children:

> To what then shall I compare the men of this generation, and what are they like? They are like children who sit in the market place and call to one another, and they say, "We played the flute for you, and you did not dance; we sang a dirge, and you did not weep." For John the Baptist has come eating no bread and drinking no wine, and you say, "He has a demon!" The Son of Man has come eating and drinking, and you say, "Behold, a gluttonous man and a drunkard, a friend of tax collectors and sinners!" (Luke 7:31-34)

Those who hopscotch rarely have both feet firmly planted on the ground; instead they always waiver between different opinions based upon what is expedient for the moment or what feels right at any given time. When the prophet Elijah confronted 450 prophets of Baal and 400 prophets of the Asherah on Mount Carmel, he asked the people of Israel, "How long will you hesitate between two opinions? If the Lord is God, follow Him; but if Baal, follow him" (1 Kings 18:19-21).

It was James who rebuked some early church members for being double-minded and, therefore, unstable in all their ways (James 1:6-8). However, today there has evolved an entire smorgasbord of religious beliefs and spiritual persuasions to fit a wide variety of individual tastes and interests. Most people desire the comfort of believing in God and an eternal heaven, but they insist on picking and choosing what suits their appetites best when it comes to the supernatural.

In short, they enjoy the pastime of spiritual hopscotch as they jump from here to there in order to accumulate beliefs they feel are valuable to them at the moment. The apostle Paul actually predicted this game of picking and choosing Scriptures and beliefs to fit one's fancy:

> The spirit explicitly says that in later times some will fall away from the faith, paying attention to deceitful spirits and doctrines of demons. ... The time will come when they will not endure sound doctrine; but wanting to have their ears tickled, they will accumulate for themselves teachers in accordance to their own desires, and will turn away their ears from the truth and will turn aside to myths. (1 Timothy 4:1; 2 Timothy 4:3-4)

Jesus addressed this, as well:

> Not everyone who says to me, "Lord, Lord," will enter the kingdom of heaven, but he who does the will of My Father who is in heaven will enter. Many will say to Me on that day, "Lord, Lord, did we not prophesy in Your name, and in Your name cast out demons, and in Your name perform many miracles?" And then I will declare to them, "I never knew you; depart from Me, you who practice lawlessness." (Matthew 7:21-23)

To put it bluntly, Jesus is telling us that hell is flooded with "religious people" and overflowing with souls who once considered themselves to be quite "spiritual," because they were religious and spiritual on their own terms, not God's. Throughout their lives they hopscotched from Scripture to Scripture and from one religious belief to another, in order to pick up what they preferred most. It was a game to them, but in the end they will discover to their horror that it was no game; God does not play games. Instead they will realize they have hopscotched all the way to hell because it was their "way" of being spiritual.

Sleepwalking to Heaven

Both the Old and the New Testaments repeatedly refer to death as a "sleep," which of course implies that eventually a person who has died will someday awaken. As the 12th chapter of Daniel declares,

> Many of those who sleep in the dust of the ground will awake, these to everlasting life, but the others to disgrace and everlasting contempt. (v. 2)

The prophet Isaiah also said,

> Your dead will live; their corpses will rise. You who lie in the dust, awake and shout for joy, for your dew is as the dew of the dawn, and the earth will give birth to the departed spirits. (Isaiah 26:19)

And it was the Son of God Himself who reminded us of these facts:

> Truly, truly, I say to you, an hour is coming and now is, when the dead will hear the voice of the Son of God, and those who hear [His voice] will live. ... Do not marvel at this; for an hour is coming, in which all who are in the tombs will hear His voice, and will come forth; those who did the good deeds to a resurrection of life, those who committed the evil deeds to a resurrection of judgment. (John 5:25, 28-29)

When Jesus went to the home of a synagogue official, named Jairus, in order to raise his daughter from the dead, Christ said to the professional mourners, "Why make a commotion and weep? The child has not died, but is asleep" (Mark 5:39). In Luke's account of this episode with Jairus' daughter, he writes:

> [Jesus] took her by the hand and called, saying, "Child,

arise!" And her spirit returned, and she got up immediately.
(Luke 8:54-55)

Repeatedly, the books of Kings and Chronicles record the death and burial of the kings of Judah and Israel with the phrase, "and he slept with his fathers and was buried." Without question, the Bible insists that it is a deceased person's body that is asleep, while his soul is very much alive and well, as it never ceases to lose consciousness. For those who commit their lives to Christ, the apostle Paul says that when the spirit departs from the corpse, it goes to be with the Lord while their body awaits its ultimate resurrection (2 Corinthians 5:1-9).

Unquestionably, the Scriptures define physical death as a sleep; however, they also refer to spiritually un-regenerated or unsaved individuals as being "dead," even though they are very much alive physically. As Paul's epistle to Timothy says, "She who gives herself to wanton pleasure is dead even while she lives" (1 Timothy 5:6). Additionally, Jesus said to a man who wanted to follow Him but needed to bury his father first, "Follow Me, and allow the dead to bury their own dead" (Matthew 8:22). Paul declared that Jesus will someday "judge [both] the living [saved] and the dead [lost]" (2 Timothy 4:1).

In view of everything the Bible has to say about death and sleep, and about being physically alive, but spiritually dead, our modern phrase, "dead man walking" or the popular TV series, *The Walking Dead*, is nothing new. The Bible has talked about this phenomenon for centuries. Today's medical terminology would categorize such people as having a sleep disorder, commonly known as sleepwalking.

Sleepwalking has been described as a sleep abnormality that causes people to get up and walk around while still sleeping. It's been said that episodes of sleepwalking typically occur when a person is in the deep stages of sleep. The sleeper is unable to respond during the event and does not remember sleepwalking. Furthermore, sleepwalking can potentially be very dangerous, due to the possibility of being injured or injuring others. The risk of tripping or falling is common for sleepwalkers, and some individuals have even been known to drive their cars while in such a state.

When it comes to walking while sleeping, there are countless sleepwalkers inside and outside of the church today. They claim to believe in Jesus, or at least acknowledge His teachings and promote some of His principles, but they refuse to repent of their sins, die to themselves, and follow and obey Him. They are spiritual sleepwalkers who have an imaginary goodness in which their trance-like state assures them they are on their way to heaven, regardless of what they believe or how they act. However, no one sleepwalks to heaven. No one gets to heaven by dreaming, and certainly no one gets saved while slumbering in the pews of a church. As Solomon put it,

> 'A little sleep, a little slumber, a little folding of the hands to rest,' then your [spiritual] poverty will come as a robber and your [need] like an armed man. (Proverbs 6:10; 24:33-34)

The only hope for spiritual and religious sleepwalkers today is to heed what Paul says in light of this:

> Therefore let us lay aside the deeds of darkness and put on the armor of light. Let us behave properly as in the day, not in carousing and drunkenness, not in sexual promiscuity and sensuality, not in strife and jealousy. But put on the Lord Jesus Christ, and make no provision for the flesh in regard to its lusts. (Romans 13:12-14)

> For this reason [the Scriptures say], "Awake, sleeper, and arise from the dead, and Christ will shine on you." Therefore be careful how you walk, not as unwise men but as wise, making the most of your time, because the days are evil. (Ephesians 5:14-16)

Sadly, spiritual sleepwalkers never make it to heaven, no matter how many of their dreams may say otherwise.

The Losing of One's Mind

"Of all the things I ever lost, I miss my mind the most." This somewhat humorous quote can occasionally be seen on bumper stickers, clothing, and elsewhere. Of course, it is just a funny way of expressing the frustrations of raising children, growing old, or simply having to deal with the stresses and strains of everyday life that can sometimes drive anyone "crazy." Contrarily, God has a great deal to say about a man's mind that should never be taken lightly. In fact, we ought to seriously consider what will be the consequences of misusing our intellect or allowing our God-given intelligence to atrophy.

First of all, the Bible tells us God made each of us to know Him, serve Him, and to "love Him with all our heart, all our soul, all our strength, and all our mind." When someone once asked Jesus which was the greatest commandment, He quoted this exact command (see Deuteronomy 6:5; Matthew 22:37; Mark 12:30; Luke 10:27).

More than anything else about us, our minds are what will determine our eternal destiny. It is the very epicenter of where we do battle with the powers of darkness because it is in our minds we gain spiritual understanding and make our choices to believe and obey God. As depicted in Romans chapter eight, if our minds are set on God and the things of God, we will surely see heaven, but if our minds are set on self-indulgence and things of the world, we may never make it into God's kingdom (vv. 5-14).

The apostle Paul warns us that when men refuse to acknowledge God, He gives them over to a "depraved mind," their "understanding becomes darkened," and their thinking turns "corrupted" (Romans 1:28; Ephesians 4:18; 2 Corinthians 11:3, KJV). A truly classic example of this can be found in the fourth chapter of the book of Daniel where God gave King Nebuchadnezzar a warning in a dream. He was cautioned to break away from his sins and start living righteously by showing mercy to the poor. However, the proud and stubborn monarch continued in his self-will and defiance of God's commands for a whole year. He refused to give God credit for anything, and rather, looked to himself as the one to be glorified.

Thus, in an instant God took away his mind—in an instant! In the blink of an eye, Nebuchadnezzar went from being the most powerful and respected man on earth to becoming a lunatic, driven into the open fields with the animals and eating grass like the wild beasts. His body was drenched with the dew of heaven, his hair matted like eagles' feathers, and his fingernails grew like birds' claws.

For seven long years, the guy was an absolute mess. He went totally insane and became ruined both socially and physically. In the twinkling of an eye, Nebuchadnezzar was transformed into a madman, and was utterly destroyed. Isn't it truly amazing how abruptly God can humble and disgrace a person who refuses to heed Him? Well, what God did to one man he can just as easily do to an entire nation.

In all honesty, would you say America has lost her mind? I'm serious. Let's avoid any knee-jerk responses to this question and simply give an honest and objective response as to whether or not our country has lost its mind. We have problems that are both innumerable and unsolvable, and throughout the world we are being humbled militarily, economically, socially, and educationally.

We have become a nation divided and conflicted at every turn. Our leaders cannot agree on anything and can solve absolutely nothing. Their only solution to every problem is to throw more money at it! We are bankrupt and there is simply no more money; nevertheless, our government continues to fabricate riches and throw dollars around like confetti, while promising the gullible masses that money will solve everything and that we can borrow our way out of debt and spend our way into prosperity.

How insane is that? In our arrogance, self-will, and rejection of God's laws, we have truly lost our mind, just as surely as Nebuchadnezzar lost his. However, after seven long years, his mind was returned to him:

> I, Nebuchadnezzar, raised my eyes toward heaven and my reason returned to me, and I blessed the Most High and praised and honored Him who lives forever. ... And my majesty and splendor were restored to me ... I was reestablished in my sovereignty, and surpassing greatness was added to me. (Daniel 4:34, 36)

It was only after King Nebuchadnezzar "raised his eyes toward heaven" that his reason returned, and his majesty and splendor were restored. Similarly, if we ever have the good grace to humble ourselves and lift our eyes to heaven, our sanity and our greatness will surely be restored to us. Then, and only then, will we see the wisdom of God's words when He promises,

> If My people, who are called by My name, will humble themselves and pray and seek My face and turn from their wicked ways, then will I hear from heaven and will forgive their sin and will heal their land. (2 Chronicles 7:14, NIV)

The Art of Snoring

Snoring can be a very unpleasant and disturbing sound for anyone trying to sleep next to someone who snores. Usually when people snore, their mouths are wide open and their soft palate has relaxed to the point where it vibrates with each breath of incoming air because they are in such a deep sleep. Hardly anything can wake them.

Some individuals have even been known to sleep through earthquakes, the roaring sounds of passing trains, or the screaming crowds at sporting events. We know from Scriptures the prophet Jonah managed to sleep through a storm that was so intense, the ship he was aboard nearly broke apart (see Jonah 1:4-5). When the captain of Jonah's vessel approached the snoring prophet, the officer couldn't believe his eyes. He exclaimed, "How can you sleep? Get up and call on your god!" (1:6, NIV).

The captain was truly amazed and completely dumbfounded that someone like Jonah could actually be asleep in the midst of a devastating hurricane. It almost appears to take a special skill to remain totally oblivious while in the center of such devastation. Well, if such unbelievable snoring could be called a talent or an art, then truly there are a multitude of deep sleepers and snoring artists today.

Just look at the incredible number of storms and the overwhelming intensity of these storms God is hurling at mankind today. Whether it be natural disasters, economic devastation, incurable disease, wars, or political confusion, God is truly trying to wake men up with all these warning sirens and forecasts of impending doom. Sadly, so many people all over the globe are in such a deep spiritual slumber, they appear to be in a coma. Like Jonah, they are utterly oblivious to the dangers that surround them.

The thunder and lightning of God's constant wake-up calls are not being heard or heeded, and an overwhelming number of people seem deaf to the voice of God's judgments because they are preoccupied with dreams of prosperity, visions of success, and fantasies of pleasure. It appears nothing can rouse them from their mindless stupor because their art of snoring has become so well-perfected.

Their only hope is to heed these words from the apostle Paul:

> Do this, knowing the time, that it is already the hour for you to awaken from sleep; for now salvation is nearer to us than when we believed. The night is almost gone, and the day is near. Therefore let us lay aside the deeds of darkness and put on the armor of light. (Romans 13:11-12)

Though the sound of a slumbering snore may be annoying to us, imagine how loud our snores must seem to God, as we have cultivated the art of drowning out and snoozing through His numerous and increasingly noisy wake-up calls.

The Goose That Gets a Sore Behind

One of Aesop's most famous fables was, "The Goose that Laid the Golden Eggs." In this popular fairy tale, a husband and wife discover they have the incredible good fortune of possessing a magical bird that lays eggs of gold, and because of the unusual talent of this gold-producing goose, the man and woman grew richer with each passing day.

Unfortunately, they decided they were not getting rich quickly enough, so they concocted a plan they thought would make them fabulously wealthy overnight. They killed the goose and cut open its entrails, hoping to find a storehouse of golden eggs that would make them instant millionaires. However, after killing the poor creature, they discovered too late that it was just an ordinary bird, and now their greed had put an end to all of their good fortune.

Interestingly, there is a somewhat different story told in the Bible. Although it is not a fable, it too possesses a moral lesson that can be applied even to today. The account is found in the first book of Samuel during the days when Israel had no king, but instead was governed by God through judges.

Over time, the people had grown tired of God's ordained leadership and demanded to have a king like all the other nations around them. In their shortsightedness they thought by having a political king (instead of a religious judge), they would become stronger and wealthier than their surrounding enemies. However, their rejection of God's government was a rejection of God Himself. As the Lord said to Samuel,

> Listen to the voice of the people in regard to all that they say to you, for they have not rejected you, but they have rejected Me from being king over them … Now then, listen to their voice; however, you shall solemnly warn them and tell them of the procedure of the king who will reign over them. (1 Samuel 8:7, 9)

Then God outlined the requirements of establishing a king and his government, along with a warning:

This will be the procedure of the king who will reign over you: he will take your sons and place them for himself in his chariots and among his horsemen and they will run before his chariots. He will appoint for himself commanders of thousands and of fifties, and some to do his plowing and to reap his harvest and to make his weapons of war and equipment for his chariots. He will also take your daughters for perfumers and cooks and bakers. He will take the best of your fields and your vineyards and your olive groves and give them to his servants. He will take a tenth of your seed and of your vineyards and give it to his officers and to his servants. He will also take your male servants and your female servants and your best young men and your donkeys and use them for his work. He will take a tenth of your flocks, and you yourselves will become his servants. Then you will cry out in that day because of your king whom you have chosen for yourselves, but the Lord will not answer you in that day. (1 Samuel 8:11-18)

Eventually the warning from God came to pass. The people began to be taxed more and more by each new king that came to the throne. The kings grew richer and richer, and their governments grew bigger and bigger. Their military grew increasingly more expensive and their administration became more bloated and inefficient. When the people cried out to God in their frustration, it was too late. They had fired the judges, or "killed the goose that laid the golden eggs," and now they were becoming bankrupt by the very king they thought would bring them prosperity.

Our country today has also put government in the place of God. We look to the state to solve all of our problems and to provide for all of our needs. From the womb to the tomb, we cry out to government instead of to God to take care of us and to protect us. We have forgotten God, and now over fifty percent of our income goes to taxes.

Israel was crying out when only ten percent of their hard-earned money went to taxes, but our government, with its insatiable appetite for more and more wealth, demands that we pay increasingly higher income tax, state tax, local tax, property tax, sales tax, vehicle tax, toll tax, excise tax, tax, tax, tax, and more tax!

It has now come full circle. The taxpayer has now become the modern-day "goose that laid the golden eggs," and like Israel of old, we have discovered too late, the goose that always lays the golden egg gets a sore behind. We have painfully learned that regardless of how sore this goose's rear end becomes, it can never lay enough golden eggs to satisfy its greedy owners. The only question now is, when will our government finally kill this exhausted bird in its foolish attempts to enrich itself?

The moral of all this should be obvious, but regrettably, most people still don't get it. The more we put government in the place of God, the more painful our behinds will become!

Stones, Snakes and Scorpions

Stones, snakes, and scorpions—three dreaded "S's" on earth. They stand for suffering, sorrow, and sadness. No one in their right mind wants these things, and no sane person ever asks for such things.

It was Jesus who said in the 7th chapter of Matthew and the 11th chapter of Luke that no father would ever give his son a stone if he requested a loaf of bread; neither would he give his child a snake if he pleaded for a fish; nor would he give the boy a scorpion if he asked for an egg.

Christ went on to say if men, who have fallen natures, know how to give good gifts to their children, how much more will God give His Holy Spirit to those who ask Him for it. He said to "ask and it will be given to you; seek and you will find; knock and it will be opened to you" (Matthew 7:7). Those words from the Son of God should ignite a fire of hope in anyone's heart who desires to ask God for that which he/she truly longs for.

In essence, Jesus has made a profound promise to all who sincerely seek God in prayer. Now here is the catch: The Scriptures tell us, "God's thoughts are not our thoughts, nor are our ways His ways, for as the heavens are higher than the earth, so are His ways higher than our ways, and his thoughts than our thoughts" (Isaiah 55:8-9). Since we cannot see the ends of the heavens, even with our most powerful and technologically advanced telescopes, it is a sure bet that God's thoughts and His ways are light-years different than our own.

That is why *faith* is so essential in our relationship with God. The apostle Paul even goes so far as to say the things of God are foolishness to our natural minds (1 Corinthians 2:14). Consequently, there may very well be times when we ask God for a loaf of bread and feel like we have been given a stone in its place. In our pain and in our loneliness and frustration, we might cry out, "Why, God? Why? Why did You give me this, when I asked for that? Why did You give me sickness, when I entreated You for health? Why did You send me grief, when I expected from You happiness? Why did You bestow upon me poverty, when I requested riches? Why did my loved one die, when I pleaded for his life? Why did You give me a difficult mate, when I implored You for a fairy tale spouse? Why, God? Why? Why? Why?" Undoubtedly, this one word has reached heaven more than any single word in history, in every language ever spoken—*why*? Because God's thoughts and His ways are vastly different from our own, that's why. Regardless of how disappointed we may be with the suffering, sorrow, and sadness that God may send to us in place of the enjoyment, prosperity and happiness we asked for, we must always remember the old saying, "God is too good to be unkind and too wise to make mistakes."

Do you recall the story in the gospels about the paralytic? (see Matthew 9:1-8; Mark 2:1-12). He was without hope and highly dependent on others. His need was obvious to everyone and his heartfelt prayer, along with the pleas of his friends, was for Christ to heal him. Well, Jesus took one look at the poor man and, prior to miraculously healing him, said, "Take courage, son; your sins are forgiven." He was brought to Christ with one desperate desire and one earnest expectation—to be healed—but the Son of God saw a much deeper need in the crippled man than anyone else could see. Jesus gazed into the man's soul and saw his need to be forgiven and for his relationship with God to be restored.

Christ knew if He simply healed the man's physical condition and not his spiritual state, the paralytic would be eternally lost, and therefore, his temporal healing would be absolutely pointless. God always looks at the deeper need when we petition Him in prayer because He wants to give what is best for us from an eternal perspective, which may involve a waiting period, sometimes misinterpreted as God's refusal.

There may be times in our lives when we must trustingly ask God for the good grace to see through the suffering inflicted by a scorpion, to discern the purpose for a sorrowful snake bite, and to realize the greater good in sadness that weighs us down like a burdensome stone. Even if we are unable to clearly see the *why*, if we sincerely believe that God is too good to be unkind and too wise to make mistakes, then the dreaded "S's" of our earthly existence will eventually become the three "S's" of our satisfaction, security, and salvation.

Plucking Chickens and Strumming Guitars

When God was giving out "ears" I thought He said "beers" and asked for a bucket! Well not really, but the truth is I can't carry a tune in a bucket, and I wouldn't know a musical note even if it hit me between my ears. My singing sounds more like the grunts of a Neanderthal accompanied by the groans of a dying mule.

Needless to say, music is not my gift and humming lullabies is definitely not a talent of mine. However there is one song that everyone can sing, regardless of how gruff and unpolished a person's vocal cords may be. Certain singing becomes a beautiful melody and a harmonic fragrance to the God of heaven—It is the song of praise and the music of thanksgiving. Genuine praise and sincere gratefulness may pass through our unrefined lips, but the words and music originate in a heart only God can see and hear.

The world's most gifted songbird in a church choir or the most talented soloist in a worship service will never be heard in heaven if their singing is motivated by self-seeking, rather than exalting the glory of Almighty God. On the other hand, some of the worst singers on the planet may be some of the most beautiful voices before the throne of the Lord of hosts. Consequently, strumming a guitar in church may be as unedifying as plucking a chicken in a barn if heartfelt praise is not what is truly being strummed and sung.

The Bible literally has hundreds of things to say about praising God. It exhorts us to praise Him in His sanctuary, to praise Him for His deeds, to praise Him with cymbals, to praise Him in our good times, to praise Him in our struggles, and to praise Him night and day. The Scriptures tell us that all of creation praises Him—from the sun and the moon, from the mountains to the stars, from the rivers to the seas, and from the insects to the angels. They all give glory and praise to the God of the universe (Psalms 148-150).

Even in our darkest hours, our deepest heartbreaks, we are to praise God and to thank Him for everything, because He is worthy to be glorified. The more sincere our praise, the more melodious our voices become to His divine ears, and the more highly He is worshipped. It was C.S. Lewis who once said,

> A man can no more diminish God's glory by refusing to
> worship Him than a lunatic can put out the sun by scribbling
> the word "darkness" on the walls of his cell.[2]

God does not need our worship or our praise. Our praise of Him is His gift to us. It is what we were created to do, and by praising Him we find our deepest joy and our richest fulfillment in life. It is what elevates our spirits and exalts our souls. The pure worship of God is what gives man His ultimate sense of well-being and purpose.

On the other hand, pigs are ungrateful creatures with no appreciation for God and His blessings. That is why Jesus said:

> Do not give what is holy to dogs, and do not throw your
> pearls before swine, or they will trample them under their
> feet, and turn and tear you to pieces. (Matthew 7:6)

People who are sincerely grateful to their Creator and who express their earnest admiration of Him in thankful worship become one with the angels—angels whose voices would mesmerize us with their beauty and hypnotize us with their glorious singing. Men and women who can truly thank God for something as ordinary as a drink of water or praise Him for their very eyesight have angelic voices, regardless of how bad their caroling may sound to the world around them.

So the next time we sing in church or give thanks before meals, we need to ask ourselves, *Am I really strumming a guitar of praise here, or am I just plucking chickens in a farmhouse?* Men may not be able to discern the difference, but an all-seeing God has no difficulty in knowing which is which.

"Love That Purifies and Transforms." *Reflections* (Nov. 2009): n. pag. *C.S. Lewis Institute*. C.S. Lewis
    Institute, Nov. 2009. Web. 3 Dec. 2013.

Ten Days of Facial Hair

In the sixth chapter of Numbers, God gives very specific instructions to anyone (male or female) who wants to dedicate themselves to God for a predetermined period of time. It was called the "Nazirite vow," otherwise known as "the law of separation." Those who took this voluntary Nazirite vow were to abstain from drinking any alcoholic beverages all the days of their separation. They couldn't even have grape juice, grapes, raisins, grape seeds, grape skins, or anything that went into the production of wine.

Furthermore, at the beginning of their Nazirite vow, they were to shave their hair; and at the end of their vow (or at the end of their separation), they were to shave their head of hair that had grown during their time of separation unto God. Then they were required to take this dedicated head of hair and place it in the fire that consumed their animal sacrifice at the completion of their vow.

Why refrain from alcoholic beverages during this time of separation and why the shaving of the dedicated hair? It actually has a very profound spiritual message—rich with symbolism and, believe it or not, relevant and applicable to everyone today.

First of all, the Bible says God gives man wine to make his heart glad (Psalm 104:15). For thousands of years, alcoholic beverages have been an integral part of celebrating and rejoicing. Whether at weddings, birthday parties, holiday gatherings, or family get-togethers, wine, beer, champagne, and liquor have been a key part of festivities.

Additionally, we know from Scripture that hair can symbolize spiritual strength and dedication to God. We see this portrayed in the lives of Samson and Samuel, as well as John the Baptist (see Judges 16:17; 1 Samuel 1:11; Luke 1:24-25). Samson and Samuel were never to cut their hair, as a sign of a life-long commitment to God. The two of them, along with John the Baptist, were never to drink wine in order to demonstrate their joy was in the Lord, not in the things of this world. Nehemiah summed this up best when he said to God's people, "The joy of the Lord is your strength" (Nehemiah 8:10).

Now here's the question, pure and simple—*What do I find the most joy in (excluding family or friends)? Is it my career? Is it my job? Is it my house, my car, my piggy bank?* The truth of the matter is that for most people, it's the television set. That's right—TV. According to Time.com, in 1990, people in their twenties watched up to six hours of TV a day. That's approximately 42 hours a week. Currently, just over twenty years later, the Time magazine reports the average American watches 58 hours of television each week. That figure translates into over two solid days a week; nearly ten days a month, which is almost four months out of a year. In a lifetime, that could easily amount to 25 total years of watching television.

Believe it or not, like it or not, admit it or not, the TV is where most people find their joy. Virtually no one gets paid to watch television, as very few people's jobs require them to watch TV. Watching TV is what people choose to do in their leisure time, instead of countless other activities. There is no way the average American would spend so much free time engaging in this pastime, unless they derived much pleasure from it.

Just do the math. If we must spend eight hours a day working and eight hours sleeping, plus a significant amount of time eating, commuting, shopping, and doing other essential time-consuming enterprises, what time do we have left for God? Virtually none! Consequently, one of the absolute best things a person could possibly do to improve their relationship with God today is to make a modern-day version of the Nazirite vow. Matthew 5:34-35 and James 4:13-15 caution us never to "swear by heaven or earth" or "vow to God" that we are going to do anything, because such foolish and rash vows will only enable the devil to get us to sin with our mouths (Matthew 4:37, NIV). Rather, we can humbly ask God for the good grace to make a vow of separation for ten days. If we fail to carry out this vow, we haven't sinned with our lips because we did not swear to God that we were going to accomplish this. We have merely asked Him for help to abstain from TV or other distractions and dedicate those ten days to drawing nearer to God.

Why ten days? Because that is the number of days Daniel and his three friends (Hananiah, Mishael, and Azariah) asked to be excluded from eating the non-kosher food that was served at King Nebuchadnezzar's table. In their determination to obey God's dietary laws, they persuaded their pagan overseer to give them just vegetables and water for ten days, rather than the appointed rations of choice food and wine from the king's menu.

They were granted their request, and at the end of ten days, they were found to be physically healthier and mentally keener than all their contemporaries. At the end of their months of training, they were found to be ten times wiser and ten times more knowledgeable than all the officials in Nebuchadnezzar's kingdom (Daniel 1). Their ten days of abstaining from the king's table put them on a path of spiritual growth and physical success for the rest of their lives.

Just ten days—not even two weeks! If we took all of the leisure time we spend watching TV in just ten days, and instead used those ten days to read God's Word, to pray, to memorize Scripture, to meditate on the Bible, and to attend Bible studies or prayer meetings, then there would be a difference in our spiritual lives—a very noticeable difference felt by us and substantially evident to others.

Hair is the symbol of spiritual strength. Though it is very difficult to detect the exact amount of hair growth in just ten days, if the average adult male failed to shave for ten days, his untrimmed facial hair would become very apparent to others and easily felt by himself. To forego shaving for one or two days may not be very apparent, but the consequences of neglecting to shave for ten days will become clear for all to see.

Facial hair—it can speak volumes without saying a word. To devote our leisure time to God for just ten days will produce amazing results. To find our joy in Christ for ten days, rather than in the television set, can be the beginning of a whole new spiritual walk. Consider how just ten days of *spiritual* facial hair growth can radically change our spiritual appearance, and take us on a deeper spiritual journey for the rest of our lives. Just ten days!

Sex—The Mystery of All Mysteries

"Sex sells!" That is the slogan of Hollywood, magazines, television, and the internet. Sex is ubiquitous. Virtually everywhere we turn, the allure of sex manages to subtly entice or overtly titillate. Men especially can be preoccupied with thoughts of sex and driven with such powerful desires in this area that they have been known to risk everything to satisfy their sexual urges. Marriages, careers, bank accounts, health and even lives have been lost because of this tremendous built-in craving deep within the psyche and make-up of all mankind.

Why is this erotic and passionate longing within the human heart so powerful, and at times, overwhelming? Both the evolutionist and the creationist may hastily respond it is due to the necessity of procreation, claiming that without this enormous drive, men and women would not reproduce, and the inevitable result would be extinction. However, this is merely stating the obvious; it does not begin to unravel the profound mystery underlying the human sex drive. The authors of the Bible (particularly the apostle Paul) have unlocked this mysterious question and have laid bare what lies at the heart of human sexuality. Paul's assertions are so poignant that on the surface they appear almost blasphemous or sacrilegious. He writes:

> Do you not know that the one who joins himself to a prostitute is one body with her? For [God] says, "The two shall become one flesh." But the one who joins himself to the Lord is one spirit with Him. (1 Corinthians 6:16-17)

The Bible repeatedly suggests the sexual union between a husband and wife is a mysterious reflection of the "one-spirit" union between God and His people, or Christ and His church. In the Old Testament, Israel is referred to as the wife of Jehovah God, and in the New Testament, the church is referred to as the bride of Christ. Paul tells us this spiritual union is a mystical phenomenon that mirrors the "one-flesh" experience of a married couple (Ephesians 5:22-33).

Furthermore, the Scriptures tell us over and over again that "God is a jealous God" who will not tolerate a rival (Exodus 20:5; 34:14; Numbers 25:11; Joshua 24:19). James declares if we claim to belong to God, and yet put anyone or anything before Him, we become "adulteresses" and are acting with hostility toward Him. He said that God "jealously desires the spirit which He has made to dwell in us" (James 4:4-5).

It was the great theologian Augustine who said, "O Lord … our heart is restless until it rests in You."[3] Just as a human heart yearns for sexual fulfillment, so the human spirit craves union with God. The devil is utterly enraged with this truth. He is so filled with contempt and driven by infernal malice toward man's one-spirit union with God that He goads and entices fallen men and women everywhere to engage in every imaginable form of sexual perversion. He delights in abasing the sex act because it mocks and degrades this spiritual ecstasy between a soul and its maker.

Whether it is fornication, adultery, homosexuality, pedophilia, bestiality, orgies, or any other sexual activity that perverts God's original design, Satan delights in promoting and encouraging these behaviors because they defile God's spiritual union with man. The more depraved the sex act, the more it mocks God's original intent and the more it pleases the powers of darkness.

Man's sex drive is so powerful because it profoundly points to the very reason he was made: to know, love and serve God with his whole heart, mind, soul and strength (Deuteronomy 6:5). Jesus said that to love God with all of one's heart, mind, soul and strength is the greatest commandment (Matthew 22:37). This is what lies at the bottom of the sex act—union with God in one's spirit. Therefore, every form of idolatry and idol worship becomes an act of spiritual infidelity.

Is this not the most profound mystery you have ever reflected upon? It truly becomes the mystery of all mysteries when we seriously contemplate the depths and implications of this reality and realize the spiritual fruit that can be produced out of this union with God.

D'Ambrosio, Marcellino. "Our Heart Is Restless." *The Crossroads Initiative*. Crossroads Productions, Inc., n.d. Web. 04 Dec. 2013.

Purple Hearts Speak for Themselves

Having been in the Marine Corps and in Vietnam, and having gone through infantry training, jungle training and 50-caliber machine gun school, I hope that my experiences will validate my perspective.

I am sure that a number of military veterans would disagree with me, but in my opinion, the Purple Heart is the highest honor a soldier could possibly receive. Although the "Medal of Honor," the "Silver Star," the "Navy Cross," the "Bronze Star," and other military decorations may rank higher than a Purple Heart, the bottom line is that a Purple Heart needs no explaining. It speaks volumes without saying a word, declaring a soldier fought brutal battles and mingled his blood with the dirt and the sweat of his comrades on the battlefield. The Purple Heart is the greatest compliment a soldier could receive because it shows he gave his all for his country, whether he lived to tell about it or not.

Yet regardless of what earthly wars men and women may have fought, it is not the real battle; it is not the real fight; it is not the real war. The epicenter of every war throughout all of history has been the spiritual war. No other combat has been fought so hard, lasted for so long, cost so much, and resulted in more casualties than the conflict between God and the devil, and the struggle between good and evil.

The battles have been innumerable and the body count without number. All the combined wars of history cannot compare with what is at stake in this spiritual warfare. It's not territory, wealth, fame or principle involved here; rather, eternal souls. Nothing is more valuable, and nothing is more costly than a human soul—absolutely nothing! It was Jesus Himself who said, "What does it profit a man if he gains the whole world and forfeits his soul?" (Matthew 16:26).

Anyone who claims to be a follower of Christ has, in essence, enlisted in God's army, and the Bible tells us, "There is no discharge in the time of war" (Ecclesiastes 8:8). Whether we like it or not, or even believe it or not, if we are walking on this planet, we are in the midst of this unseen war. The only remaining question is, on whose side are we fighting in the age-old conflict? We are either an asset or a liability to Christ in this war; He said if we are not with Him, then we are against Him (Matthew 12:30). There is no demilitarized zone in this supernatural warfare, and anyone who deserts their God-given post has gone over to the enemy's side.

Thus, it was the apostle Paul who said if we are to stand firm in this battle, we need to put on the full armor of God because "our struggle is not against flesh and blood, but against the rulers, against the powers, against the world forces of this darkness, against the spiritual forces of wickedness in the heavenly places" (Ephesians 6:12).

Furthermore, Paul told Timothy to "suffer hardship with [him] as a good soldier of Christ Jesus," and "[not to entangle] himself in the affairs of everyday life, so that he may please the one who enlisted him as a soldier" (2 Timothy 2:3-4). Paul then went on to tell Timothy that he himself had fought the good fight, and because of his sacrifices as a soldier, Jesus was going to award him with a crown of righteousness (4:7-8). In addition, Jesus said,

> Blessed are you when people insult you and persecute you, and falsely say all kinds of evil against you because of Me. Rejoice and be glad, for your reward in heaven is great; for in the same way they persecuted the prophets who were before you. (Matthew 5:11-12)

Jesus also promised a crown of life to his followers who were martyred for His name's sake. This martyr's crown is heaven's Purple Heart. It is the ultimate decoration in this spiritual war because without saying a word, it says you gave your all for Christ. It silently proclaims you were there when the battles were being fought, and you have the wounds and scars to prove it.

The most decorated war hero on earth is soon forgotten, along with his many medals for bravery, but a heavenly Purple Heart will never lose its significance. Its glory will never fade because there is no greater honor or privilege than to give your all for Christ in this epic conflict between good and evil.

A Beauty Pageant for the Feet

Unless someone has a real foot fetish, chances are most people don't look at another person's feet. Beauty contests are never about feet; rather, every other part of the human body. Hair, face, arms, breasts, hips, abdomen and legs are evaluated and judged—but certainly not feet. Virtually no one notices them. Shoes, maybe. But feet?
Never!

God looks very closely at a person's feet, however, and has something to say about them. For instance, the Lord said through His prophet Isaiah:

> How lovely on the mountains are the feet of him who brings good news, who announces peace and brings good news of happiness, who announces salvation, and says to Zion, "Your God reigns!" (Isaiah 52:7)

The apostle Paul paraphrased these words of Isaiah when he asked in Romans 10, how will people know about God and His salvation unless someone proceeds on their feet and tells others of the good news of redemption? He said, "How beautiful are the feet of those who bring good news of good things!" (vv. 14-15).

In short, God says anyone who goes forth and shares the good news of the gospel has beautiful feet. Secondly, God looks closely at the feet of men and women because their feet have everything to do with their walk. The Bible relates a lot about a person's life to a walk.
For example,

"Walk by the spirit" (Galatians 5:16)

"Walk humbly" (Micah 6:8)

"Walk in My instruction" (Exodus 16:4)

"Walk in My statutes" (Leviticus 26:3)

"Walk before Me in truth" (1 Kings 2:4)

"Walk in the Light" (1 John 1:7)

"Walk by faith" (2 Corinthians 5:7)

"Walk in love" (Ephesians 5:2)

"Walk as children of Light" (Ephesians 5:8)

Dozens of other Scripture verses speak of a person's walk, including such negative statements like, "The wicked strut about on every side," "The fool walks in darkness," and, "Even when the fool walks along the road, his sense is lacking and he demonstrates to everyone that he is a fool" (Psalm 12:8; Ecclesiastes 2:14; 10:3).

Walking denotes making definite progress, in a definite direction, at a definite pace. Our walk is simply either taking us to heaven or leading us to hell. Is it any wonder, then, that God's beauty pageant has everything to do with feet, while the beauty contests of men focus on everything but feet? Likewise, the Lord said to Samuel, "Man looks at the outward appearance, but the Lord looks at the heart" (1 Samuel 16:7). God gazes at a man's heart because He knows wherever a man's heart is, his feet will surely follow. The ancient Chinese adage says it all when it declares, "The journey of a thousand miles begins with a single step." Every soul's eternal destiny is determined by its feet.

While the judges and spectators at a beauty pageant or a Miss America contest evaluate each contestant from the ankles up, God is looking at the feet—because therein lies one's true beauty or flaws in the eyes of heaven.

Muscles and a Mustache

Imagine saying to a woman, "You have everything a man would want—muscles and a mustache!" Obviously no man in his right mind would say such a thing to a woman, and no woman in her right mind would perceive such a statement as a compliment. Why? Because it's an insult, and unless a woman truly desires to be a man, she is not likely to want to look like a man.

God made men to be physically bigger, faster, and stronger than most women because He has ordained and equipped men for leadership. He has fashioned men to defend, to protect, to provide, and to decide. Furthermore, God has commanded that men's strength be used in servitude and their manhood be rooted in self-sacrifice. Even within the church, the Bible clearly states that men are to lead and women are to follow (see 1 Timothy 2:11-14; 1 Corinthians 14:34-37).

Throughout the ages, though, women have often demonstrated more spiritual strength than men. Women stood at the foot of the cross when almost all the apostles ran away in fear, they were the first ones at the tomb of the risen Christ, and they were the first ones to believe in His resurrection and witness to men about it (see John 19:23-27; Matthew 28:1-10; Luke 24:1-11). It was to a woman that Christ first appeared after He rose from the grave; it was very often women who provided for Jesus' needs, and at Christ's trial before Pilate, only a woman had the courage to come to Jesus' defense (see John 20:11-17; Luke 8:1-3; Matthew 27:19). Lastly, only a woman understood what Jesus meant when he talked about His death (see Matthew 26:12).

Let's face it, women have often been the backbone of the church. They have proven themselves to be more spiritual than most men and have been less intimidated than men when it comes to sharing their faith and filling the pews at church. So on Judgment Day, don't be surprised if more women than men are honored by God because even though Peter calls women the "weaker vessel" they often show more spiritual muscles and manly attributes than men (1 Peter 3:7, KJV).

Consequently, if you ever hear a "foolish" man say to a beautiful woman that she has muscles and a mustache, he may very well be right if she is mightier in spirit than he is—and she may very well take it as a compliment!

.

Can a Corpse Dig Its Own Grave?

The expression "dead man walking" originated within America's prison system many years ago when a man condemned to die was escorted from his prison cell, wearing handcuffs and shackled in leg irons, and with guards surrounding him, he would be taking his last steps on earth to his place of execution. As he passed the jail cells of other imprisoned men, they would call out to one another, "dead man walking!" He was still very much alive, but he was as good as dead because his time had run out.

Another sad reality is there have been a number of people throughout history who were forced to dig their own graves just before they were executed. This happened time and again under Nazism where Jews, political prisoners, and so-called "enemies of the state" were forced to dig the very hole in which they were about to be buried. In essence, they were dead men digging their own graves.

Of interest, too, are the many examples given in the Bible, depicting "dead men walking." People can be very much alive physically, yet at the same time, be very dead spiritually. Once there was a man who very much wanted to follow Jesus but said he first needed to bury his father. Christ looked right at him and said, "Follow Me; and let the dead bury their dead" (Matthew 8:21-22). When Paul wrote to Timothy about promiscuous women he said, "She who gives herself to wanton pleasure is dead even while she lives (1 Timothy 5:6); he also said to Timothy that Christ was someday going to "judge the living and the dead" (2 Timothy 4:1). He furthermore told the Romans to present themselves "to God as those alive from the dead" (Romans 6:13).

Jude referred to some wicked men in the early church as being "doubly dead" and Paul wrote to the Ephesians telling them to "arise from the dead and Christ will shine on you" (Jude 12; Ephesians 5:14). John tells us in the book of Revelation that he "saw the dead, the great and the small, standing before the throne" of judgment, and that hell will eventually give up its dead (or its unsaved souls) and they will be judged (Revelation 20:12-13).

So you see? It is very possible for a dead person to dig his own grave. Even on a purely physical level we can see the truth of this. If someone says, "He is digging his own grave," we understand he is engaging in an activity that will eventually kill him. Well, spiritually dead people constantly engage in sinful activities that will lead them to "the second death," which is eternal separation from God in hell.

Therefore, whenever someone rejects Christ, he is surely a dead man walking, and anyone refusing to repent of his sins is a corpse digging its own grave.

The Naked Evolutionist

Perhaps the biggest hoax ever perpetrated upon mankind is Darwin's theory of evolution. If it is not the greatest scam to which the world has ever succumbed, it certainly ranks among the top ten most colossal frauds in history. Is this not a bold statement? This is the kind of volatile claim that provokes some of the most vicious reactions imaginable. To come right out and declare, "Darwinism is nothing but a massive Ponzi scheme which swindles everyone who buys into it!" is to invite hostility and ridicule from every corner—including jeers from some within the church—and to be labeled as a fool or an ignoramus (on the same level as the simpletons who once believed the world was flat or the sun revolved around the earth). They are silenced with laughter and intimidated with derision.

Do you know why everyone who disagrees with the theory of evolution is hushed with scorn and muted with vicious antagonism? It is because Darwinism has been dressed up in "science" and cloaked in "academia"; it has been fitted with the gown of "scholarship" and attired with the clothing of "knowledge." As a result, few dare dispute the claims of evolution, in utter fear of being called stupid or labeled as idiotic.

However, before I continue with this assertion, let me digress for ten seconds and make it abundantly clear that the evolution to which I am referring is macro, not micro. Macroevolution (Darwinism) is the process of evolving from one species into another species; whereas, microevolution can be seen every day, everywhere. Cross a red rose with a white rose and you get a pink rose; cross a mother's genes with a father's genes and the fertilized egg will produce a hybrid of the parents. This is microevolution, and that's not what I am disputing. The fraud of macroevolution dressed up in the fashionable clothing of "science" and outfitted in the costume of "higher education" is what I'm refuting.

We have all heard about the fairy-tale king with no clothes. Remember? This was the very vain and pompous emperor who was obsessed with wearing the finest, most luxurious clothes in the world. Every time he would purchase a new set of clothing, he would summon his entire kingdom to watch him parade up and down the street and applaud his one-man fashion show. One day, a very clever and deceitful tailor rode into town and convinced the foolish king that he could make for him the most fabulous clothes the world had ever seen. He conned the emperor into believing that his new clothes were so dazzling and so impressive that only sophisticated, cultured, and very intelligent people could see them, and anyone who was stupid, unrefined and ignorant would be unable to observe them.

Well the rest of the story is history. The proud and gullible ruler summoned everyone in his kingdom to view his very unique and stunning vestments. Everyone was informed ahead of time that his garments were so splendid and so majestic that only people who were refined and enlightened could see them. So this dupe goes strutting up and down the street in his birthday suit, and no one dares say that the fool is buck naked, lest they appear stupid in the midst of so many "intelligent" people. It takes the innocence and brutal honesty of a little child to blurt out, "He ain't got no clothes on!" to open eyes and inspire the rest of the crowd to see and state the obvious.

Similarly, the so-called "evidence" to support the theory of macroevolution is so feeble and manufactured that its claims are truly laughable. The only possible way to prop up the foolish theories of Darwinism is to dress them up in the impressive clothing of "science." However, Darwinism is not good science; it is junk science! It's the curtain that the Wizard of Oz hides behind while he intimidates anyone who dares to disagree with him. Pull back the curtain of junk science, and we discover there are no transitional fossils—not one! Virtually every claim of macroevolution is propped up with words like "perhaps," "likely," "possibly," and "it appears." Darwinism is riddled from beginning to end with assumptions, hypotheses, speculations, and suppositions.

On the other hand, genuine science supports the evidence for intelligent design and creationism.[4] Junk science is nothing more than imaginary clothing that is outfitted for a fool. As long as the gullible masses are intimidated into going along with the naked charade of evolution, it's going to require someone who is not afraid to be called "ignorant" to open the eyes of those around him.

See *Darwin's Black Box: The Biochemical Challenge to Evolution* by Michael Behe (The Free Press, 1996).

Other books on this subject I would also recommend are *The Human Difference* by John Allan (Lion Publishing Corporation, 1989), *When Science Fails* by John Hudson Tiner (Baker Book House Company, 1974), *Creation or Evolution?* by the staff at Plain Truth Ministries (Plain Truth Ministries

—Worldwide, 1996)

My Favorite Color Is Black

The only reason black is my favorite color is because no one has invented a darker one. Does this sound a bit morbid or depressing? Well, it should. Black is the color people traditionally wear at funerals and associate with burial ceremonies; there is even a whole subculture today of young people who enjoy dying their hair jet-black, and wearing black makeup and black clothing. They like to be referred to as "Goths" or "Gothic" because of the medieval gloom and sinisterness it projects. They often wear chains and/or sport tattoos of skeletons, swastikas, or skulls and crossbones because they delight in shocking people with their offensive appearance and bizarre behavior. Anything associating them with death, especially the color black, makes them stand out and they relish the attention it generates.

Did you know the Bible actually commends people who think much about death and who reflect often on dying? I am not talking about Goths, however, who merely have a fetish about death in order to attract attention to themselves. Indeed, the Bible is referring to those who look at life through the spectacles of death and who seriously ponder the reality of the grave.

The wisest of all wise men, King Solomon, once wrote,

> A good name is better than a good ointment, and the day of one's death is better than the day of one's birth. It is better to go to a house of mourning [funeral parlor] than to go to a house of feasting [partying] because that is the end of every man, and the living [spiritual person] takes it to heart. Sorrow is better than laughter, for when a face is sad a heart may be happy. The mind of the wise is in the house of mourning, while the mind of fools is in the house of pleasure. (Ecclesiastes 7:1-4)

Our culture suggests it is morbid and unhealthy to meditate on death and to contemplate dying, but God says to do it, and do it often. He says only a fool thinks of the here and now, and only a person lacking sense ignores the inevitability of his own death. Shallow people think often of partying, while deep people habitually reflect upon the Grim Reaper and his stare. Perhaps this is the reason black is my favorite color—the one most often associated with death—because death is something we always need to be mindful of, not in a morbid or unhealthy sense, but in a sober and serious way.

Go ahead and select a black outfit to wear at the next funeral, realizing it is not just a sign of mourning for the dead; it's a color we should perhaps wear more often as a reminder of our own impending demise. After all, the Scriptures admonish, "It is appointed for men to die once and after this comes judgment" (Hebrews 9:27).

The Memory of a Flashbulb

If you were to hear a random phone number right now, what are the chances you would be able to repeat it a minute later? You probably couldn't do so, simply because we all have the memory of a flashbulb. As fast as it takes to blink an eye, or as quickly as it takes for the light to flash on a camera, is about how rapidly we can forget things. You don't think so? When someone is introduced to you, how quickly does his or her name escape you? Can you recall the text of last Sunday's sermon or how about the name and theme of the last book you read or movie you saw?

Chances are we have already forgotten these things. At best, we would really need to concentrate in order to remember even half of what transpired. It is truly astounding, isn't it? Some people may boast of having a photographic memory, but even what they manage to recall is often very selective and very short-lived. God knows just how terrible the human attention span can be; thus, He gave the people of Israel some very strict orders and very sound advice regarding this:

> These words, which I am commanding you today, shall be on your heart. You shall teach them diligently to your sons and shall talk of them when you sit in your house and when you walk by the way and when you lie down and when you rise up. You shall bind them as a sign on your hand and they shall be as frontals on your forehead. You shall write them on the doorposts of your house and on your gates.

> Then it shall come about when the Lord your God brings you into the land which He swore to your fathers, Abraham, Isaac, and Jacob, to give you, great and splendid cities which you did not build, and houses full of all good things which you did not fill, and hewn cisterns which you did not dig, vineyards and olive trees which you did not plant, and you eat and are satisfied, then watch yourself, that you do not forget the Lord who brought you from the land of

Egypt, out of the house of slavery. (Deuteronomy 6:6-12)

God cautioned His people that they must exercise memorization techniques both day and night, or they would surely forget Him. He warned that the memory of Him would be especially bad in times of prosperity and happiness. Why? Because wealth, success and material things make us feel independent from God, and when we have an abundance and our bellies are full, we are likely to think to ourselves, *Who needs God, and why should I obey Him?*

This is exactly what has happened to America. This country was once the most prosperous and powerful nation on earth, but our success and materialism have veiled our dependency on Him. Look at us now—we no longer read, study, or meditate upon His Word every day, so we have forgotten Him—exactly what he admonished us would happen. And the devil knows, "Out of sight, out of mind!" So he has done a thorough job stamping out God and His Word everywhere! Christ and the Bible have been run out of our schools, out of our courts, out of our businesses and our homes, and in some cases, even out of our churches—all because we no longer exalt His Word by regularly reminding ourselves of what He has told us. Even if we do claim to believe in the Bible, many of us refuse to take it seriously.

Consequently, the only way we can truly remember God, especially in times of prosperity, is to take seriously the words of Jesus Christ when He said, "Man does not live on bread alone, but on every word that proceeds out of the mouth of God" (Deuteronomy 8:3; Matthew 4:4).

It was Agur who said in the book of Proverbs,

> Two things I asked of You, do not refuse me before I die:
> Keep deception and lies far from me, give me neither
> poverty nor riches; feed me with the food that is my portion,
> that I not be full and deny You and say, "Who is the Lord?"
> or that I not be in want and steal, and profane the name of
> my God. (30:7-9)

This man knew if he received more than just the essentials in life, he would likely forget God and say, "Who is the Lord?" Look at the pharaoh of Moses' day—he was the richest, most powerful and most influential man on the planet, and when Moses told him the Lord said to "let My people [Israel] go," Pharaoh just sneered and said, "Who is the Lord, that I should obey Him?" (Exodus 5:2,

NIV). That's what happens to almost all men who become rich and prosperous —They forget God and have no interest in what He has to say. The Bible does tell of several men who were the exception to this; among others, they were Job, Daniel, and Joseph. Unlike them, however, most men and most nations will forget God when their appetites are satisfied and their prosperity is renowned.

So the next time you can't remember a phone number that was just told to you, let it serve as a reminder that we have the memory of a flashbulb, and that's just how quickly we can forget God and what He has said. In a flash He will leave our minds if we fail to take the diligent steps He told us to, especially when our stomachs are full.

The New Math

Perhaps similar analogies have been used by others, but this illustration is worth repeating, especially since our present day educational system is so intent on this new form of calculating. I call it "the new math of science."

Just imagine enrolling in a math class where on the very first day of instruction, the professor proclaims to his students, "There is no number twelve." This is the first thing he tells his class, and for an entire week this is all he teaches his pupils. "Twelve does not exist—it's a fabrication. Only an ignorant, foolish, and superstitious simpleton believes there is a number twelve." Day after day, the professor virtually brainwashes and intimidates his class into repeating this "scientific mantra" that number twelve has never existed, does not exist, and will never exist.

After months of this type of mathematical lecturing, the tutor then gives his students their final exam. The test includes a number of computations, such as 8+4, 6+6, 11+1, 17-5, 100-88, 35-30+7, and 24÷2, all equating to the same number. Now the response cannot be 12 because "the number 12 does not exist." Anyone who dares to answer "12" will automatically fail the class. Do you see what is happening here? The answer has been eliminated before the question is even asked. Therefore, the answer just becomes relative to whatever anyone wants it to be (as long as it doesn't amount to the number 12).

Well, this is the new math of many scientists, teachers, and philosophers today. This new math insists that the God of the Bible (or the God of Creation) "does not exist"; therefore, whatever conclusions to the meaning or purpose of life people devise are all of equal value—everything is relative. Although this relativism may have been around for centuries, it all adds up to the "new math."

Of course the rebuttal to all of this reasoning is that numbers do not lie and that mathematics is a proven science of numbers, while the existence of God cannot be verified by any scientific method. However, that is just the point. The possibility of intelligent design *can* be demonstrated mathematically when dealing with the mathematical laws of probability. Consider how the existence of some subatomic particles can only be deduced mathematically (though they cannot be seen, even by some of our most powerful microscopes); likewise, we can deduce the existence of an intelligent creator because the mathematical probability of all of life coming into existence by pure chance is so astronomically remote as to be impossible.

Did you know the word "number" is used almost 300 times in Scripture? Additionally, when the numbers become inconceivable, God compares their incalculable figures to the uncountable stars in the heavens, dust of the ground, and sands of the seashore (Genesis 15:5; 22:17; Jeremiah 33:22; Revelation 20:8). God is a God of numbers. Jesus divulges to us that even the hairs on a person's head are all numbered (Matthew 10:30; Luke 12:7). It is not just that someone might have 250,000 strands of hair, but that each and every strand has a number assigned to it by God!

By applying the laws of mathematical probability, the existence of an intelligent designer can be verified by numbers. Furthermore, any professor who declares that God does not exist is on the same level as a mathematician foolish enough to insist that the number twelve is non-existent. Both have ruled out the answers before the questions are even posed. Now how smart is that?

The Poorest Millionaire

Money! Most people can't stop thinking about it, talking about it and imagining having lots of it. Its allure is everywhere, and there is absolutely nothing on earth men have not done for money. People will lie, cheat, steal, kill, compromise their morals, alter their values, and prostitute their very lives for money. The poor crave it, the middle class strive for it, and the rich want more of it. Even old, wise Solomon said, "Money is the answer to everything" (Ecclesiastes 10:19).

God Himself has a lot to say about money. Time and again He warns of its tenacity and deceitfulness:

> He who loves money will not be satisfied with money, nor he who loves abundance with its income. (Ecclesiastes 5:10)

> Those who want to get rich fall into temptation and a snare and many foolish and harmful desires which plunge men into ruin and destruction. For the love of money is a root of all sorts of evil, and some by longing for it have wandered away from the faith and pierced themselves with many griefs. (1 Timothy 6:9-10)

> Riches are deceitful and can choke out the spiritual lives of people. (Matthew 13:22)

> It is easier for a camel to go through the eye of a needle, than for a rich man to enter the kingdom of God. (Matthew 19:24)

> Do not weary yourself to gain wealth, cease from your consideration of it. When you set your eyes on it, it is gone. For wealth certainly makes itself wings like an eagle that flies toward the heavens. (Proverbs 23:4-5)

Literally dozens of other Scriptures deal with the issues of money, wealth, and riches, because few other things in life can so powerfully compete against our relationship with God. Money has become a god that rivals almost all other gods. It doesn't matter if it's the American dollar, the Russian ruble, the Japanese yen, or the euro of many countries; money in any language is an all-powerful idol that men worship and for which many will do almost anything when it comes to paying homage to her.

Man's only hope of escaping wealth's seduction is to "learn the secret of being content" (Philippians 4:11). Being appreciative and truly thankful for what God has given us in life is our only hope of escaping the deceitful charms and hypnotic draw of this seductress. Nothing but gratefulness can empower us to break free of her forceful grip and suffocating embrace—nothing else. Unless we learn to sincerely appreciate God and recognize all He has done for us, then our chances of averting the powerful grip of this goddess of riches are slim to none. Consequently, it's always good to take inventory of God's blessings.

The first thing we need to ask ourselves is, *Have I anything in life I would not be willing to part with for a million dollars?* Would you be willing to give up your eyesight for a million dollars? Would you be willing to forego your hearing for a million dollars? How about your arms, legs, health, or children or your mental faculties? Just how many things do you possess in life that you would not be willing to surrender for a million dollars, or ten million dollars, or even a billion dollars?

Even the poorest of the world's poor have been blessed by God with features they would not be willing to give in exchange for any sum of riches. To that end, we are all extremely rich, even the most destitute among us. We just need the good grace to see it and a grateful heart toward God to appreciate it.

Spiritual Liposuction

Cosmetic surgery has become a multibillion-dollar industry where people are literally flocking to have nose jobs, bigger lips, smaller ears, larger breasts and enhanced sexual organs. From head to toe, the promise of surgical reconstruction awaits anyone who can afford the cost of the procedure.

People put such tremendous emphasis upon outward appearance nowadays that they are willing to pay anything, endure any pain, and invest any amount of time in order to improve their looks. In the midst of all of this nipping and tucking, the surgical procedure of liposuction has become very popular and commonplace. Furthermore, every research and latest survey tells us that most Americans are overweight and obesity is epidemic, even among children. We are told even the majority of American dogs are overweight!

It doesn't take a genius with a PhD to know why obesity is on the rise. We can blame our excess baggage on our genes all day long, but, apart from a hormonal imbalance, the unpleasant reality is people are putting on the pounds because we either eat too much or exercise too little (or both).

Diet books always become bestsellers, but regardless of what they promise, there is no really successful diet known to man other than reducing calories and increasing mobility. Liposuction is becoming more and more prevalent because it surgically removes excess fatty tissue without the painful cost of exercise and without the self-denial of dieting. It's the magic bullet when it comes to instant weight loss and looking trim. No other procedure guarantees such immediate results.

On the other hand, it's too bad no one has yet invented a similar technique for spiritual flabbiness and obesity of the soul. If people constantly feed on junk food and overindulge when it comes to sleeping, eating, and drinking, the consequences are going to be apparent to all. If our spiritual lives are characterized by constantly feeding on the junk food of television and the enticements of the internet, then our souls are going to eventually show it. If we continuously indulge our fleshly appetites with self-gratification and worldly amusements, then our spirits are obviously going to reflect this. In other words, if we seldom exercise the core of our being with spiritual disciplines, then our bloated, out-of-shape inner man will become very evident. The apostle Paul said,

> Do you not know that those who run in a race all run, but only one receives the prize? Run in such a way that you may win. Everyone who competes in the games exercises self-control in all things. They then do it to receive a perishable wreath, but we an imperishable. Therefore I run in such a way, as not without aim; I box in such a way, as not beating the air; but I discipline my body and make it my slave, so that, after I have preached to others, I myself will not be disqualified. (1 Corinthians 9:24-27)

Paul tells us that bodily discipline has its advantages and rewards in this temporal life, but the spiritual disciplines are what are most important in regards to our eternal lives. There are no shortcuts, though—no instant procedures or magic bullets—when it comes to spiritual fitness and godly attractiveness. It's discipline, discipline, discipline! "[Working] out [our] salvation with fear and trembling" (Philippians 2:12) involves hard labor. Endurance and perseverance are necessary to grow spiritually, and it takes discipline and self-denial to become mighty in spirit.

There is no spiritual liposuction for the flabby soul, and there is no quick method to becoming Christ-like in our spiritual lives. The strength and fitness of a soul depend solely on the amount of discipline we exert when it comes to prayer, Bible study, fellowship, good works, and "walking" humbly with the Lord Jesus Christ. Self-control, not wonder pills, will fashion us into dynamic warriors in the ranks of heaven.

Ancient Boundary Marks

No less than four times in the Old Testament does God forbid anyone from moving the boundary marks (or landmarks) of another person's property (Deuteronomy 19:14; 27:17; Proverbs 22:28; 23:10). Through the casting of the lot, God determined which land, and how much of it, was to be given to each tribe, each clan, and specifically every family of Israel. God's people were then to mark off their allotted portions of land with markers, and those boundary markers were never to be moved.

If your neighbor had a creek, a well, or a fertile patch of ground on his estate, you were never to move the land markers of his or your property line in order to appropriate for yourself what rightfully belonged to someone else. To do so would bring a divine curse upon you, for God would severely judge anyone who engaged in such dishonesty (see Deuteronomy 27:17).

Well, thousands of years have come and gone. All the ancient boundary markers of God's people, Israel, have been eradicated due to wars, natural disasters, neglect and the never-ending encroachment of the wilderness. One thing, however, has not changed throughout the centuries: God's ancient boundary marks of morality. God is the same yesterday, today, and tomorrow, and therefore His ethical standards continue to mark off the boundaries He has set in regards to right and wrong and what is good and evil in His sight.

The world has historically attempted to move God's moral markers; even more so today, as there is a growing groundswell of people all around who are moving His property lines in every which way. This is especially blatant in the area of homosexuality and gay marriage. From the Old Testament to the New, God has clearly condemned this lifestyle. Genesis 19:1-29; Leviticus 18:22; 20:13; Romans 1:26-27; 1 Corinthians 6:9; 1 Timothy 1:10; 2 Peter 2:6; and Jude 7 divulge His ancient boundary marks in regards to this immoral behavior. Therefore, anyone who dares shift or remove these divine landmarks comes under a heavenly curse.

I must now briefly address the inevitable argument surely to be used in countering what I am saying about God's moral landmarks. God's moral laws are not the same as God's ceremonial laws. The ceremonial laws were not boundary markers; rather, beacon lights pointing us to Christ. As Paul tells us in Galatians 3,

> Before faith came, we were kept in custody under the law, being shut up to the faith which was later to be revealed. Therefore the law has become our tutor to lead us to Christ, so that we may be justified by faith. But now that faith has come, we are no longer under a tutor. (vv. 23-25)

In other words, the ceremonial laws—such as forbidden foods, Sabbath observances, cleansing rituals, mandatory executions, and dress codes—were the tutors pointing us to faith in Jesus Christ. These laws have been fulfilled in Christ. No longer are people to be given the death sentence for breaking the Sabbath, committing adultery or engaging in any number of forbidden activities. However, the spiritual principles still apply and God's moral laws are still intact. His moral laws are His land markers and they have not changed and are not to be moved. Paul stated these clearly as well:

> Or do you not know that the unrighteous will not inherit the kingdom of God? Do not be deceived; neither fornicators, nor idolaters, nor adulterers, nor effeminate [crossdressers], nor homosexuals, nor thieves, nor the covetous, nor drunkards, nor revilers, nor swindlers, will inherit the kingdom of God. (1 Corinthians 6:9-10)

> We know that the law [boundary mark] is good, if one uses it lawfully, realizing the fact that law is not made for a righteous person, but for those who are lawless and rebellious, for the ungodly and sinners, for the unholy and profane, for those who kill their fathers or mothers, for murderers and immoral men and homosexuals and kidnappers and liars and perjurers, and whatever else is contrary to sound teaching. (1 Timothy 1:8-10)

Needless to say, God's moral standards have not changed. They are His ancient boundary marks that are never to be moved or altered in any way. Not long ago I was listening to a radio talk show discussing whether or not gay marriage should be legalized in the state of California. A homosexual person on the program absolutely insisted marriage between two people of the same gender should be legalized because they love one another, and therefore should not be denied that "right."

A caller phoned in and asked the homosexual advocate if polygamy should also be legalized, since individuals in that lifestyle could love each other as well. This champion of gay rights then said, "No! Polygamy should not be legalized because it does not involve two committed people." *Well, why not?* was my immediate thought. See, if God says that something is wrong and someone else comes up and says, "I am telling you that God is wrong!" then he has just moved God's ancient boundary mark. Thus, he is in no position to prohibit anyone else from moving it in a different location, regardless of how far out that location may be.

Once the landmark has been uprooted and moved, then it should be allowed to be moved by anyone and for any reason. A pedophile should be allowed to marry a child, a dog owner should be permitted to marry his pet, a narcissist should be granted authorization to marry himself, and a polygamist should have the right to marry multiple partners. They could all use the same homosexual argument that "they love each other, and failure to include them would be hateful, discriminatory, and intolerant."

To say the least, this will undoubtedly inflame hostility from the homosexual community; however, they must admit the airtight logic of this argument. They cannot defiantly move God's moral standards to include their lifestyle and then deny anyone else their "right" to do the same. Once the boundary line has been moved, it's up for grabs for anyone and everyone to move it again, and again and again. Their justifications for doing so should apply to anyone in any lifestyle; it's only fair. Wouldn't you agree? To argue the contrary would be hypocritical and disingenuous at best, and downright "hateful and intolerant" at worst.

Marriage Is the Perfect Storm

How many jokes have you heard about marriage? Wisecracks abound about the oldest institution in human history. Here are just a few examples of what I am talking about:

> "When a man steals your wife, there is no better revenge than to let him keep her."

> "Husbands and wives are like two sides of the same coin—they can't face each other, but they still stay together."

> A desperate old maid put an ad in the classifieds saying, "Husband wanted." The next day she got a thousand responses from women saying, "You can have mine!"

> "I had some words with my wife and she had some paragraphs with me."

> "I've had bad luck with both my husbands. The first one left me and the second one didn't."

> "My wife and I were happy for twenty years. Then we met!"

> First Guy: "My wife made me a millionaire!"
> Second Guy: "Oh really? How did she do that?"
> First Guy: "Before I met her, I was a billionaire!"

> First Guy: "My wife is an angel."
> Second Guy: "You're lucky; mine is still alive!"

We may snicker or chuckle at these but underneath, dwells a sobering reality: Men and women are so different that handcuffing them together for a lifetime can become a breeding ground for conflict and a formula for disaster. Doesn't sound very romantic, does it? Sadly, it is often the case. Men and women were created unalike—anatomically, mentally and emotionally. If God designed male and female differences to complement one another, where did all the conflict come from? Why are over fifty percent of the marriages today destined to become shipwrecked, and so many other marriages something to be endured, rather than enjoyed?

It is because of mankind's fall. The first married couple on earth chose to do things their way instead of God's way. Their rebellion did not make them into "gods" (contrary to what Satan promised); rather, their disobedience opened up a Pandora's box of troubles they could not have imagined possible.

Not only did man's work become laborious and sweat-producing, but also henceforth, women would experience pain during childbirth. To make matters worse because of this mutiny, now someone had to be in charge and someone had to submit. Before the fall there was a leaderless coexistence between the man and the woman—nothing but harmony and cooperation, selfless giving and mutual edification. They were always on the same page, heading in the same direction and walking hand in hand at the same pace, but all of this harmonious unity came to a screeching halt once they defied their creator's command.

God announced to the woman her desire would be for her husband, and that he would rule over her (see Genesis 3:16). The word "desire" is the same word God used when he warned Cain about his hatred toward his brother, Abel. He said, "Sin is crouching at the door, and its *desire* is for you, but you must master it" (4:7).

The "desire" that God was speaking of to both Eve and Cain was the desire to control. Eve now desired to control Adam and sin desired to control Cain. Is this not a formula for calamity, when the husband is to rule over the wife and the wife's desire is to control the husband? Because all men and women have fallen natures, they are naturally selfish, egotistical, proud, lustful, covetous, and stubborn. Like it or not, this is the very unflattering and unpleasant truth; even an honest atheist, who takes a candid look at himself and the world around him, would be compelled to admit this.

Ultimately, marriage boils down to two sinners being thrown together, each with different backgrounds and experiences, wants, needs, and expectations. On top of this, one is going to try to rule and the other is going to try to control. So, good luck with that! This scenario equals "the perfect storm." Even if the marriage manages to avoid the shipwreck of divorce, it is still destined to be a very stormy voyage.

Hence, what is the secret of cultivating a happy marriage? We could flippantly reply it is "religion," but we'd be mistaken because many religious people get divorced while a number of nonreligious people manage to achieve somewhat happy marriages. In reality, the secret is to carry out the principles God sets forth in His Word regarding husbands and wives. People do not have to believe in the Bible, nor own it or read it, nor even know that the Bible exists before they can carry out its principles. And although God gives a number of principles for husbands and wives by which to live, only two are needed to sustain a happy and fulfilling marriage:

1. "Husbands ought also to love their own wives ... as he loves himself" (Ephesians 5:28, 33).

2. "[A] wife must see to it that she respects her husband" (v. 33).

A great deal of research and a number of bestselling books have concluded that most married men desire sexual fulfillment, an attractive spouse, a woman who admires him and enjoys doing what he thinks is fun, and a mate that diligently takes care of the household. A woman who sincerely tries to do this in her marriage (whether she believes in God or not) is putting into action the biblical principle of respecting her husband.

On the other hand, a woman craves affection, conversation, honesty, financial security, and domestic support. Consequently, if a husband truly strives to love his wife the same way he loves himself, he is putting into practice a scriptural principle that can produce a happy marriage (whether he is religious or not).

Due to our fallen natures and inherently different needs, storms in marriages are as inevitable as storms in nature. Nevertheless, storms do not always necessarily destroy, drown, or shipwreck couples; they can strengthen, season, and mature them. Even the "perfect storm" can be navigated and survived by employing the two aforementioned essential principles guaranteed to keep any marriage afloat, which will cater to smooth sailing more often than not.

The Darkest Light

Quick! Think of half a dozen opposites! True/false, right/wrong, up/down, sorrow/joy, good/bad, and light/dark spring to my mind immediately. Regarding this last one, would you believe light can actually be dark, and dark, light?

According to Jesus Christ, this is very possible. He said,

> The eye is the lamp of the body; so then if your eye is clear, your whole body will be full of light. But if your eye is bad, your whole body will be full of darkness. If then the light that is in you is darkness, how great is the darkness. (Matthew 6:22-23)

It's true: Some brilliant light can, in reality, be extremely dark. Any cult and false religion in history amount to nothing more than dark-light. Every false prophet, false teacher, and false doctrine is in essence darkness parading around as light.

Some darkness can be so intense that light is not only incapable of penetrating it, but every ray of brightness is swallowed up by the inescapable force of darkness' grip. Black holes do exactly this. When the thermonuclear fire of a massive star begins to exhaust its energy, it is in danger of turning into a nova or a supernova. When this happens, a star will actually explode, and because of its incredible size, its gravitational pull will cause the star to collapse. Its force of gravity becomes so intense that it caves in on itself. All the atoms and molecules constituting that star rapidly press together in a ball so dense and so tightly compacted that not even light can escape its ferocious pull, and can subsequently begin to draw every other source of light around it into its horrible blackness.

This is dark-light—and "how great is the darkness." No wonder it is so difficult to reach a Muslim, Hindu, or Buddhist; a witch, medium, or cultist; or an atheist, with the light of the gospel. They devour every ray of light to which they are exposed and concoct it into night. Job relates, "They make night into day, saying 'the light is near,' in the presence of darkness" (Job 17:12). Even people who profess to believe in the God of heaven can rashly transform the light of the gospel—the truth of God's Word—into utter gloom. It's akin to possessing 20/20 vision, yet in the absence of light, one is totally blind.

There is, nonetheless, a very severe judgment in store for anyone who turns day into night and daybreak into nightfall:

> Woe to those who call evil good and good evil; who substitute darkness for light and light for darkness; who substitute bitter for sweet and sweet for bitter! (Isaiah 5:20)

> He who justifies the wicked and he who condemns the righteous, both of them alike are an abomination to the Lord. (Proverbs 17:15)

Jesus said His followers are to be the "light of the world" (Matthew 5:14). Failing to become light truly makes us darkness, and we actually contribute to the blackness surrounding us. As the apostle Paul put it,

> You were formerly darkness, but now you are Light in the Lord; walk as children of Light (for the fruit of the Light consists in all goodness and righteousness and truth), trying to learn what is pleasing to the Lord. Do not participate in the unfruitful deeds of darkness, but instead even expose them; for it is disgraceful even to speak of the things which are done by them in secret. But all things become visible when they are exposed by the light, for everything that becomes visible is light. For this reason it says, "Awake, sleeper, and arise from the dead, and Christ will shine on you." (Ephesians 5:8-14)

The Universe Thrown Into Reverse

Have you ever wondered about the potency of God, asking yourself, *Just how powerful is God? Exactly how "almighty" is He?* Well, God's power is so far beyond our comprehension that our finite minds are utterly incapable of wrapping our intellect around it. This is why faith is absolutely essential in our relationship with Him. In fact, the Bible says, "Whatever is not from faith is sin," "without faith it is impossible to please [God]," and that we literally cannot be saved apart from faith (Romans 14:23; Hebrews 11:6; see Ephesians 2:8).

Contrary to popular opinion, having such faith is far from being stupid, weak, or gullible. This faith is based on reason; yet it still boils down to "the assurance of things hoped for and the conviction of things not seen" (Hebrews 11:1). Just look at the vastness of our universe and everything it contains; it is truly mind-boggling. Who can comprehend how it all came into being out of nothing? None of us can. That is why God places such a premium on faith and even goes as far as equating faith with righteousness (see Genesis 15:6; Romans 4:3, 22).

With this thought in mind, imagine sitting in a cosmic stadium where we are about to witness the most incredible miracle this universe has ever experienced. It is so unbelievable that even being eyewitnesses to this event, we still would not believe our eyes. Our limited minds would immediately scramble to try to minimize or explain away what just occurred in our sight because our restricted intelligence would tell us that no one—not even God—could be so powerful.

This miracle is recorded in 2 Kings 20 and Isaiah 38. It was when King Hezekiah was dying and pleading to God for his life. Moved with compassion, God sent His prophet, Isaiah, to the king and told him that he would recover from his sickness. As confirmation, Hezekiah asked what sign God would give him. In response, Isaiah asked Hezekiah whether he wanted the shadow of Ahaz's sundial to go back ten steps of stairs or forward ten steps. Hezekiah said that since it was nothing for the shadow of the sundial to advance ten degrees (the equivalent of forty minutes), to ask God to make it go back—and so it did. Slowly the shadow retreated ten steps.

Unless we simply convince ourselves that God moved the shadow like a man would move a chess piece or the hands on a clock, then what we are witnessing is truly beyond human comprehension. Our earth is spinning on its axis at 1,040 miles an hour. It is revolving around the sun at almost 67,000 miles an hour. Our galaxy is moving millions of miles per hour, and our universe is expanding at a velocity that now exceeds the speed of light. We set our watches and calculate our calendars by the rotation of the earth and the position of the stars.

Now, for the shadow of Ahaz's sundial to go back ten degrees, it meant the entire universe would have to be thrown into reverse. Yet no one so much as even felt it! If you were in a speeding vehicle and it suddenly got thrown into reverse, the kinetic energy of your forward motion would catapult you right through the windshield. Accordingly, to reverse time (or to move the sundial back forty minutes) requires an unfathomable power.

For anyone to claim that the movement of the stars and planets were not involved in this miracle, they are forgetting what happened in the days of Joshua when he asked God to make time stand still, so that he and his men would have the sunlight they needed in order to defeat their enemies. Joshua said,

> 'O sun, stand still at Gibeon, and O moon in the Valley of Aijalon.' So the sun stood still and the moon stopped, until the nation avenged themselves of their enemies. ... And the sun stopped in the middle of the sky and did not hasten to go down for about a whole day. There was no day like that before it or after it. (Joshua 10:12-14)

What kind of power is that? It's the same power that stopped the wind and halted the kinetic motion of the waves on the Sea of Galilee, and when the apostles witnessed it they said, "What then is this, that even the wind and the sea obey Him?" (Mark 4:37-41). A further inquiry could be, "Who then is this, that even the stars and the planets obey Him?" The same God who became this Man on the Sea of Galilee will someday make the entire universe disappear in His presence:

> Then I saw a great white throne and Him who sat upon it, from whose presence earth and heaven fled away, and no place was found for them. (Revelation 20:11)

Power that can create this universe, stop its motion, reverse its movement, and then make this universe vanish is power beyond all understanding. No wonder faith is so essential in knowing God, because His power is incomprehensible.

Whenever we check the time, we can be reminded that it certainly can be turned back, but only with the power of an omnipotent God. Without question, it is this Almighty Being who created our incredible space-time continuum who can thereby control it and dissolve it with just a word.

It's Not That Complicated

"It's complicated!" That's a well-worn phrase that can be either very accurate or very deceiving, depending on the context in which it is used. To most people computers are complicated, so are physics, chemistry, molecular biology and the DNA molecule. Life can be complicated and so can relationships. One thing, however, is not complicated: truth—especially the truth about God and His moral standards. The reason this truth is not that complicated is because God has put the knowledge about Himself within us and then has demonstrated His invisible attributes—His eternal power and divine nature—through what He has made. Therefore men are without excuse when they deny what God has made self-evident within them (Romans 1:18-20).

The sad reality is when men do not want to obey God, they then develop a real knack for getting themselves confused, and they manage to (deceitfully) complicate almost everything God has said in His Word. Mark Twain said it best when he stated, "It ain't the parts of the Bible that I can't understand that bother me, it's the parts that I do understand."[5] There are a number of things written in Scripture I personally do not want to believe. I don't want to believe that certain behavior is sinful or that my own goodness cannot get me to heaven. I don't want to believe there is only one way to be saved. I don't want to believe in a personal devil. And I most certainly do not want to believe in an eternal hell where unrepentant sinners go and are tormented forever!

It takes a truly courageous and determined person to espouse everything God has said in His Word. It doesn't take a rocket scientist to understand what the Bible says, but it does take boldness as well as humility to accept it. Knowing full well that most people do not have the intellectual honesty and the fearlessness to believe God, Paul wrote:

> Preach the word; be ready in season and out of season; reprove, rebuke, exhort, with great patience and instruction. For the time will come when they will not endure sound doctrine; but wanting to have their ears tickled, they will accumulate for themselves teachers in accordance to their

own desires, and will turn away their ears from the truth and will turn aside to myths. (2 Timothy 4:2-4)

The Spirit explicitly says that in later times some will fall away from the faith, paying attention to deceitful spirits and doctrines of demons. (1 Timothy 4:1)

Furthermore, in 2 Thessalonians 2, Paul predicted that in the latter days there would be a worldwide apostasy, or falling away, from the truth because people take pleasure in doing evil. John records Jesus saying that men prefer darkness rather than the Light because their deeds are evil (John 3:19).

For this reason, Jesus foretold that one of the signs preceding His imminent return would be a multitude of false prophets and religious teachers who would mislead many, even some who once believed what God has said (Matthew 24:4-5). Paul even went so far as to predict Satan would be allowed to deceive men with powerful signs and false/deceptive wonders because people refuse to believe what the Bible proclaims (2 Thessalonians 2:9-12).

So you see? God's Word is really not that complicated. It's simply that we really don't want to believe it. We would much rather believe a lie because a lie is what convinces us that we can believe, do, and profess whatever we want and still be saved and get to heaven. It's that simple.

If anyone asserts that the Bible is complicated, realize it is because he or she wants to complicate it. It would be like taking a simple paperclip and adding fifteen moving parts to it and then including with it an instruction manual written in a foreign language. Now that's complicating things, wouldn't you say? And we all have a real genius for doing just that—complicating things—especially when it comes to what God has plainly said.

Khurana, Simran. "Religion Quotes by Mark Twain." *About.com Quotations*. About.com, n.d. Web. 03 Dec. 2013.

Leaven That Will Kill You

"He is so broad-minded that his brains have fallen out." Perhaps you have heard this sarcastic saying before, but whether it's familiar or not, it speaks volumes. In our society, broad-mindedness and acceptance have become politically correct virtues, and anything that smacks of traditional values or biblical morality is considered hateful, bigoted, and intolerant. Nevertheless, the Bible refers to anything morally corrupting or doctrinally incorrect as "leaven."

In the Old Testament, God instituted an annual observance called the "Feast of Unleavened Bread." The tradition began with the very first Passover recorded in Exodus 12. The Passover was the ritual of killing a lamb and applying its blood on the top and sides of the door of each family's house. At midnight God passed through the land of Egypt, and the firstborn of the household was slain by the Lord if that house failed to have the lamb's blood around the door. God "passed over" any home displaying the lamb's blood. These families were to eat the roasted lamb that very night, standing up, fully clothed, and with their staff in their hand. They were to eat it in haste with unleavened bread and bitter herbs, and they were prohibited from consuming leaven for an entire week.

This ritual was very rich in symbolism and most significant in what God was saying to His people Israel. It all prefigured Jesus Christ as the Lamb of God and the need to be under His shed blood in order to escape the consequences of hell for one's sins. In short, these instructions were our tutor teaching us some very profound spiritual truths. When we accept Christ as our Lord and Savior, we need to get out of the world (or Egypt) in a hurry—hence, fully clothed, with staff in hand, and eating quickly. The bitter herbs are to remind us of our bitter slavery to sin and our bondage to Satan (or Pharaoh).

The seven-day feast of unleavened bread included the day of Passover and tells us that when we give our lives to Christ, we need to abstain from all morally corrupting influences for the rest of our lives. If we claim to be Christian, then everything spiritually contaminating must be gotten rid of, for it will surely destroy our relationship with God—be it pornography, tarot cards, occult books, Ouija boards, astrology, false doctrine, immoral behavior—it's all leaven that will ruin us spiritually.

Today, more than ever before, people want to "have their cake and eat it too." They want to eat the Paschal Lamb (accept Christ as Savior) and continue to feed on leaven (false teachings and sinful behavior). However, the apostle Paul deals with this kind of mindset head-on in his first letter to the Corinthian church. There was a man in the assembly of Corinth who was sleeping with his stepmother. The Corinthian church accepted him in the name of tolerance and arrogantly believed their broad-mindedness made them more loving and merciful churchgoers.

Paul was absolutely livid over this situation and demanded the church leaders and members of the congregation throw this wicked man out of their fellowship immediately:

> You have become arrogant and have not mourned instead, so that the one who had done this deed would be removed from your midst. ... Your boasting is not good. Do you not know that a little leaven leavens the whole lump of dough? Clean out the old leaven so that you may be a new lump, just as you are in fact unleavened. For Christ our Passover [Lamb] also has been sacrificed. Therefore let us celebrate the feast, not with old leaven, nor with the leaven of malice and wickedness, but with the unleavened bread of sincerity and truth.
>
> I wrote you in my letter not to associate with immoral people; I did not at all mean with the immoral people of this world, or with the covetous and swindlers, or with idolaters, for then you would have to go out of the world. But actually, I wrote to you not to associate with any so-called brother if he is an immoral person, or covetous, or an idolater, or a reviler, or a drunkard, or a swindler—not even to eat with such a one.
>
> For what have I to do with judging outsiders? Do you not judge those who are within the church? But those who are outside, God judges. Remove the wicked man from among yourselves. (1 Corinthians 5:2; 6-13)

Today, many churches refuse to do what Paul commands. Instead, pedophiliac priests are moved from congregation to congregation; Protestant churches are ordaining homosexual bishops; and other denominations are promoting gay lifestyles, abortion "rights," and additional heretical teachings. Paul tells us this is all "leaven" and that it needs to go. Otherwise it will negatively affect "the entire lump of dough": in other words, the entire church.

It's very interesting to note that when the Corinthian church obeyed Paul and excommunicated the immoral man, this discipline brought the man to repentance. Consequentially, Paul told the church in his second letter to bring the man back into their fold, lest Satan overwhelm him with discouragement and despair (see 2 Corinthians 2).

The bottom line is that spiritual leaven is truly corrupting, contagious, and lethal. It will destroy our souls and eventually damn us, even if we claim to be under the blood of the Lamb.

Bull in a China Shop

It was wise, old Solomon who once said, "Where no oxen are, the manger is clean, but much revenue comes by the strength of the ox" (Proverbs 14:4). An ox is an extremely powerful animal and has the potential of being very destructive or very productive, depending on the situation in which it finds itself.

If you put a 1,000-pound ox in a small room filled with delicate glassware, chances are there will be one horrific crash after another—especially if the beast becomes spooked or threatened in any way. Harness that same creature to a millstone, and there is a good chance he can do the work of a dozen men.

The apostle Paul quoted Moses when he said, "Do not muzzle an ox while it is treading out the grain," meaning just as an ox needs to be fed while it works, ministers who work hard in serving the Lord should be paid well for their labor (1 Timothy 5:18; Deuteronomy 25:4, NIV). In the process of trying to accomplish something for the honor and glory of God, these hard workers may often make mistakes, sometimes saying or doing the wrong things. After all, they are only human. At least they are attempting to do something for the Lord's sake.

Remember Jesus' parable in Matthew 25 when the master entrusted three of his slaves with his money? The first and second servants doubled their master's currency, while the third simply buried his coin and returned the un-invested cash when he was audited by his master. It's possible the two industrious servants made a number of mistakes or experienced failures in their attempts to enrich their lord. They may even have been criticized by others who disagreed with their methods of using their entrusted talents. Perhaps in their clumsy attempts to achieve something worthwhile, they resembled a bull in a china shop. In the end, though, they were greatly praised and richly rewarded by the one whose opinion truly mattered.

On the other hand, the servant who did nothing with his master's money made no mistakes because he took no risks, and therefore was safe from the criticism and the mockery of others. This servant had clean hands and never stained his garments with perspiration. Well, where there is no ox, the manger may be clean, and while doing nothing for his master, the servant may have made no mistakes. Yet in the final accounting, he discovered too late that his master was not interested in a stable that was unsoiled; rather, in a valuable return on his money:

> You wicked, lazy slave. ... You ought to have put my money in the bank, and on my arrival I would have received my money back with interest. Therefore take away the talent from him, and give it to the one who has ten talents. For to everyone who has, more shall be given, and he will have an abundance; but from the one who does not have, even what he does have shall be taken away. Throw out the worthless slave into the outer darkness; in that place there will be weeping and gnashing of teeth. (Matthew 25:26-30)

Work hard and take risks for the Lord Jesus Christ because "much revenue comes by the strength of [an] ox," and armchair critics will be greatly criticized by the One whose criticism matters most.

Old School

The prophets of the Old Testament are sometimes referred to as "old school" prophets because a great deal of their preaching strongly emphasized the wrath and judgment of God. From Moses to Malachi, we read example after example of God's anger, as well as His discipline, judgment, and chastisement of the wicked and of His unrepentant people. He is often referred to as the "God of thunder and ice." Even some of our modern-day preachers have referred to the God of the Old Testament as being little more than a "big bully."

Not surprisingly, many atheists and other unbelievers today delight in attacking the Bible and the God of ancient Israel for seemingly condoning much bloodshed recorded in the Hebrew Scriptures. Here is one such example:

> The God of the Old Testament is arguably the most unpleasant character in all fiction: jealous and proud of it; a petty, unjust, unforgiving control-freak [sic]; a vindictive, bloodthirsty ethnic cleanser; a misogynistic, homophobic, racist, infanticidal, genocidal, filicidal, pestilential, megalomaniacal, sadomasochistic, capriciously malevolent bully.[6]

This quote comes from the bestselling book entitled <u>The God Delusion</u>, written by the famed atheist, Richard Dawkins. Dawkins' words capture the thoughts and sentiments of many people today, including a growing number of professing Christians within the church. They assert their God is not the God of the Old Testament, but rather, the God of the New Testament. They claim that the love, compassion, and forgiveness demonstrated by Jesus Christ in the New Testament are characteristic of the kind of God in whom they can put their faith —but they cannot trust in the God who destroyed the world with a flood and incinerated Sodom and Gomorrah with a firestorm.

The truth of the matter is, the God of the Old Testament is indeed the same God as in the New, and the "old school" prophets were no different from the New Testament prophets. We can easily find the love of God in the Old

Testament as well as the wrath of God in the New Testament. However, a major difference has evolved with many of our modern-day prophets (or preachers). They have become so mild mannered, soft-spoken and sentimental that they have chosen to ignore all of the unpleasant realities of the New Testament writings. God, however, has not changed. Just listen to some of the preaching of the "new school" prophets:

John the Baptist

> Repent, for the kingdom of heaven is at hand. (Matthew 3:2)

> You brood of vipers, who warned you to flee from the wrath to come? Therefore bear fruit in keeping with repentance. ... The axe is already laid at the root of the trees; therefore every tree that does not bear good fruit is cut down and thrown into the fire. (Matthew 3:7-8, 10)

Paul

> Because of your stubbornness and unrepentant heart you are storing up wrath for yourself in the day of wrath and revelation of the righteous judgment of God. ... There will be tribulation and distress for every soul of man who does evil, of the Jew first and also of the Greek. (Romans 2:5, 9)

> You who are full of all deceit and fraud, you son of the devil, you enemy of all righteousness, will you not cease to make crooked the straight ways of the Lord? Now, behold, the hand of the Lord is upon you, and you will be blind and not see the sun for a time. (Acts 13:10-11)

Peter

> God did not spare angels when they sinned, but cast them into hell and committed them to pits of darkness. (2 Peter 2:4)

Peter goes on to say that just as God destroyed the world with a flood and incinerated Sodom and Gomorrah with fire from Heaven, He will again destroy all unrepentant sinners when He returns. This sinful world will be burned up, as the elements will melt with intense heat along with the wicked (2 Peter 2 and 3).

Jude tells us basically the same things in his epistle. James 5 also proclaims the judgment of God upon evildoers, and John, the "Apostle of Love," describes God's coming wrath and punishment in ways never before witnessed in all human history (see the book of Revelation).

As for Jesus Christ—the God of all mercy and compassion—listen closely to some of the things He had to say:

> Repent, for the kingdom of heaven is at hand. (Matthew 4:17)

> Unless you repent, you will all likewise perish. (Luke 13:3)

> Whoever causes one of these little ones who believe in Me to stumble, it would be better for him to have a heavy millstone hung around his neck, and to be drowned in the depth of the sea. (Matthew 18:6)

Eight times Jesus says "woe" to the scribes, the Pharisees, and the religious leaders of His day. He frequently calls them "hypocrites" and "blind guides." He angrily refers to them as "whitewashed tombs," "murderers," "serpents," and "brood of vipers" and irately asks them how they can possibly "escape the sentence of hell" (Matthew 23:1333). He even denounced them as being sons of the devil (John 8:44).

He said, "Every careless word that people speak, they shall give an accounting for it in the day of judgment" (Matthew 12:36). To the unrepentant cities of Chorazin, Bethsaida and Capernaum, He disclosed that they would be brought down to hell for rejecting the great light they were given (Matthew 11:20-24; Luke 10:12-15).

In righteous anger, Jesus made a whip and violently overturned swindlers' money tables in the temple, and when He returns, His "eyes [will be] a flame of fire" (John 2:15; Revelation 19:12). At that time, He will slay more men than all the despots of history combined (see Revelation 14:20; Matthew 25:31-32, 41).

Old school? No one was more old school than Jesus Christ. No one spoke more of hell than He, and no one warned of it more than He. Consider these hard words emitted from Jesus' lips:

> If your hand or your foot causes you to stumble, cut it off and throw it from you; it is better for you to enter life crippled or lame, than to have two hands or two feet and be cast into the eternal fire. If your eye causes you to stumble, pluck it out and throw it from you. It is better for you to enter life with one eye, than to have two eyes and be cast into the fiery hell. (Matthew 18:8-9)

If there is no hell, then what did Christ die for—to save us from the grave? The saint dies right along with the sinner. No, it is hell from which His shed blood saves us, not death.

This is why Jesus Christ and the New Testament prophets are "old school"—because God has not changed. He is the same yesterday, today, and tomorrow. The God of love and compassion is still the God of holiness and justice. I daresay, without a flood of old-school prophets in the pulpits today, we will continue to be on a collision course with an all-consuming fire of holiness. "Old school" is what the world needs now like never before.

Dawkins, Richard. *The God Delusion*. Boston: Houghton Mifflin, 2006. Print.

Heaven's Rain

"All sunshine and no rain make a desert." In their efforts "to rain in the desert," how often do Christians feel their work for the Lord is so fruitless and unproductive as to be in vain? Day after day, month after month, and year after year, they may toil in preaching sermons, teaching Bible studies, instructing children, witnessing to the lost, and counseling the afflicted; yet their efforts seem so futile.

Although last week's sermon or last month's good deed done in the Lord's name may have been long forgotten, like last year's rainfall, it doesn't mean one's labor for Christ has been pointless or unfruitful. Paul reminds us of this when he says,

> Neither the one who plants nor the one who waters is anything, but God who causes the growth. Now he who plants and he who waters are one; but each will receive his own reward according to his own labor. (1 Corinthians 3:7-8)

The apostle Peter exhorts us to "long for the pure milk of the word, so that by it [we] may grow in respect to salvation" and he tells us to "grow in the grace and knowledge of our Lord and Savior Jesus Christ" (1 Peter 2:2; 2 Peter 3:18).

Crops cannot grow without rain, and people cannot grow spiritually without others watering them with God's Word and ministering to them in the name of Jesus Christ. We may have long forgotten last month's dinners or last week's beverages, but that doesn't mean they served no purpose. They both promoted growth and sustained life—so does heaven's rain, and the smallest deed done out of love for God will not lose its reward and will not have been done in vain (see Matthew 10:42).

As the author of Hebrews so eloquently acknowledged,

> God is not unjust so as to forget your work and the love

which you have shown toward His name, in having ministered and in still ministering to the saints. (Hebrews 6:10)

Truth Is Stranger Than Fiction

One of the most profound declarations made in all of human history can be found in the fifth chapter of the gospel of John. It is so outlandish that any rational person is left with only one of two conclusions: either this man is utterly insane or He is who He claimed to be—none other than God Almighty. There are no other options here. Though someone might argue that the guy had to be joking, that would be intellectually dishonest because this man was obviously not kidding. He was deadly serious and His listeners knew it! Here's what He said:

> Truly, truly, I say to you, an hour is coming and now is, when the dead will hear the voice of the Son of God, and those who hear will live. Do not marvel at this; for an hour is coming, in which all who are in the tombs will hear His voice, and will come forth; those who did the good deeds to a resurrection of life, those who committed the evil deeds to a resurrection of judgment. (John 5:25, 28-29)

Isn't that outrageous and unbelievable? Yet Jesus turned right around and demonstrated conclusively that He possessed the power to perform this impossible feat. Right in front of both friends and enemies, He called forth a man who had been dead for four days! This cadaver had already begun to decompose and to give off a stench, and despite being wrapped from head to toe with the grave clothes of a mummy, he clearly heard the voice of Jesus Christ and obeyed at the Lord's command, "Lazarus, come forth!" (see John 11).

Profound, isn't it? Billions of people who have died in the past and who will die in the future will someday hear the voice of Jesus Christ—the Son of God—and will come out of their tombs, catacombs, sepulchers, and mausoleums. They will come forth from the watery graves of the oceans that have concealed their remains for centuries. No one who has ever died will be overlooked; no one will escape this resurrection, regardless of how long they have remained buried—no one!

The atheists and scoffers will mock this coming reality, stating it is physically impossible for the remains of a decomposed or incinerated body to live again; yet the apostle Paul called such skeptics of the resurrection "fools" (1 Corinthians 15:35-36).

They are fools because they refuse to believe that God has the ability—the incredible power—to raise all who have died throughout the ages of history. God's tremendous power will call forth all the deceased multitudes that have disappeared within the portals of time and decay, and they will rise again. The Law of Conservation of Matter states that matter can be neither created nor destroyed (except in certain cases of quantum physics and special relativity). Consequently, the authority of God's words will summon all the still-existing atoms and molecules that made up each departed human being and will resurrect them in a heartbeat.

There is an old saying, "Truth is stranger than fiction." Can you think of anything more bizarre than the resurrection of all mankind from the dead? You would be hard-pressed to come up with something more peculiar—yet true—than this. The applicable question now is, "Which resurrection will I be part of—the resurrection of the righteous and the saved or that of the unrighteous and the lost?" You may want to consider this the next time you view a body in an open coffin, understanding that although the corpse cannot hear you, it is not deaf; regardless of how deep it may be buried or how decomposed it may become, it is not oblivious to the voice of God. The dead will someday heed the words of Jesus Christ and come forth. Is this truth not stranger than fiction?

Betting on a Dead Horse

Let's face it, gambling can be a very fun form of entertainment for many people. Whether it is the thrill of betting on a winning horse, a sporting event, or an ideal poker hand, gambling can give a person a rush, especially if the one who wagers happens to win big.

Choose a winning lottery ticket; win big at a slot machine; get lucky in a mutual fund; or have your investment in a stock, bond, or 401K pay off handsomely and people's reaction will always be the same—excitement, joy, and a sense of triumph. It's all gambling, though. Regardless of how wise the investment or how foolish the bet, no matter if it's a blue-chip stock or an illegal dog fight, the bottom line is, when there is money involved, it's a gamble and a risk; there is a possibility to lose, and in some cases, to lose big!

Do you know what the biggest gamble in life is, the biggest wager any human being could possibly make? It is the gamble of one's soul. That is the ultimate bet, where everyone has the exact same ante and stands to win or lose an eternal fortune. In essence, it is betting on God's Word, wagering whether or not God really means what He says. This wager has no hedge bets, side bets, or insurance bets. It's just an all-out wager where winner takes all and loser loses all.

Either there is a heaven and a hell or there isn't. Either Jesus Christ is "the way, the truth and the life" or He isn't. Either there is a final judgment and life after death or there isn't. There is no third option here—only true or false. It doesn't depend upon a person's interpretation of the Bible or the odds stacked in favor or against the claims made in the Scriptures. People are betting on it one way or another. They are gambling with their immortal lives, and all those who refuse to bet have already placed their bets.

It is the same thing as if a ship at sea were sinking, and all the passengers and crew were in sharp disagreement as to whether or not the ship was truly in peril. Every passenger and crewmember that gets into a lifeboat is betting the vessel is on its way to the bottom of the sea; all voyagers and ship personnel who stay onboard are betting the vessel is not about to sink. Any others who have an I-don't-know attitude or a wait-and-see approach have unwittingly wagered on the side of all those who chose to stay onboard. They do not have the luxury of being an uninvolved spectator because, metaphorically speaking, the ship is the world, and they are onboard whether they like it or not.

If, contrary to what the Bible proclaims, this world is all there is and there is no life after death, nor final judgment and heaven or hell, then to remain onboard makes absolutely no difference. However, the lifeboat, representing Jesus Christ, is available to all who trust in Him. Personally, I would bet my soul that the Bible is true and Jesus Christ is the only way to heaven. I would wager everything that, unless I repent of my sins and commit my life to Him, I will be eternally lost. If I lose this bet, then my wager has been a foolish one at worst. If I win the bet, then I've gained more than I could ever imagine.

As with horse races or penny-ante poker, life can be a gamble, only the eternal stakes are infinitely higher, and regardless of what the God-mockers may say, if we are betting on a dead horse we have no chance of winning, and we will lose an eternal fortune.

The Lying Atheist

Atheists have been around for centuries, and the only thing new about these "free thinkers" is that they are rapidly growing in number and are becoming more vocal and influential with each passing day. Lawsuits by atheists are accruing against Christians and any semblance of Christianity. Our 21st century is witnessing a surge of best-selling books by hard-core atheists who mock the existence of God and scoff at the claims of the Bible. Along with their growing number is their swelling support. The media, academia, and the entertainment world have become the biggest cheerleaders for the modern infidel.

Do you want to hear the brutal truth about atheists? As offensive as it may sound, the raw and sobering truth is all atheists are simply bold-faced liars. This brazen statement is not meant to insult or belittle; it is merely meant to state the truth in such a way that any tactfulness, diplomacy, or politeness cannot do without diminishing the harsh reality—that all atheists are patent liars. They lie to everyone and anyone, but most of all, they lie to themselves. Recall what the apostle Paul wrote in chapter one of Romans, verses 18-22:

> For the wrath of God is revealed from heaven against all ungodliness and unrighteousness of men who suppress the truth in unrighteousness, because that which is known about God is evident within them. For since the creation of the world His invisible attributes, His eternal power and divine nature, have been clearly seen, being understood through what has been made, so they are without excuse. For even though they knew God, they did not honor Him as God or give thanks, but they became futile in their speculations, and their foolish heart was darkened. Professing to be wise, they became fools.

Their foolishness motivates them to invent "futile speculations" in order to explain God out of existence. Consequently, these self-deceivers manufacture the foolish lie of evolution to counter the idea of a Creator God and then "profess themselves to be wise" (again, I don't mean this as an insult; but I will not compromise the truth for the sake of being polite).

Psalm 14:1 says, "The fool has said in his heart, 'There is no God.'" A person who lies to others may do so for a multitude of self-serving reasons, but the person who deceives himself must be considered a fool. Now, why would someone be so foolish as to lie to themselves (especially in matters that have such severe consequences, both in this life and the next)? The reason is not in the least bit complicated, perplexing, or sophisticated. It's simply because atheists do not want to obey God. That's it—pure and simple. Strip away the countless layers of their "intellectual" arguments, and what lies at the bottom of their "foolish speculations" is rebellion—an all-out revolt against God's authority and His laws. If someone claims to be an atheist, I basically just laugh and say, "You're not an atheist at all. What you are is a 'God-hater.' You cannot stomach the thought of God because you do not want to submit to Him; you just don't have the courage and intellectual honesty to admit it."

In reality, atheists are obsessed with God; He constantly occupies their thoughts as they try to explain Him away. In essence, they have tried to become God, in order to feel free to do what they want, say what they want, and believe whatever they want. Their lie has freed them from Him, and they desperately want their lie to free others from Him as well. That's what makes their life so pathetic; they are willfully lying to themselves, yet deep within their beings, they know they have deluded themselves with an untruth and that their atheistic house of cards is built on shifting sand.

God Is Blind

Did you know that God is blind? Sounds like blasphemy, doesn't it? But it is true—God's vision is totally obstructed when it comes to the shade of a man's skin. In other words, the all-seeing God of the universe is color-blind. He is oblivious to the pigmentation of a man's skin, doesn't notice an individual's social status, is unconcerned with someone's economic standing, and is not impressed with whatever power or influence a human being may possess. God is totally blind to all of these things—these same things on which men everywhere place such a premium. Jesus said to the wealthy and influential leaders of His day, "That which is highly esteemed among men is detestable in the sight of God" (Luke 16:15). The Creator of all men clearly says,

> There will be tribulation and distress for every soul of man who does evil, of the Jew first and also of the Greek, but glory and honor and peace to everyone who does good, to the Jew first and also to the Greek. For there is no partiality with God. (Romans 2:9-11)

We are experiencing an accelerating hypersensitivity in regards to race today. Unsubstantiated accusations of racism threaten corporations with lawsuits, paralyze the military and police forces, and cripple schools. Ordinary citizens are instantly silenced when the "race card" is played. No word other than racism has such power to stop all discussion, end all debate, and stigmatize any and all who dare to disagree.

Unfortunately, the instigators today vilify anyone (including their own) who promotes personal responsibility rather than victimhood and who demands individual integrity versus playing the blame game. In the end, they will stand before a righteous God and discover too late that repentance, not race, will be the determining factor in His court of eternal justice. He is blind—color-blind! He is no respecter of persons and there is no partiality with Him. This all-consuming fire of holiness will gaze right through the color of a man's skin and look deep into his soul. He will judge him according to his actions (acceptance of Christ as Lord and Savior) and will not be swayed by passion or pity or be influenced by gender or ethnicity on that fateful day. The only "R word" that will matter is "repentance," not "race."

The most bigoted person will not dare play the race card in God's presence because they will see clearly that the color of a man's skin means absolutely nothing to Him. They will transparently recognize that He cannot be fooled. Instead, "There will be tribulation and distress for every soul of man who does evil, of the Jew first and also of the Greek" (Romans 2:9).

Martin Luther King's dream where all men "will one day live in a nation where they will not be judged by the color of their skin but by the content of their character" will become a reality before the holiness of a sightless God.[7] It will truly be an eye-opener to all men who do evil—to Jew and Gentile, black and white, male and female, rich and poor, literate and illiterate. Men must realize God cannot see and therefore will not be influenced by status or moved by pigment when he metes out "tribulation and distress" to all the unrepentant of mankind.

King, Martin L., Jr. "I Have a Dream." Speech. Lincoln Memorial, Washington, DC. 28 Aug. 1963. *American Rhetoric*. American Rhetoric. Web. 03 Dec. 2013.

The Foolish Wise Man

If there ever was a man who epitomized the spirit of wisdom, it was King Solomon. God appeared to him in a dream and promised him anything his heart desired. The young king replied to the Lord,

> Now, O Lord my God, You have made Your servant king in the place of my father David, yet I am but a little child; I do not know how to go out or come in [or, do the simplest thing]. Your servant is in the midst of Your people which You have chosen, a great people who are too many to be numbered or counted. So give Your servant an understanding heart to judge Your people and to discern between good and evil. For who is able to judge this great people of Yours? (1 Kings 3:7-9)

The Lord was so pleased with Solomon's request that He made him a promise:

> Behold, I have done according to your words. Behold, I have given you a wise and discerning heart, so that there has been no one like you before you, nor shall one like you arise after you. (v. 12)

What a gift, what a privilege—to be given more wisdom and insight than any man who lived before him and any person who would be born after him! What an advantage he possessed over the rest of mankind, and as if that blessing were not enough, God gave him countless riches, great glory, and legendary fame as well. Furthermore, Solomon enjoyed perfect health and lived a long life. What man could ask for more? His glory was so unmatched that even Jesus made reference to it when he spoke of the lilies of the field (see Matthew 6:28).

Would you believe this great king slowly became a conflicted man whose wisdom eventually evaporated with the years and whose glory faded with the sunset? At the end of his days, Solomon became spiritually shipwrecked and died an ignominious failure. He lost his connection with God because his passion for women eventually drove him mad. His judgment became impaired due to his insatiable desire for sexual variety. His sensual appetites compelled him to do anything to experience the pleasures the female body could offer. In exchange for erotic fulfillment, Solomon was willing to listen to the persuasions of his pagan wives and build altars to their gods, in addition to burning incense to their idols. He accumulated a thousand different sexual partners through marriage, and a number of his playmates pressured him to compromise his relationship with God. Consequently, he died a cynic and a fool.

Even the first century Jewish historian, Josephus, tells us that Solomon was driven mad because of his lust for women, and the author of the book of Kings informs us that Solomon's stupidity eventually lead to the division of his glorious kingdom (1 Kings 11).[8] Although Peter tells us that women are the weaker vessel, the shores of history are strewn with the wreckage of men, both great and small, who have been brought low by the power of a woman (1 Peter 3:7).

A woman can be weaker physically, but men can truly become weak and feeble in their presence. A woman's seductive powers can overcome the strongest of men, and their charms can bring low the mightiest of the mighty. A man's vulnerability can readily be seen in his weakness for the weaker vessel—a woman's seductive spell brought Adam to ruin and another's enchantments paralyzed the strength of Samson. Women's sexuality has destroyed kingdoms and damned untold millions. This is why God warns men to turn away from the seducing influence of an adulterous woman, by saying,

> Now therefore, my sons, listen to me, and pay attention to the words of my mouth. Do not let your heart turn aside to her ways, do not stray into her paths. For many are the victims she has cast down, and numerous are all her slain. Her house is the way to Sheol [hell], descending to the chambers of death [the realm of the spiritually dead]." (Proverbs 7:24-27)

Solomon affirmed, "A wise man is strong, and a man of knowledge increases power," but not even his strength as a wise man could match the strength of an alluring woman (Proverbs 24:5). Only the power of Christ's spirit can enable the strongest of strong men and the wisest of wise men to overcome the power of the weaker vessel. Solomon was a wise man who died a fool, and his foolishness stands as a dark warning for all men: "Let him who thinks he stands, take heed that he does not fall" (1 Corinthians 10:12). Men have a prevailing weakness in their sexual desire for women; but Jesus said, "My grace is sufficient for you, for [My] power is perfected in weakness" (2 Corinthians 12:9).

So if the wisest of wise men could ultimately die a fool, how much easier is it for lesser men to do the same? As weak as men are in the company of the weaker gender, the Lord assures them,

> No temptation has overtaken you but such as is common to man; and God is faithful, who will not allow you to be tempted beyond what you are able, but with the temptation will provide a way of escape also, so that you will be able to endure it. (1 Corinthians 10:13)

Only a foolish man could think he is stronger than an attractive woman, because her proven strength has reduced even the most glorious of wise men and the mightiest of mighty men into groveling fools.

Josephus, Flavius. "Book VIII, Chapter 7, Paragraph 5." *The Antiquities of the Jews*. Trans. William Whiston. Blacksburg, VA: Unabridged, 2011. N. pag. Print.

Magic Mirror on the Wall

One of the greatest cartoon classics of all time is the story of *Snow White and the Seven Dwarves.* It is a childhood fairy tale that begins to unfold as a very conceited queen stands daily before her mystical mirror and asks, "Magic Mirror on the wall, who is the fairest of them all?" She is a wicked woman who places enormous importance upon her physical beauty and cannot tolerate the thought of anyone rivaling her outward appearance.

Day after day and year after year, she inquires of her all-seeing mirror as to who is the most attractive woman in her kingdom, and day after day she is content to be told what she wants to hear—that there is no one who can compete with her elegant reflection. As the decades pass and her preoccupation with her looks continues, she is eventually informed of what she most feared: there is a young woman whose fairness and beauty far exceeds her own. This candid statement from her magical looking glass ignites a firestorm of rage and jealousy in this prideful and resentful queen.

Her jealousy and her outrage know no bounds as she plots and schemes to destroy this beautiful young girl named Snow White. Well, as in almost all fairy tales, it concludes with a happy ending where the heroine is rescued and the vicious villainess meets a terrible end.

Although this story is just make-believe, there is actually a similar analogy in the Bible that is anything but a childhood fantasy; however, the scriptural account speaks of there being *two* enchanted mirrors. One mirror reveals the cold, naked truth, while the other speaks incredible lies and falsehoods; one mirror tells man what he desperately wants to hear, while the other mirror tells him what he desperately needs to hear—the truth. One is God's Word, while the other is man's heart; one is the Lord's assessment of man, and the other is man's estimation of himself. The Bible says "we see in a mirror dimly," as if seeing spiritual things through a dark glass, so we would do well to look more intently than we may be in the habit of doing (1 Corinthians 13:12).

When the Israelites first came out of Egypt, God gave Moses all of the instructions for building the tabernacle and all of its furnishings. The Lord said to Moses,

You shall also make a laver of bronze, with its base of bronze, for washing; and you shall put it between the tent of meeting and the altar, and you shall put water in it. Aaron and his sons shall wash their hands and their feet from it; when they enter the tent of meeting, they shall wash with water, so that they will not die; or when they approach the altar to minister, by offering up in smoke a fire sacrifice to the Lord. So they shall wash their hands and their feet, so that they will not die; and it shall be a perpetual statute for them, for Aaron and his descendants throughout their generations. (Exodus 30:18-21)

What is most interesting and insightful about this laver (or water basin) is that it was made with melted-down *brass mirrors* donated by the women of the congregation (Exodus 38:8).

The water symbolically pointed to the Word of God, just as Paul tells us,

Christ also loved the church and gave Himself up for her, so that He might sanctify her, having cleansed her by the washing of the water with the word, that He might present to Himself the church in all her glory, having no spot or wrinkle or any such thing; but that she would be holy and blameless. (Ephesians 5:25-27)

In short, God's Word is a mirror that reflects a crystal-clear image of man's sinful state and his utter need to be cleansed with the blood of Christ and to be perpetually washed or sanctified with the purifying power of Scripture. Note, too, the laver the priests were required to wash in was made of bronze. Brass metal (or bronze) always points to "judgment" throughout the Bible, and failure to wash in this reflective pool of water was grounds for execution (see Exodus 30:21). The symbolism of the brass tub fashioned out of women's bronze mirrors is truly powerful in its spiritual meaning, isn't it?

Man's fallen nature is unquestionably sinful and evil, and before a holy and righteous God, even the best of men are "wretched and miserable and poor and blind and naked" (Revelation 3:17). No man wants to be told this, let alone believe it, but unless he has the moral courage and intellectual honesty to look into this mirror of God's Word and agree with its divine assessment of him, he is destined to be deceived by the blackness of his own heart.

Man's heart is fallacious—a dishonest mirror that cannot be trusted. It is a dark pool whose flattering reflection draws men into a world of make-believe and lies. God said through His prophet Jeremiah,

> The heart is more deceitful than all else and is desperately sick; who can understand it? I, the Lord, search the heart, I test the mind, even to give to each man according to his ways, according to the results of his deeds. (Jeremiah 17:910)

The Bible declares the human heart is the most deceitful and wretched thing in this physical universe. Men are like Narcissus in Greek mythology: Narcissus was a beautiful young man who fell in love with his own reflection as he stared into a pool of water. He could not take his eyes off of himself and eventually pined away due to neglect as he became transfixed with admiration for his own image. Narcissus' reflection was his great undoing, and man's deceitful heart is the greatest tool in the hands of a deceitful devil.

It is man's deceitful heart that convinces him he is basically good in the midst of all his evil deeds. It is man's deceitful heart that assures him all is well between him and God when, in actuality, he is at war with God. It is man's deceitful heart that tells him his immoral lifestyles are approved by God and suggests to him that "good is evil and evil is good." It is man's deceitful heart that persuades him he evolved from apes (rather than being brought forth from the hand of the Creator) and enables him to justify his every act of greed and injustice. It is man's deceitful heart that whispers to him that God really did not mean what He said and really did not say what He meant. Likewise, it is man's deceitful heart that makes him believe there is no judgment and there is no hell, and that if there is a heaven, he is sure to go there.

Yes, a man's heart is his own worst enemy. It is his worst moral compass. Yet, sad to say, most men are deceived, and they don't have the good grace or spiritual insight to see it, nor do most people even care. Who is the most deceitful or dishonest person who ever lived in all of history? Who is the greatest con artist the world has ever known? Well, regardless of who it may have been (or who it still may be), the heart of that untrustworthy flimflamming scoundrel is no less dependable, sincere, or truthful than the heart of a man who is considered the absolute best among men.

If we stare earnestly enough into the reflective pool of God's Word, we will clearly see the truth about what the Bible says concerning our sinful and wretched condition. James says,

> If anyone is a hearer of the word and not a doer, he is like a man who looks at his natural face in a mirror; for once he has looked at himself and gone away, he has immediately forgotten what kind of person he was. But one who looks intently at the perfect law, the law of liberty, and abides by it, not having become a forgetful hearer but an effectual doer, this man will be blessed in what he does. (James 1:23-25)

We may detest what God's "mirror on the wall" tells us, but it is this mirror of His reflective word that has the ability to transform us into images of His Son Jesus Christ—and that is a reflection worth admiring.

Shining Pews and Roasting Marshmallows

Napoleon's French foreign minister, Talleyrand, famously said, "You can do anything with bayonets, except sit on them."[9] Well, I am inclined to say this man lacked a great deal of imagination. The truth of the matter is that church members sit on their swords all of the time. I am talking about their spiritual weapon, the one we call the Bible and the one God says is our "sword." The author of Hebrews declared that

> the Word of God is living and active and sharper than any two-edged sword, and piercing as far as the division of soul and spirit, of both joints and marrow, and able to judge the thoughts and intentions of the heart. (Hebrews 4:12)

Furthermore, the apostle Paul advised Timothy,

> Be diligent to present yourself approved to God as a workman who does not need to be ashamed, accurately handling the word of truth. (2 Timothy 2:15)

He also said to the Ephesians' church to "take up the sword of the spirit, which is the Word of God" when doing battle with the forces of darkness, and when warring against the powers of evil that are all around us in this supernatural conflict and spiritual warfare (Ephesians 6:10-17).

Jesus Christ, more than anyone, knew how to use the sword of God's Word. When the devil came to tempt Him in the wilderness with three different temptations, Christ defeated him each time with His scriptural sword. However, here is a real sobering insight about Jesus' conflict with Satan which is recorded in the fourth chapter of the gospel of Matthew: The devil himself began to quote Scripture to the Son of God in order to get Him to stumble and to sin against His Father.

Imagine that—the archenemy of God knows the Bible! As a matter of fact, the devil probably knows the Scriptures better than anyone on earth. No doubt, he can quote them backwards and forwards and in every language and dialect known to both men and angels. Obviously, this should give everyone a clue that there is a right way and a wrong way to apply the sword of God's Word. Cults misuse and misquote the Bible all the time—so do nonbelievers and atheists; so do Muslims, Buddhists, Hindus, and even Satanists—and unfortunately, so do many churchgoers who do not know how to effectively wield the "Sword of the Spirit."

It takes study and practice, study and practice, and more study and practice to diligently learn how to do battle with the sword of God's Word. I'm not trying to be anyone's judge, but pure logic would suggest that if every professing Christian with a Bible really knew their Scriptures and how to use them, there wouldn't be so many lost souls before us, or so much unrestrained evil around us. This is not an unfounded speculation; Jeremiah describes this sobering truth when he says, "'Is not My word like fire?' declares the Lord, 'and like a hammer which shatters a rock?'" (Jeremiah 23:29).

God's Word is a powerful weapon. It is a flamethrower and a mighty hammer that shatters and destroys. Yet it appears that many church members today are goaded by the powers of darkness to just shine the pews on Sunday with their posteriors and to counterintuitively use their swords for roasting marshmallows, rather than assaulting and invading the kingdom of the evil one.

This opinion is in no way intended to judge or offend; it is merely an objective observation of what so many of we churchgoers do with the Word of God today. We use the Sword of the Spirit to promote social agendas, promise prosperity, and simply beat the air with fluff and sentimentality. We use our Swords to press flowers, adorn coffee tables, fill bookshelves, or store birth certificates and marriage licenses. We carry our Bibles with us to church services, if we feel so inclined or if the pastor encourages us to do so, but have little knowledge of what it is saying to us.

The truth is that most professing Christians couldn't recite the Ten Commandments, or name the twelve apostles, or explain the Sermon on the Mount, or even say with certainty how many books there are in the New Testament. The truly sad fact is that too many pastors, ministers, priests, and laypeople today view the Bible as simply a "literary work" which should never be taken literally. They believe it is just a nice collection of fables, legends, poetry, and parables that need not be taken seriously, let alone studied diligently or obeyed faithfully.

If we are going to be effective warriors for God in this titanic duel between good and evil, we must do much more than merely shine pews and roast marshmallows. We need to obey God and study His Word with all diligence, in order to know exactly what it is we profess to believe. We need to know exactly how to reach the lost with the message of salvation and be able to confront heretics, expose false prophets, and put demons to flight. If we do not learn how to use the Word of God skillfully, then we become like soldiers in the midst of battle without loaded weapons. We become easy targets for the enemy and become more of a liability than an asset to our Supreme Commander.

We Christians must realize that in the end, Christ is not going to be interested in how shiny we made His pews or how many marshmallows we roasted with His Sword, but how diligently and effectively we did battle for His name's sake and how obediently we carried out His every command.

Bonner, Bill. "Sitting on Bayonets." *LewRockwell.com*. LewRockwell.com, 1 June 2004. Web. 03 Dec. 2013.

Managing an Outhouse

"The toil of a fool so wearies him that he does not even know how to go to a city" (Ecclesiastes 10:15). In other words, a fool is so lacking in common sense and sound judgment that he is unable to accomplish even the simplest of tasks.

How difficult do you think it would be to run an outhouse? It's just a small structure that encloses a seat with a hole in it. So how complicated do you think it would be to manage or take care of such a shack? Let's be honest, it wouldn't take a whole lot of brains to master such an unsophisticated chore; but according to Solomon, a fool would somehow be incapable of overseeing something as simple as a hole in the ground.

Well now, how complicated do you think it is to govern a metropolis, preside over a state, or rule a nation? Unquestionably, it would require tremendous wisdom, understanding, and intelligence to effectively and proficiently run a country with millions of people, enormous operating expenses, multitudes of problems, and ever-changing circumstances. Now imagine the overwhelming majority of a nation's leaders having no godly wisdom or heavenly understanding because they have no fear of God, which is the beginning of true wisdom (Proverbs 9:10). Their leadership becomes foolishness because, without God's guidance, they become fools.

In 2 Chronicles 15 and 16, God sends two different prophets to a king of Judah by the name of Asa. God tells Asa through His prophet Azariah,

> The Lord is with you when you are with Him. And if you seek Him, He will let you find Him; but if you forsake Him, He will forsake you. (2 Chronicles 15:2)

Then a second prophet, Hanani, told King Asa this:

> The eyes of the Lord move to and fro throughout the earth that He may strongly support those whose heart is completely His. (2 Chronicles 16:9)

America has forsaken God and consequently, He has forsaken her. God has been kicked out of her schools, courts, government, businesses, many of the homes and in some cases, even out of the churches. People only want to keep Him around as some cuddly mascot, as long as He stays in His place and doesn't put any demands on them. Some may want to retain His name in the pledge of allegiance and keep His name on dollar bills but refuse to obey Him, and therefore He has forsaken them. The nation's problems grow worse and troubles multiply by the minute, but still it doesn't wholeheartedly turn back to God. Consequently, every attempt to solve difficulties only exacerbates the troubles. Wise men in leadership positions are lacking because so few leaders have a genuine fear and reverence for God.

Therefore, one shouldn't be a bit surprised if the leaders are incapable of intelligently running their nation and producing commonsense solutions to the country's problems, because God has deprived them of the ability to so much as manage a simple hole in the ground. This statement paraphrases the very words of Jesus Himself when He said, "Apart from Me you can do nothing" (John 15:5).

Eenie-Meenie-Miney-Mo

Did you ever hear about the foolish church member who always read his Bible in a very lazy and moronic way? Every day when he sat down to read the Scriptures, he would just close his eyes and plop open his Bible to any random page, and then, with his eyes tightly shut, he would simply stab his fingertip on the exposed page. Whatever Scripture verse his bony limb landed on is what he believed God was saying to him that day.

After weeks of practicing this scriptural roulette, a day came when his ridiculous method of Bible study went like this—haphazardly flipping pages, he jabbed his finger on a verse that said, "and [Judas] went away and hanged himself" (Matthew 27:5). Thinking that God couldn't be talking to him through this verse, he closed his eyes again and flipped to a different page, landing his finger on a verse that said, "Go and do the same" (Luke 10:37). Believing there was no way God was telling Him to go out and hang himself, he tried his luck again with the finger pointing. Turning to a new page, he blindly poked a verse that said, "What you do, [go and] do quickly" (John 13:27). Well the senseless man ignored this command, as well, and is still poking around in the Word of God to find what he wants to hear and believe.

Rather than diligently studying the Bible in order to see the relevancy of what the Lord is saying in his life, he merely plays a game of "Eenie-Meenie-Miney-Mo." Unfortunately, there are a number of professing Christians today who take this approach to studying the Bible. Very few church members have ever taken the time or made the effort to read the Word of God from cover to cover. But it was Jesus who told Satan, "Man shall not live on bread alone, but on every word that proceeds out of the mouth of God" (Matthew 4:4).

In addition, Paul tells us to study our Bible in such a way that we will not be "ashamed" when we stand before the Lord (2 Timothy 2:15). People in cults will be utterly ashamed when they stand before the God of heaven while He rebukes them for the ways in which they perverted, denied, and distorted His words in order to get Scripture to say things that God never intended. Furthermore, lethargic and indifferent Christians will be embarrassed when they are divinely reproved for the casual and offhanded manner in which they responded to the words of their Creator. If we do not read God's Word diligently and in its entirety, then we fail to get the full counsel of the Lord and fail to grasp the importance of what God is saying. Consequently, we become hamstrung when it comes to defending the faith and growing to our fullest spiritual potential.

God does not play games when He speaks, and we should not play games when it comes to listening to Him. Reading the Bible is not an entertaining pastime of "Eenie-Meenie-Miney-Mo"; rather, it is a very serious study of what our Creator has to say to us. It was Jesus who said, "Heaven and earth will pass away, but My words will [remain forever]" (Luke 21:33).

Only a lunatic or God Almighty could say such a thing and mean it. This is why reading the Bible should never become a game of "pick and choose," or a sport of twisting and distorting what the Bible declares and what the Son of God has proclaimed. To do so will surely incur the wrath of a God who has made Himself synonymous with His every word.

The Mouth of a Jackass

Of all the countless species on earth, only two creatures (outside of man) have communicated with human language. One was a serpent and the other, a jackass. In their communicating with man, the crafty reptile spoke the words of Satan, while the dumb animal spoke the words of God. Unfortunately for mankind, the viper's words were heeded, and sadly for one man, the words of a donkey were not.

The Gentile prophet by the name of Balaam developed a famous reputation for pronouncing blessings and curses on both men and nations from the mouth of the Lord. His fame grew so great that a Moabite king by the name of Balak promised the prophet great riches and rewards if he would simply come and curse the people of God. However, God told Balaam that he was not to curse Israel. King Balak kept tempting the man of God to denounce the Jews, and in doing so, he would make the seer a very wealthy and powerful man.

The prophet was truly conflicted. He wanted to follow and obey God, but he was desperate to please the king and thereby receive his compensations. While riding his donkey to meet the king of Moab, God considered slaying the prophet with a flaming sword at the hand of an angel because of his double-mindedness. In God's mercy and compassion, though, He resolved to give Balaam a warning by speaking to him through the mouth of a jackass.

Three different times Balaam's mule saw the angel of the Lord with his flaming weapon, and each time, the terrified animal refused to go near the glory of this divine messenger. Unaware of the angel's threatening presence, on the third time that the donkey refused to go in the direction of the angel, Balaam began beating it out of extreme anger and total frustration. Amazingly, the mule asked its infuriated master three distinct questions. The prophet was so enraged that instead of being shocked into a dumbfounded silence, he angrily answered each of the mule's questions. The conversation (found in Numbers 22:28-30) went as follows:

> **Donkey:** What have I done to you that you have struck me these three times?

Balaam: Because you have made a mockery of me! If there had been a sword in my hand, I would have killed you by now.

Donkey: Am I not your donkey on which you have ridden all your life to this day? Have I ever been accustomed to do so to you?

Balaam: No.

Once the dialogue ended, God opened the stubborn prophet's eyes and he, too, saw the divine being with a burning sword. The angel of the Lord told him if it weren't for the donkey's avoidance of him, he would have killed the headstrong man and let the beast live. Balaam promised God he would say and do only what He told him, and nothing else. In the end, however, Balaam figured out a way to "technically" obey God, while at the same time please the king of Moab. His attempts to "have his cake and eat it too" only led him to die the death of the wicked (see Joshua 13:22). Balaam's spiritual two-step so disgraced him before heaven that he is mentioned three different times in the New Testament as a dark warning to others to avoid the "way of Balaam," the "error of Balaam," and the "teaching of Balaam" (2 Peter 2:15, Jude 11, Revelation 2:14).

Thousands of years have come and gone, yet nothing has really changed, because human nature has not changed. God is constantly speaking His words today through pastors, ministers, and priests in order to direct His people and to save the lost. Nonetheless, when stubborn and self-willed people refuse to listen to His voice, He will often use a jackass as a last resort to get people turned around and to listen to Him.

I am not a pastor, neither a minister nor a priest. As a matter of fact, I have often been referred to as the equivalent of a "horse's rear end" or an ignorant "bull in a china shop," but it doesn't really matter whether people view me as being a jackass or a dumb ox. What matters is whether or not God is using laypeople like me as a last resort in order to keep stubborn souls from plunging headlong into the fate of His wayward prophet. So, the next time we think a prophet of sorts is nothing but a jackass, we need to ask ourselves if God just might be trying to tell us something through the mouth of an obstinate mule.

The Spiritual Invasion

Did you know there is nothing in the physical universe that does not have a spiritual counterpart, or point back to God in some way? A plant contains life, an insect has consciousness, an animal can think, and a man possesses reason. Even a stone can reflect back to God by the mere fact that it exists and would cry out if Christ's disciples were silenced (see Luke 19:40). From a drop of life-giving water to stellar galaxies, the glory of God can be perceived everywhere man looks.

To the spiritually minded, God can even be recognized in His judgments. When a nation loves, honors, and obeys God, that nation is blessed and prospers in a multitude of different ways. However, when a country forsakes the Lord and dishonors Him with idolatrous and sinful practices, then He will plague them with a host of problems intended to bring them back to Him in repentance. Consequently, the more obstinate and stiff-necked a land becomes, the more numerous and severe the curses will become until a country is broken, often beyond repair. I call these curses "spiritual invasions," as God uses various types of invasions to get our attention.

Take, for example, the complicated and perplexing problem of illegal immigration. It is a hot-button issue, troubling both Europe and America. Europe was once the cradle of civilization but is now almost completely secularized, and Europeans mostly view God with indifference or contempt. They have endured the devastation of two world wars, and now their very way of life is threatened by innumerable immigrants flooding their shores, particularly from the Muslim world.

As the difficulties and tensions mount over this delicate and sensitive concern, the label of "racism" is invariably used to halt all discussion and paralyze any debate in regards to finding workable solutions. This divisiveness is a form of God's judgment, and we have no hope of ever manifesting wise and common-sense decisions until we recognize God's hand in this and seek Him for wisdom.

In the writings of Moses, God told His people Israel that if they forsook Him and began to act with hostility toward Him, the following would be the end result:

> A people whom you do not know shall eat up the produce of your ground and all your labors, and ... you shall bring out much seed to the field but you will gather in little, for the locusts will consume it. ... The alien who is among you shall rise above you higher and higher, but you will go down lower and lower. He shall lend to you, but you will not lend to him; he shall be the head, and you will be the tail. So all these curses shall come on you and pursue you and overtake you until you are destroyed, because you would not obey the Lord your God by keeping His commandments and His statutes which He commanded you. ... Therefore you shall serve your enemies whom the Lord will send against you. ... The Lord will bring a nation against you from afar ... a nation whose language you shall not understand ... [and it] shall eat the offspring of your herd and the produce of your ground until you are destroyed, who also leaves you no grain, new wine, or oil, nor increase of your herd or the young of your flock until they have caused you to perish. ... Then you shall be left few in number, whereas you were as numerous as the stars of heaven, because you did not obey the Lord your God. (Deuteronomy 28:33, 38, 43-45, 48-51, 62)

During the Revolutionary War on April 18, 1775, Paul Revere made his historic ride throughout the towns and villages of Concord and Lexington, warning the American people that the British were coming. His words were meant to sound the alarm to mobilize people to take defensive action against an invading army.

Today the United States has more than 7,500 miles of border (5,525 miles along its northern border and 1,954 miles along its southern border). It has been estimated that as many as 525,000 undocumented immigrants cross its border each year, 25,000 from the Canadian side and up to 500,000 from the Mexican side.[10]] [11]

Conservatively, there now appears to be between 8 and 12 million people who are in the U.S. illegally, while a more realistic estimate places the figure between 15 and 20 million.[12] Although America's present economic woes have slowed the influx of people breaking into the nation, the numbers are still climbing.

In spite of this alarming situation, an increasing number of liberal activists (along with social and religious organizations) defend and promote this practice. The illegal "invasion" of millions of people (and the millions more on their way) is simply not a healthy situation for any country. In short, it is bankrupting America. Their numbers are overwhelming schools, courts, jails and prisons, and social services, especially the welfare programs. Nevertheless, this phenomenon has become the proverbial elephant sitting in the living room that no one wants to notice or mention, lest they be labeled as "racist," "hateful," or "intolerant." As a nation, America has become paralyzed when it comes to addressing this issue with any kind of resolve. In essence, it has become just one more complicated situation that continues to grow worse and for which there is no solution, as people continue to engage in pointless hand-wringing and meaningless rhetoric.

With each passing day, the undocumented immigrants within the U.S. borders are rising higher and higher as they continue to obtain more positions of power and influence, because God is allowing it. Soon their vast numbers—many in key positions, influencing almost every decision and policy—along with America's inability to respond, will guarantee that they will be ruling the nation, all because of one spiritual reason: God's judgment on a nation that has turned away from Him.

There are a few lone voices that have become modern-day Paul Reveres, but their warnings are falling on deaf ears because of the spiritual invasions. From the White House to the State House, the political leaders have become paralyzed with political correctness and hamstrung with a spirit of foolishness. They are blinded with special-interest money, intoxicated with power, and driven by self-interest. Their inebriation with authority (their own, not God's) has impaired their judgment, distorted their understanding, and clouded their reasoning—and, again, the cause is spiritual.

Essentially, America has become incapable of making commonsense decisions because she has forsaken God, and every undocumented immigrant in the country should rejoice over this. They should rejoice in the fact that America is at war with the Almighty because the house they have broken into will someday be given to them.

Illegal Immigration: Border Crossing Deaths Have Doubled Since 1995; Border Patrol's Efforts to Prevent Deaths Have Not Been Fully Evaluated. Rep. no. GAO06-770. Washington, DC: United States Government Accountability Office, 2006. Print.

"Canada-United States Border." *Wikipedia*. Wikimedia Foundation, 28 Nov. 2013. Web. 03 Dec. 2013.

Elbel, Fred. "How Many Illegal Aliens Are in the U.S.?" *The American Resistance*. The American Resistance Foundation, 2005. Web. 03 Dec. 2013.

Clowns Abound

Go to a rodeo and you'll see a couple of clowns; go to a fair and you'll see a few more; go to a circus and you'll see clowns all around; but you'll see even more at Mardi Gras, a place where clowns abound. Fat Tuesday in New Orleans becomes alive with an endless procession of merry-making clowns. Regardless of where you go, you can immediately recognize clowns by their outlandish costumes, their layers of ridiculous make-up, and their riotous antics. They are clumsy buffoons, entertaining jesters, boorish comedians, and silly tricksters.

Everyone knows that the clowns' bizarre behavior is just an act, a show intended to ignite laughter through a performance highly comical and disconnected from reality. Conversely, an alarming number of clowns today are not easily recognized, and are anything but funny. They hide behind painted smiles and ordinary costumes, and their antics are not meant to amuse, but to abuse. They are what Jesus referred to as wolves in sheep's clothing. He cautioned, "Beware of the false prophets, who come to you in sheep's clothing, but inwardly are ravenous wolves" (Matthew 7:15).

When the disciples of Jesus asked Him, "What will be the sign of Your coming and the end of the age?" the first thing Christ warned about, and the thing that led the list of all the end-time signs, was an exponential increase in false teachers, false prophets, and false messiahs. Jesus admonished them,

> See to it that no one misleads you. For many will come in My name saying, "I am the Christ" and will mislead many. ... At that time many will fall away and will betray one another and hate one another. Many false prophets will arise and will mislead many. (Matthew 24:4, 10-11)

He similarly reproved them in the gospels of Mark and Luke:

> See to it that you are not misled; for many will come in My name, saying, "I am He," and "The time is near." Do not go after them. (Luke 21:8; see also Mark 13:5-6)

The apostle Paul similarly warned,

> The Spirit explicitly says that in the later times some will fall away from the faith, paying attention to deceitful spirits and doctrines of demons. (1 Timothy 4:1)

> The time will come when they will not endure sound doctrine; but wanting to have their ears tickled, they will accumulate for themselves teachers in accordance to their own desires, and will turn away their ears from the truth and will turn aside to myths. (2 Timothy 4:3-4)

Peter also warned of this:

> False prophets also arose among the people, just as there will also be false teachers among you, who will secretly introduce destructive heresies, even denying the Master who bought them ... and in their greed they will exploit you with false words. (2 Peter 2:1, 3)

In 2 Corinthians 11 and in Galatians 1, Paul implores Christians to be very discerning because there is another Jesus, a false gospel, and a different spirit that can lead people away from the simplicity and pure devotion to Christ. He was angry and amazed that some people were so quickly deserting the Lord Jesus due to the influence of false teachers and deceitful prophets.

Paul was so livid about these false prophets that he said even if an "angel of light" were to preach anything different than what the believers learned from him, such an angel was to be eternally accursed or damned. Then Paul repeated this pronouncement of damnation on any false teachers, in order to emphasize the seriousness of his warnings (Galatians 1:6-9).

When Paul was saying farewell to the Christians at Ephesus, the last thing he said to them was,

> Be on guard for yourselves and for all the flock, among which the Holy Spirit has made you overseers, to shepherd the church of God which He purchased with His own blood. I know that after my departure savage wolves will come in among you, not sparing the flock; and from among your own

selves men will arise, speaking perverse things, to draw away the disciples after them. Therefore be on the alert, remembering that night and day for a period of three years I did not cease to admonish each one with tears. (Acts 20:28-31)

God goes to great lengths, both in the Old Testament and the New, to warn men of the dangers of false teachers and the perils of misleading prophets. They are wolves in sheep's clothing; and today, as predicted, they are coming out of the woodwork and multiplying like locusts.

Clowns pretend to be something they are not and are humorous because of it. False prophets profess to be one thing, but in actuality, they are something totally different, and in the eyes of heaven, they are anything but funny. Their false words, their deceptive behavior, and their misleading clothing can be so convincing that they even manage to delude themselves with their own lies. But of them, Jesus said,

Many will say to Me on that day, "Lord, Lord, did we not prophesy in Your name, and in Your name cast out demons, and in Your name perform many miracles?" And then I will declare to them, "I never knew you; depart from me, you who practice lawlessness." (Matthew 7:2223)

Clowns abound! Everywhere we look we can see people pretending to be something they are not. Our only hope of not being carried away with this present deluge of religious clowns is to heed these words of Paul:

We are no longer to be children, tossed here and there by waves and carried about by every wind of doctrine, by the trickery of men, by craftiness in deceitful scheming; but speaking the truth in love, we are to grow up in all aspects into Him who is the head, even Christ. (Ephesians 4:14-15)

Young and Dumb

When we are young, we are dumb. There are no exceptions. We may like to think this fact of life does not apply to us (especially when we are young), but the youth of every generation are simply lacking in a great deal of wisdom. Only experience can bring wisdom, because acquiring it is a process. The bumper sticker touting, "Hire a teenager while he still knows everything," demonstrates how adamantly a young person would revolt at being called "dumb." I was certainly no exception. The apostle Paul summarized this truth nicely:

> When I was a child, I used to speak like a child, think like a child, reason like a child; when I became a man, I did away with childish things. (1 Corinthians 13:11)

Due to the fact that young people lack a great deal of insight, they are prone to do foolish and reckless things that can have far-reaching consequences: posting nude photos of themselves on the internet, drag racing in the rain, joining gangs, using drugs, getting drunk, or doing any of the myriads of things that can impair their futures—and even lead to premature death. In short, their lack of wisdom puts them and others at great risk when it comes to foolish behavior with regrettable results.

God fully realizes the dangerous pitfalls of being young and the severe outcomes that youthful actions can produce. Therefore He essentially communicates to the youth, "Look, even though you are very young, and even though you are very dumb, if you just listen to My instruction and do what I tell you, you can avoid an awful lot of negative consequences in your life. But you must pay close attention to what I am telling you; and if you do, you will not only escape many disasters, you will become wiser than all your teachers and all your friends as well."

Solomon's book of Proverbs is perhaps the best instruction manual God has written for young people and is useful for them in the following ways:

> To know wisdom and instruction, to discern the sayings of understanding, to receive instruction in wise behavior,

righteousness, justice and equity; to give prudence to the naive, to the youth knowledge and discretion. ... Fools despise wisdom and instruction. (Proverbs 1:2-4, 7)

Solomon later goes on to say,

Wisdom shouts in the street, she lifts her voice in the square; at the head of the noisy streets she cries out; at the entrance of the gates in the city she utters her sayings: "How long, O naive ones, will you love being simpleminded? And scoffers delight themselves in scoffing and fools hate knowledge? Turn to my reproof, behold, I will pour out my spirit on you; I will make my words known to you." (Proverbs 1:20-23)

Solomon warns the "young and dumb" that if they refuse to listen to wisdom, "calamity [will come upon them] like a whirlwind," and they will eventually find that "distress and anguish [will overtake them]" (Proverbs 1:27) He says those who hate knowledge and spurn wisdom's reproof will be killed by their waywardness and destroyed by their complacency toward God (Proverbs 1:28-32). On the other hand, God says if a young person pays close attention to wisdom and inclines his heart to understanding, and if he cries out for discernment, he will be given wisdom, knowledge, and understanding and will be protected from poor choices and many foolish decisions (2:1-15).

According to Solomon, the Spirit of wisdom is calling out to people everywhere, especially to the young and dumb, and the longer a young person refuses to heed her voice, the more likely the immature adolescent will slowly turn into an old fool. That's why the wisest of wise men says to "remember also your Creator in the days of your youth, before the evil days come and [you no longer enjoy living]" (Ecclesiastes 12:1). Unfortunately there are many middle-aged fools and a number of foolish senior citizens who have grown into aged simpletons because they have ignored the cries of wisdom. This is not said with any kind of self-righteousness or judgmental spirit; it is simply what God warned would happen to men and women who grow old without Him.

A person can have a high IQ, be very successful in his career, or accumulate a great deal of wealth, yet still be classified "a fool" because his indifference to the words of God deprives him of spiritual enlightenment and heavenly wisdom. In contrast, someone who is young and dumb but listens to wisdom can avoid many of the pitfalls that often ensnare the naïve; such wisdom can even help avoid future behavior that would destroy marriages, fortunes, reputations, and careers.

Therefore, if you are young and want to become wise, make the Word of God (especially what He has to say in the writings of Solomon) an absolute priority in your life—because being young and dumb is inevitable, but being old and stupid is a choice.

The End of Cockroaches

Will cockroaches inherit the earth? Some people seem to think so, due to how incredibly hearty these creepy critters are. They can easily live a month without food and can exist up to two weeks without water; they can even have their heads cut off and still survive for days! How resilient is that? Female cockroaches can actually reproduce without a male, and all of their offspring turn out to be female. Amazing, isn't it?

Cockroaches are found in the most inhospitable of environments. From barren deserts to the polar icecaps, these ugly devils can dwell where most other creatures would perish in a heartbeat. Rumor has it cockroaches could survive the nuclear fallout of an all-out atomic war. The fruit fly and the parasitoid wasp (as well as a foul-smelling bacterium called *Deinococcus radiodurans*) can actually absorb much more radiation than a cockroach; nevertheless, the cockroaches' adaptability and their survival instincts are truly legendary.[13], [14]In short, don't ever expect to find cockroaches on anyone's most-endangered species list. Certainly if there were any creatures that could survive a catastrophic global disaster, the cockroach would be among the top ten contenders to inherit the earth.

However, the Bible describes a number of coming calamities that will be so life-threatening that not even a cockroach has a chance of surviving. The apostle Peter predicted,

> The present heavens and earth are being reserved for fire, kept for the day of judgment and destruction of ungodly men. ... The heavens will pass away with a roar and the elements will be destroyed with intense heat, and the earth and its works will be burned up. ... The heavens will be destroyed by burning, and the elements will melt with intense heat! (2 Peter 3:7, 10-12)

Jesus also foretold that in the coming days,

> There will be signs in the sun and moon and stars, and on the

earth dismay among nations, in perplexity at the roaring of the sea and the waves, men fainting from fear and the expectation of the things which are coming upon the world; for the powers of the heavens will be shaken. (Luke 21:25-26)

He further warned, such dreadful things are coming upon this world and all of mankind that men cannot even imagine it:

There will be a great tribulation, such as has not occurred since the beginning of the world until now, nor ever will. Unless those days [are shortened], no life [will survive]; but for the sake of the elect those days will be cut short.

(Matthew 24:21-22)

In other words, the only thing that will ensure the survival of both men and cockroaches is if Jesus Christ Himself comes back at the very closing minutes of human history and puts an abrupt end to the cascading natural disasters and the horrific nuclear destruction on earth.

Christ and His apostles have promised that devoted Christians will be spared the coming destruction and approaching sorrows. But for those who are left to experience these coming judgments, if they find themselves huddled in a hole with a cockroach, they should know ahead of time that neither one of them will crawl out of their ditch alive, if not for Christ's promise to return and rescue them. If even a resilient cockroach doesn't stand a chance of surviving without Christ, what makes man think that he can survive without Him?

Kunkel, Joseph G. "Are Cockroaches Resistant to Radiation?" *The Cockroach FAQ.* U. Massachusetts Amherst, 9 Mar. 2012. Web. 04 Dec. 2013.

Ramanujan, Krishna. "Research Reveals Key to World's Toughest Organism." *Phys.org.* Phys.org, 19 Oct. 2009. Web. 04 Dec. 2013.

The 900-Pound Gorilla

"What does a 900-pound gorilla do?"
"Anything it wants to!"

Ain't that the truth? A gorilla is so powerful and intimidating that only a fool would dare to provoke it. Imagine having a 900-pound gorilla sitting in your living room. If you were forced to live with this threatening creature, you would very likely walk cautiously around him; you wouldn't dare make eye contact nor do anything to call attention to yourself. Tiptoe! Whisper! Keep your focus down! Whatever you do, don't sneeze or awaken him, and above all, don't confront him! In a nutshell, don't disturb this grunting, slobbering ape because if you do, you will most likely live to regret it (that is, if you manage to live at all).

Well, as ridiculous as this scenario may sound, people everywhere do this with the 900-pound gorilla called "death." Death is something we don't want to mention, we don't want to talk about, and we definitely don't want to confront. We want to do everything in our power to skirt around it and pretend it doesn't exist. To most men, death is frightening, alarming, and dismaying, and the last thing anyone wants to do is deal with it. However, the Bible says the truly wise person will think much about death. They will look death right in the eyes and stare at it closely, and most of all, they will prepare to confront it (see Ecclesiastes 7:2-4).

Death is truly the 900-pound gorilla sitting in our living rooms. It will not be moved and it will not go away, regardless of how much we try to delay it or how much we attempt to avoid it. Nevertheless, the wise man will deal with it head-on because he knows "death has been swallowed up in victory" and the "sting of death" has lost its power (1 Corinthians 15:54-55). He knows that Christ has defeated death, and therefore when he puts his faith in Jesus he will surely live forever, because Christ said,

> I am the resurrection and the life; he who believes in Me will live even if he dies, and everyone who lives and believes in Me will never die. (John 11:25-26)

For the committed Christian, the terrible glare of the 900-pound gorilla of death is gone forever. It has been removed from our living rooms, and we can live our lives to the fullest because of our victory through Jesus Christ. Consequently, we are enabled to

> be steadfast, immovable, always abounding in the work of the Lord, knowing that [our] toil is not in vain in the Lord. (1 Corinthians 15:58)

The bottom line is simply that fools pretend the 900-pound gorilla is not in their living rooms, ignoring it at all costs, but the wise man will take this drooling ape by the hand and show him the door. The sage can do this because he knows that death no longer has power over him.

The key question now is, "Am I a wise man or a fool?" The 900-pound gorilla will surely elicit a response, one way or the other.

Heart of Stone

Most people understand what is meant when someone is accused of having a "heart of stone." It simply means such an individual is unfeeling, unmoving, and totally insensitive to the desires or needs of someone else. A person with a heart of stone is callous and indifferent, and at many times, just plain hostile to the loving overtures of another.

The heart is mentioned almost a thousand times in Scripture. God is constantly talking about the heart because it is the essence of a person's soul. In it reside a man's emotions and affections. Someone who has his heart set on God and the things of God will someday see Him. The individual who has his heart set on the world and the things of the world will never see heaven, and because the heart of man is so important, God never ceases to address it.

It was Jesus who said, "Where your treasure is, there your heart will be also" (Matthew 6:21). Furthermore, the greatest commandment is to "love the Lord your God with all your heart." (Matthew 22:37; Deuteronomy 6:5). Solomon said to "watch over your heart with all diligence, for from it flow the springs of life" (Proverbs 4:23). Jesus even went so far as to say, "Blessed are the pure in heart, for they shall see God" (Matthew 5:8).

On the other hand, Jeremiah declared, "The heart is more deceitful than all else and is desperately sick" (Jeremiah 17:9). Christ also said, "Out of the heart of men proceed the evil thoughts, fornications, thefts, murders, adulteries, deeds of coveting and wickedness, as well as deceit, sensuality, envy, slander, pride and foolishness" (Mark 7:21-22; Matthew 15:19).

Look at Pharaoh during the time of Moses. No less than eight times the Bible says, "God hardened Pharaoh's heart" (Exodus 7:3; 9:12; 10:1, 20, 27; 11:10; 14:4, 8). The Scriptures also tell us that Pharaoh hardened his own heart at least eight times (Exodus 7:13, 14, 22; 8:15, 19, 32; 9:7, 34).

People may very well take issue with the fact that God hardened Pharaoh's heart. Even the apostle Paul mentions people who fault God for solidifying the heart of the Egyptian king (see Romans 9:18-19). However, what we need to understand is the *way* in which God hardened Pharaoh's heart; the Lord simply shined His divine light upon him. After all, as Charles Spurgeon said it, "The same sun which melts wax hardens clay."[15] Consequently, it is not God who is to blame for someone developing a heart of stone; rather, it is the obstinate and stiff-necked person himself.

When Christ raised Lazarus from the dead, we are told that many of the Jews came to believe in Jesus—but in contrast, Caiaphas and the chief priests decided the resurrection of Lazarus was the last straw, and from that time on, searched for a way to kill the very Son of God (John 11). God's sunlight shone upon their hardened hearts to the point where they were not only determined to murder Jesus, but even plotted to put Lazarus back in the grave because his resurrection was causing so many people to look to Christ as their promised Messiah (John 12:10-11).

This powerful miracle prompted some people's hearts to soften and believe, while the same miracle caused other people's hearts to harden like concrete; God's sunlight melted some and petrified others. So, when Jesus says, "Behold I stand at the door [heart] and knock; if anyone hears My voice and opens the door, I will come in to him and will dine with him, and he with Me," it is up to us, not Him, to open the door (Revelation 3:20).

In summary, a receptive heart to the voice of God will carry a person all the way to heaven, while a hardened heart to the call of Christ will surely sink an individual like a millstone all the way to the depths of hell. The choice is ours, not God's, for "where your treasure is, there your heart will be also."

"The Same Sun Which Melts Wax Hardens Clay." Web log post. *Puritan Quotes (Wordpress)*. The Puritan Quoter, 12 Nov. 2010. Web. 04 Dec. 2013.

Morning Comes at Night

> Watchman, how far gone is the night? Watchman, how far gone is the night? The watchman says, "Morning comes but also night. If you would inquire, inquire; come back again." (Isaiah 21:11-12)

This is a very interesting way God pronounces judgment against those who hold Him in contempt and those who are enemies of His people. A watchman was like a modern-day police officer. His job was to watch for any sign of danger or evil, and to sound the alarm in order to protect innocent lives and to confront the hazards at hand. The watchman is to be ever on the alert for dangers ranging from the perils of fire to the threat of wild beasts, and from the onslaught of invading armies to the coming of natural disasters.

However, when the question is asked of the watchman, "How far gone is the night?" he replies with a contradictory statement that says, "Morning comes but also night." In careful analysis of these verses, we see the watchman is saying that there is coming a glorious morning for some and a terrible night for others. When he says, "If you would inquire, inquire; come back again," he is encouraging people to keep watching with anticipation and to always be prepared for what is coming. It may seem to take a long time, but rest assured, this coming light and approaching darkness will soon arrive. It will not delay, even though it seems so long in getting here.

The end of the world as we know it is rapidly approaching and will be here before we realize it. Then it will be a glorious morning for some and a horrible night for others; some will be delivered at daybreak while others will be devastated by nightfall. It was Jesus who said to "be on the alert, for you do not know which day your Lord is coming" and to "keep on the alert at all times, praying that you may have strength to escape all these things that are about to take place, and stand before the Son of Man" (Matthew 24:42; Luke 21:36). He told the Christians at the church in Philadelphia that because they persevered in obedience to His Word, He would "keep [them] from the hour of testing … which [was] about to come upon the whole world" (Revelation 3:10).

This is now the twilight hour—the most dangerous time of the day. It is the gray twilight just before morning as well as just prior to evening. It is the time when objects are most difficult to discern—an hour when the distances of things are hardest to evaluate; according to insurance companies, the occurrences of auto accidents increase during this critical interval. It is also a period when the greatest number of suicides and other fatalities take place—right before dawn and at dusk.

We are now in the interim when we need to be most alert and to inquire, "Watchman, how far gone is the night?" This is no season to doze and no age to sleep because the danger is imminent and the rewards, immediate. Are we slumbering as if no danger exists, or are we preparing as if time is of the essence? The consequences of our actions, or the results of our inaction, will determine whether or not we will escape the coming darkness of despair and judgment. The choice is ours and it would behoove us to never stop asking, "Watchman, how far gone is the night?" because morning will surely come at evening and nightfall, at dawn.

Slow-Motion Train Wreck

Ask little children what they want to be when they grow up, and their answer will range anywhere from being a fire fighter or famous actor to becoming President or a renowned athlete. Kids dream of popularity and success, and they fantasize about fame and fortune. No children in their right minds say when they grow up they want to live on death row; be a drug addict or an alcoholic; or become a child molester, a mass murderer, or a derelict lying in a gutter.

Well, if no rational child aspires to grow up and become a person whose life is characterized by increasing dysfunction, then why do so many innocent children develop into adults whose existence demonstrates a host of major malfunctions? They drop out of school and become prostitutes, dope addicts, criminals, and an array of unproductive members of society. Everywhere we look we can see people whose lives have become shipwrecked and destroyed by poor choices with negative consequences.

Again, the obvious question is, "Why do so many virtuous children grow up to become such dysfunctional adults?" Undoubtedly, the reasons can vary greatly and at times be complicated. However, there is a Chinese proverb that says, "A journey of a thousand miles begins with a single step." In other words, no one goes to bed at night and wakes up with a ruined life (unless, of course, they are hit by a natural disaster or are terribly victimized by criminals or disease). The truth is that a dysfunctional and unproductive life is almost always the accumulative result of a lifetime of poor choices and bad decisions. Paul the apostle said it best when he wrote under the inspiration of God's Spirit:

> Do not be deceived, God is not mocked; for whatever a man sows, this he will also reap. For the one who sows to his own flesh will from the flesh reap corruption, but the one who sows to the Spirit will from the Spirit reap eternal life. Let us not lose heart in doing good, for in due time we will reap if we do not grow weary. So then, while we have opportunity, let us do good to all people. (Galatians 6:7-10)

Do you see? It's really not that complicated or difficult to understand. Just as surely as God has established physical laws, He has instituted spiritual laws as well. If anyone sows to the wind, he will in time surely reap the whirlwind. Anyone who thinks he can jump off a ten-story building and fly away is a fool, for the law of gravity will drop him like a heavy stone on the concrete below; and anyone who thinks he can disregard the counsel of God will eventually end up with a ruined life and nightmarish eternity. But it all happens ever so slowly. Like a seed planted in the ground, it can take months or even years before we see the fruit of our choices.

A lifetime of ignorant decisions and poor choices does not produce instant destruction; it's more like a slow-motion train wreck, resulting in one devastating impact after another because of multiple foolish decisions. Bystanders look on in stunned disbelief when they realize there is little they can do to halt the devastation or the acquired damage that others (especially their loved ones) may bring upon themselves through their habitual sowing to the wind.

Only God can salvage such a ruinous mess, but He will not change a thing unless people humbly look to Him in prayer and resolve that with His grace they are going to change. The transformation will surely be long and painful because "as the twig is bent, so grows the tree." It will take years of hard work and godly discipline to clean up the accumulative messes from the poor choices in one's life, but God can salvage anything, including the demolition of a slow-motion train wreck. He can still take our childhood dreams and turn them into productive realities, if we only let Him—by making Him, instead of ourselves, the Lord of our lives.

Bottled Water

Water sold in plastic bottles is somewhat of a recent phenomenon. When bottled water first appeared in supermarkets and in vending machines, many people in America thought it was a joke. Why pay good money for an ordinary and abundant product that practically anyone could get out of a faucet for virtually nothing?

Well a couple of decades after bottled water first arrived on store shelves, it has now become an amazing money-making enterprise. There are so many brands, sizes, and health claims of bottled water that it is almost impossible to keep up with the promotions of this multibillion-dollar industry.

Would you believe God has been in the bottled-water business for thousands of years? It was the ancient psalmist who wrote, "You have taken account of my wanderings; put my tears in Your bottle. Are they not in Your book?" (Psalm 56:8).

Imagine that. God saves all of the tears of His people in a bottle! He does not forget their heartbreak, disappointment, grief, and pain. How many tears do you think have been shed since human history began? No one could possibly number them, yet God is so moved by His people's tears that He will not permit one drop to disappear into the ground or to evaporate into thin air.

If God is so stirred by the weeping of men, why does He allow tears to form at all? It was David who gave us the answer to this perplexing question when he said, "My tears have been my food day and night, while they say to me all day long 'Where is your God?'" (Psalm 42:3). David also declared, "You have fed them with the bread of tears, and You have made them to drink tears in large measure" (80:5).

No one drinks salt water, whether it is bottled or not, because consuming seawater will eventually drive a person mad and will surely kill him. But the salty tears God gives us to drink through our sorrows and our sufferings actually become nourishment for our souls. Our tears deepen us, they enrich us, and they mature us. Our tears drive us to God for His comfort, and they bring us to our knees in quiet desperation. Nothing feeds our spiritual growth like bitter tears.

Nothing transforms us into images of Christ the way weeping does. It is pain, not happiness, that deepens men; and it is sorrow and tears, not pleasure or laughter, that strengthen mankind.

The shortest verse in the New Testament is "Jesus wept" (John 11:35). His tears speak volumes. He entered the arena of human grief so much that His tears, almost more than anything else, identified Him with men and women everywhere and throughout all time. Tears are the universal language in a world torn apart with differences. We can find comfort whenever those drops of saline solution fall from our eyes, as we remember they are being stored in a bottle that God will pour out before us in His presence. Then He will explain why every drop was shed for an eternal purpose and for our good and His glory.

The only human tears that are shed in vain are the ones that men themselves pour out of God's bottle. They refuse to feed upon them. They reject God's transforming effects of tears, so their eternal nourishment escapes them, and they are therefore destined to weep forever in an eternal place of "weeping and gnashing of teeth" (Matthew 13:42). They are unlike the sinful woman who came to Jesus and washed His feet with her sobbing; not one of her painful tears escaped God's bottle because she was transformed by her weeping (Luke 7:36-50).

When we purchase water in a bottle, we can be reminded that God has His own bottled water, and His vessel of human tears will truly quench our eternal thirst—if only we allow His infinite wisdom and love to transform us through those captured tears.

Fluff in the Rough

It doesn't take a PhD to recognize the growing problems and escalating dangers facing our world today. Like never before in history, mankind faces a flood of insurmountable difficulties and a deluge of unsolvable problems. In spite of such incredible troubles, it is truly astonishing to hear the important questions with which so many people occupy themselves, such as:

"Is it true that blondes have more fun?"

"Who is competing in the Super Bowl?"

"Who is the greatest athlete, most famous celebrity, richest

CEO, or most talented rock band?"

"How is the weather outside?"

These questions are fine, in and of themselves, but such inquiries in the face of so much global unrest and so many social ills are truly shallow and shortsighted, to say the least. Even more baffling is the growing number of churches today that are preaching gospels of health, wealth, and prosperity, and promoting social agendas in the midst of such spiritual darkness. So much of what is being preached in the pulpits today is simply fluff in the face of so much spiritual darkness and impending doom.

Preachers of the "prosperity gospel" will argue that people need an upbeat and positive message because times are so difficult and trying. They say people don't need to be told they are sinners and in need of repentance; rather, that they are basically good people in need of prosperity and improved self-esteem. These preachers and teachers of positive thinking will constantly cherry-pick Scriptures in order to support their claims that if you just send them enough money, God will bless you abundantly with riches and success, and with happiness and fulfillment! However, social gospels, prosperity gospels, and self-esteem gospels are not the real gospel. The true gospel is the "good news" that is epitomized in the words of John. These 25 little words are the greatest, most powerful, most wonderful 25 words ever spoken in sequence. You can essentially distill the entire Bible down into these few words:

> For God so loved the world [man], that He gave His only begotten Son [Jesus], that whoever believes in Him [obeys him] shall not perish [go to hell] but have eternal life [enter heaven]. (John 3:16)

That's the gospel, the good news in a nutshell! It tells of God's love, man's sinfulness, the need to repent, and the necessity to commit our lives to Jesus Christ in order to be saved from the fires of hell. Any other gospel is merely fluff, and those who disseminate them are beating the air with false hopes and a deceptive message. Such gospels cannot save anyone. As God said through Jeremiah the prophet, "Harvest [time] is past, summer is ended, and [still] we are not saved" (Jeremiah 8:20).

Fluff cannot produce salvation, only repentance can. Whether it's fluff in the world or fluff in the church, it's never going to sink below the shallow and superficial interests. If we are to be saved, we have got to go deeper and live in the depths of truth and get to the bottom of spiritual realities where God's words are truly weighty and transforming, not fluffy and delusional. Indeed, we need a heavy message in the midst of so much hot air if people are truly going to be given lasting prosperity and eternal self-esteem.

The Fate of Slugs

Slugs and snails are remarkable creatures. The only difference between these mollusks with soft bodies is that snails have hard, spiral shells for protection, while slugs have no such safeguard. They are equally notorious, however, for their slow, leisurely movements. They move so slowly that they project the image of having an abundance of time. Nothing can hurry their movements, not even the threat of death or the hazards of danger. Their lazy plodding has given rise to the word "sluggard," and the Bible has some very definite instructions for people whose lives characterize the existence of a slug. God directs,

> Go to the ant, O sluggard, observe her ways and be wise, which, having no chief, officer or ruler, prepares her food in the summer and gathers her provision in the harvest. How long will you lie down, O sluggard? When will you arise from your sleep? "A little sleep, a little slumber, a little folding of the hands to rest"—your poverty will come in like a vagabond and your need like an armed man. (Proverbs 6:6-11)

Of the sluggard the Bible also declares, "Like vinegar to the teeth and smoke to the eyes, so is the lazy one to those who send him" (Proverbs 10:26). In other words, a sluggard can be extremely irritating to those who are depending upon him to get an important job accomplished. Moreover, Solomon says, "The soul of the sluggard craves and gets nothing, but the soul of the diligent is made fat"; and, "The sluggard does not plow after the autumn, so he begs during the harvest and has nothing" (13:4, 20:4). A lazy person will constantly make excuses for his slothfulness and will always justify his indolence, as disclosed in Proverbs 26:16, "The sluggard is wiser in his own eyes than seven men who can give a discreet answer."

In Proverbs 24, Solomon repeats God's instruction, noting again the warning to sluggards:

I passed by the field of the sluggard and by the vineyard of the man lacking sense, and behold, it was completely overgrown with thistles; its surface was covered with nettles, and its stone wall was broken down. When I saw, I reflected upon it; I looked and received instruction. "A little sleep, a little slumber, a little folding of the hands to rest," then your poverty will come as a robber and your want like an armed man. (vv. 30-34)

A lazy person will seldom, if ever, amount to much in regards to being successful. For example, sluggards will drop out of school and invent every justification they can for doing so, except that they are lazy. Then they will proceed to turn to the government to support them or will engage in criminal activity to make a living. If they have children, they will very likely pass on their lethargy to them and future generations as well. Consequently, they are destined to wake up in a prison or to live in poverty and "beg during the harvest," just as Solomon foretold.

Would you believe a spiritual sluggard is so nauseating to Christ that He said He would "spew [him] out of [His] mouth" (Revelation 3:16, Amp)? Those are extremely harsh words. They are offensive and are bound to provoke a negative reaction, but we must never forget, it was the Son of God who said this, not a son of Adam. The only hope for a slothful soul is to follow Christ's advice and "buy gold from Him refined by fire" (v. 18).

In other words, it's going to be very costly to be transformed from a slow-moving sluggard into an industrious and hard-working servant of God, but it will be extremely worth it in the end. Anyone who loses a great deal of excess weight through a rigorous routine of exercise and discipline would say that all of their hard work was worth it, once they've reached their desired goal. Likewise, the spiritual rewards for a sluggard are countless if he is willing to train himself and submit to the strenuous disciplines of God's Spirit.

Paul refers to our spiritual life as a "race":

Do you not know that those who run in a race all run, but only one receives the prize? Run in such a way that you may win. Everyone who competes in the games exercises self-control in all things. They then do it to receive a perishable wreath, but we an imperishable. Therefore I run in such a way, as not without aim; I box in such a way, as not beating the air; but I discipline my body and make it my slave, so that, after I have preached to others, I myself will not be disqualified. (1 Corinthians 9:24-27)

Additionally, the author of Hebrews says there is a great cloud of witnesses watching us run this race, so we are admonished to

lay aside every encumbrance and the sin which so easily entangles us, and let us run with endurance the race that is set before us, fixing our eyes on Jesus, the author and perfecter of faith. (Hebrews 12:1-2)

Slothfulness is a sin. It was listed by the early church fathers as being one of the "seven deadly sins" sure to damn a soul. A spiritual sluggard, apathetic to the things of God, is in danger of waking up in hell. His fate is sealed and his destination is certain, yet guidelines to preventing spiritual complacency can be found in both the Old and the New Testaments. "Whatever you do, do your work *heartily*, as for the Lord rather than for men," and as Peter says, be *diligent* in our relationship with Christ (Colossians 3:23; 2 Peter 3:14). Lastly, recall how God said He made us to know, love and serve Him with all of our *strength* (Deuteronomy 6:5).

Consequently, the fate of a slow-moving slug in the face of life-threatening danger is obvious, and the eternal fate of spiritual sluggards will be nothing short of fatal as well.

Fat Guy in a Red Suit

Merry X-mas! Season's Greetings! Happy Holidays! Yuletide solstice! Joyful Kwanzaa! Happy Hanukkah, Ramadan, winter break, and dream tree! These are a few of the politically correct salutations people use in order to camouflage the true meaning of Christmas. Let's admit it, a growing segment of humanity can't stomach the thought of publicly honoring Jesus at Christmas, even though He is truly the reason for the season.

People just want Christmas without Christ, gifts without the Giver, and celebrations without Jesus, because they want salvation without repentance, heaven without hell, and God without commandments. That is why Christmas has now been reduced to simply getting excited about a fat guy in a red suit doing the 100-yard dash with a bag of clanging junk on his back. Whatever you do, don't mention Christ! Don't invoke His name! By all means, don't have a nativity scene displayed in the open, lest someone be offended or some attorney throw a lawsuit at you.

Why is there so much animosity toward Jesus at Christmas? Clearly, it is because "our struggle is not against flesh and blood, but against the rulers, against the powers … and against the spiritual forces of wickedness [of this age]" (Ephesians 6:12). Otherwise, it shouldn't bother anyone if someone wants to express a belief in the Bible; it would elicit no response unless deep down, something (our spirit) gets stirred within to cause an emotional response.

It makes sense that Satan would utterly hate Christmas, because Christ's birth heralds the beginning of his end. Jesus coming into this world announced the devil's upcoming defeat and proclaimed that a new ruler, a new age, and a new kingdom were about to be born. It was the prophet Isaiah who foretold of this coming new King and of this coming new government when he predicted *over 700 years before* the birth of Jesus,

> A child will be born to us, a son will be given to us; and the government will rest on His shoulders; and His name will be called Wonderful Counselor, Mighty God, Eternal Father, Prince of Peace. There will be no end to the increase of His

government or of peace, on the throne of David and over his kingdom, to establish it and to uphold it with justice and righteousness from then on and forevermore. The zeal of the Lord of hosts will accomplish this. (Isaiah 9:6-7)

No wonder this two-horned devil wants to stamp out Christmas, in light of Isaiah's proclamation. It is no mystery why he has duped so many gullible people in our schools, courts, businesses, and government institutions into going along with his charade of political correctness and his convoluted arguments about the "separation of church and state," prohibiting any reference to the Lord practically anywhere.

However, all those who foolishly insist on ridding Christmas of the name of Christ will, in the end, be forced to bend their knees and confess with their mouths that Jesus Christ is Lord (see Philippians 2:10-11). At that time they are going to desperately wish they had honored the name of Jesus during their lifetime (acknowledging Him on His birthday is a start). I personally have nothing against Old Saint Nick; he is a fine entertainer and a jolly guy to have around when celebrating the birth of God's Son. Santa Claus is a nice tradition— as long as we realize he is just a fat man in a red suit doing the 100-yard dash, and not the reason for the season. So with resounding joy, I bid you, "Merry Christmas!"

Death of the Grim Reaper

Death—the king of terrors, the ruler of intimidation and the sovereign of dismay. His icy stare has been around for millenia and is seen and known in every culture on earth. He beckons from the graveyards of the world, waits at the threshold of every home, and manifests his ominous presence among every living creature on earth. No one can escape his presence or ignore his call. He can be seen standing over the cribs of infants and at the bedsides of the aged. His horror can be seen in the eyes of a drowning man and the face of a burning soldier. He can be heard calling from a distance, or seen striking from a blind side.

It has been said that "nothing is certain but death and taxes"; however, even taxes do not possess the long reach and the inflexibility of death. Death reigns supreme; he has no equal. Where did this coldblooded monster come from? What Pandora's box did this repulsive menace crawl out of? Is there no hope of ever defeating him and exterminating his terrible existence?

From Greek mythology to Marvel comics and from the black plague to the scourge of AIDS, death has been depicted as the Grim Reaper. He is portrayed as a cold figure with a lengthy sickle in one hand and an hourglass in the other. He is clothed in a long, black, hooded robe, and his hourglass tells him when a person's time is up. He then uses his razor-sharp blade to cut down every unfortunate individual and steal away their soul without the slightest twinge of mercy or compassion.

Perhaps his ominous appearance originated from hooded monks praying at the bedside of the dying or from the Old World farmers who used to cut down their standing grain while dressed in dark clothing and pointed hoods. Regardless of how his hooded persona originated, the bad news is that the Grim Reaper is truly an angel from hell, unleashed by the foolishness and pride of one man and one gullible woman. God Himself warned them never to unlock the door labeled, "the tree of the knowledge of good and evil" (Genesis 2:16-17). He told them if they ever disobeyed His command, this angel of the night would surely destroy them and cut down every last one of their innumerable descendants. Despite this, they freed this diabolical killer; now no one can escape him and no one can defeat him.

The good news, however, is that God felt such sympathy and compassion for a world condemned to be ruled by this king of terrors, that He sent a little baby to defeat him. Imagine that! God sends an infant to slay a giant, a newborn to annihilate an ancient destroyer. This boy was destined to do mortal combat with this murderer and was going to lose his life in the process of killing this killer. Even though this Man-child was destined to die in a morbid conflict, the power of this angel from hell would never be able to keep Him in His grave.

This creature from the bowels of the netherworld is destined to die himself in the "second death," which the Bible calls "the lake of fire." The prophet John says death and hell will be thrown into the lake of fire, along with Satan, all his demons, and damned souls (Revelation 20:14-15). There, the Grim Reaper will never again see the light of day or cut down the life of another man, woman, or child.

This God-sent baby (His divine Son and the only perfect man) has told all the sons of Adam and all the daughters of Eve that if they want to live forever, they must believe and follow Him. Otherwise, the angel of death, this Grim Reaper, was sure to imprison them forever in outer darkness where there would be never-ending "weeping and gnashing of teeth" (Matthew 13:42).

Death may still be very much "alive and well" today, but its demise is certain and its burial is a fact. Death is going to die. The Grim Reaper is going to be slain and will be entombed forever, because of this Man-child, this God-man, this Savior named Jesus Christ. He conquered death with his own dead body, and now man can live forever in his own body.

As for this hooded angel from hell, the Bible says, "Death is swallowed up in victory. ... O death, where is your sting?" (1 Corinthians 15:54-55).

Baloney Factories

When someone is accused of being "full of baloney," everyone realizes it is just an expression—a slang way of saying a person is foolish and that his talk is exaggerated. Such an individual is not literally stuffed with sausage or full of lunchmeat; rather, they are overflowing with preposterous ideas or idiotic notions.

Well, listening to so much of what's being said today in every nation on earth, it makes you wonder if people are manufacturing their beliefs in a baloney factory. From the concepts of reincarnation to self-realization, gurus to avatars, mind sciences to soul travel, and prosperity gospels to social gospels, the different teachings and various beliefs are far-reaching. In most cases, these varying persuasions are diametrically opposed. They do, however, have one thing in common: Their metaphysical beliefs differ from what God has clearly said and, therefore, they are all full of baloney. In other words, their religions, their creeds, and their teachings have been manufactured in baloney factories and not from the inspiration of God's Spirit.

Lest what I am saying sound mean-spirited, let me assure you that I am merely paraphrasing what God Himself has said through His prophet Jeremiah:

> The prophets are as wind, and the word is not in them. (Jeremiah 5:13)

> The prophets are prophesying falsehood in My name. I have neither sent them...nor spoken to them; they are prophesying to you a false vision, divination, futility and the deception of their own minds. (14:14)

> Thus says the Lord of hosts, "Do not listen to the words of the prophets who are prophesying to you. They are leading you into futility; they speak a vision of their own imagination, not from the mouth of the Lord. ... I did not send these prophets, but they ran. I did not speak to them, but they prophesied. But if they had stood in My council,

then they would have announced My words to My people and would have turned them back from their evil way and from the evil of their deeds. ... I am against the prophets," declares the Lord, "who use their tongues and declare, 'The Lord declares.' Behold, I am against those who have prophesied false dreams," declares the Lord, "and related them and led My people astray by their falsehoods and reckless boasting; yet I did not send them or command them, nor do they furnish this people the slightest benefit," declares the Lord. (23:16, 21-22, 31-32)

Jeremiah had to contend vigorously for the truth of God's Word in the midst of so many false teachers and religious heretics of His day. Baloney factories were everywhere, and the manufacturers were promoting their wares on almost every street corner. The baloney business was booming because there were so many gullible buyers who were eager to purchase the pre-packaged lies and the tasty falsehoods of countless peddlers.

Six centuries later, the apostle Paul warned the people of his day not to be flimflammed by these merchants of rehashed hash:

Do you not know that the unrighteous will not inherit the kingdom of God? Do not be deceived; neither fornicators, nor idolaters, nor adulterers, nor effeminate, nor homosexuals, nor thieves, nor the covetous, nor drunkards, nor revilers, nor swindlers, will inherit the kingdom of God. (1 Corinthians 6:9-10)

These words of Paul stand in stark contrast to the words of the baloney vendors of today, and people need to realize these are the words of God, not mine. If it were up to me, I'd tell everyone that it doesn't matter what anyone believes or how anyone acts—I'd tell everyone they are basically good and that God will bless them in all of their lifestyles and in all of their different worldviews. But know for certain, I would be full of baloney. Baloney would be oozing out of my ears as I tell others things that God has clearly not said and things He has absolutely declared to be untrue.

It would be wise to ask God for discernment when listening to someone who claims to be speaking for Him, and then ask yourself, *Is God really speaking through this person, or is he imparting what was just thrown together in a baloney factory?*

How Big Is Your Nose?

Do you know what the church and the world desperately need today? It is people with big noses. God gave man a nose in order to smell fragrances and to detect and discern odors. Did you know that without the ability to smell, we would be incapable of tasting? You doubt it? Well, try this out on a friend—blindfold him and block his ability to smell by pinching his nose completely shut. Now give him an onion to bite into, but tell him it is an apple. He will not be able to detect it is an onion because his sense of smell has been greatly impaired.

Now, would you believe for every physical reality there is a spiritual parallel? Our eyes, ears, hands—in fact, our entire physical anatomy—have spiritual counterparts or corresponding similarities. Indeed, one of our most-needed spiritual organs today is a nose—a very, very big nose. Our spiritual nose is our discernment—our ability to detect which things are from the world, the flesh and the devil, versus those from God, His Spirit, and His Word. It's the skill in distinguishing between what is true and what is false, and the ability to ascertain the attitudes and motives of people. It's the power to recognize the gray areas between good and evil and the difference between a halftruth and a blatant deception.

Discernment is one of the gifts from God, and in my opinion, it is an absolutely essential gift (1 Corinthians 12:10). Paul lists the gift of prophesy (or preaching) as being one of the greatest gifts, but preaching without discernment can easily become heretical teaching or degenerate into the "doctrine of demons" (1 Timothy 4:1). The apostle further enumerates the gifts of miracles, healings, tongues, interpretation of tongues, as well as the gifts of faith, service, exhortation, giving and mercy (1 Corinthians 12:4-10; Romans 12:6-8). The Bible also lists the seven spirits of God, which are gifts as well: the Holy Spirit; the spirits of wisdom, knowledge, understanding, strength, and counsel; and the spirit of the fear of the Lord (Isaiah 11:2).

In the midst of the prevalent spiritual deception and apostasy today, the gift of a big nose (i.e., the gift of discernment) is utterly necessary for detecting the truth about God and for Christian growth, more so than any of the other gifts. A gigantic nose is vital when so much of what is being taught and believed today is false and demonically driven. This falling away from the truth today was also predicted by Paul when he said, "The Spirit explicitly says that in later times some will fall away from the faith, paying attention to deceitful spirits and doctrines of demons" (1 Timothy 4:1).

In the book of "The Song of Songs," Solomon (who is a type of Christ) describes the physical features of his beloved wife. If he were not speaking in spiritual terms, what he says about her would in no way be considered a compliment to a woman, because he says, "Your nose is like the tower of Lebanon, which faces toward Damascus" (Songs 7:4). Imagine telling your spouse or girlfriend she has a nose so big that it looks like a "tower." I seriously doubt if she would find your assertion to be flattering. However, to say that her soul has an enormous capacity to discern what is true and what is false, and to recognize the real spirit behind what is being taught and believed, is truly beautiful in the eyes of God and would be welcomed praise.

Damascus is the oldest existing city in history, and it has been perpetually occupied by the age-old enemies of God's people. So to say, "you have a nose like the tower of Lebanon that faces toward Damascus," is spiritually saying that you have the uncanny ability to detect from whence God's enemies are coming. We don't wrestle against flesh and blood, but against incredible forces of wickedness and spiritual powers of darkness (see Ephesians 6:12). Therefore, a big nose is exactly what we need to discern their influences.

During the time of Moses, the people of God had such tiny spiritual noses that they viewed almost everything God was doing for them as something about which to cry and complain. God fed them with a diet of nutritious and delicious manna, but they grew tired of it and murmured constantly about it. Instead, they demanded meat to eat while at the same time despising God's miraculous provisions. So God said, "Fine." He said He would give them so much meat to eat that it would be coming out of their nostrils (Numbers 11:19-20). He sent them quail by the millions, and because the people had no way of preserving their prey, the dead birds they had amassed quickly became rancid. Consequently, many people got sick to the point where they were vomiting them back up. They were even expelling them through their noses! Perhaps God hoped the regurgitated birds would enlarge their nostrils to the point where their discernment would finally improve.

However, if they possessed much bigger spiritual noses to begin with, they would never have gotten sick. They would have discerned the love of God in their blessing of manna, and would have appreciated His care instead of despising it. Thus, if people today have tiny spiritual noses, their lack of smell will prohibit them from tasting how detrimental the things they feed upon are. From pornography to false teachings and from godless entertainment to sacrilegious beliefs, people are someday going to be vomiting these things back up due to their inability to smell.

Now whenever you notice a person with a big nose, pray that God will give you an even bigger one—a much bigger one—in your spirit, because what the world and the church desperately need today are more people with big noses— very, very big noses!

What's My Excuse?

Arguably, less than fifty percent of professing Christians in America attend church with any kind of regularity, and in Europe, less than ten percent of the population attend church regularly.[16] What is most interesting about this growing trend of rarely or seldom attending church services is that this practice is in direct violation of what God has clearly commanded in the book of Hebrews:

> Let us consider how to stimulate one another to love and good deeds, not forsaking our own assembling together, as is the habit of some, but encouraging one another, and all the more as you see the day [of Christ's return] drawing near. (Hebrews 10:24-25)

What is also very revealing are the myriads of excuses people give to justify their failure to obey God in this matter, which range from having to work, to not wanting to associate with the "hypocrites" that go to religious services, to it being too hot or too cold, to it raining outside, to being too cozy inside! Excuses, excuses, excuses! Why so many excuses? It all began approximately six thousand years ago when God asked Adam about his disobedience to His clear command in the Garden of Eden; Adam excused himself by blaming the woman, and the woman excused herself by blaming the serpent (Genesis 3:9-12). Their excuses were formulated in such a way as to release themselves from any guilt or responsibility concerning their actions.

Sixty centuries have come and gone and nothing has changed. The first two excuses were only the initial drops in what has now become an ocean of lame rationalizations and flimsy justifications for disobeying God. Men everywhere, in every generation, have contrived some of the most elaborate and asinine excuses in order to release them of their responsibility before the God of heaven. When it comes to excusing one's spiritual shortcomings, there is nothing like a little reality check to put things in perspective. For example, in the gospel of Luke, Jesus gives the parable of a dinner where a man prepares a great feast and then tells all those who were invited,

"Come; for everything is ready now," but they all alike began to make excuses. The first one said to him, "I have bought a piece of land and I need to go out and look at it; please consider me excused." Another one said, "I have bought five yoke of oxen, and I am going to try them out; please consider me excused." Another one said, "I have married a wife, and for that reason I cannot come." (Luke 14:17-20)

When the generous host heard of everyone's excuses, he became angry and determined that none of those who were invited would taste of his dinner. Instead, he brought in the poor, the crippled, the blind, and the lame so that his banquet hall might be filled and the celebration would go on as scheduled.

Now here is the reality check—had the man who was giving this elaborate dinner said to all of His invited guests, "Come; for everything is ready now, and everyone who comes to my dinner will be given a bag with $1,000 in it," how many of these same invited guests would all of a sudden have found the time and the willingness to go to the dinner? Virtually every single invitee would enthusiastically show up for the feast, and you can be sure not one of them would be late!

Hypothetically, what would have made the difference? It certainly wouldn't have been the host, or the appointed time, or the guest list or the dinner; these things all would have remained the same. The difference is obvious—the money. It wasn't a love for the host, or a desire to celebrate with him, or a longing to taste his dinner and be in his presence. All of their lame excuses would evaporate in a heartbeat had they been guaranteed a sack of riches in exchange for their attendance.

To paraphrase an old saying, "Excuses are like navels because everybody's got one," especially when it comes to attending church, going to Bible studies, participating in prayer groups, evangelizing, or serving Jesus Christ. However, if a church or Bible study group advertised a promise to give everyone who shows up at their service or class $1,000, there would be a sea of people waiting at their doorsteps. I imagine some people would even be willing to crawl to church, if necessary, for such a reward. Unfortunately, it's not because the Lord's Word is being preached, or His Spirit is in their midst, or for the purpose of growing closer to God; no, it's because their real god— money—showed up. Now every lame excuse they could concoct becomes nonexistent. There is nothing like the promise of riches to scour away the thin veneer of man's pitiful excuses when it comes to his relationship with God.

Whenever we conjure up an excuse for not going to a Bible study class or church service in the future, we ought to contemplate whether or not we'd find a way to attend these gatherings if we were promised a sack of riches for doing so. If the honest answer is "yes," then our justifications for disobeying God just become lame excuses before heaven. Ouch!

"New Statistics on Church Attendance and Avoidance." *Barna Group*. The Barna Group, Ltd., 3 Mar. 2008. Web. 04 Dec. 2013.

The $19,000 Lunch

The New York Post once printed an article about a Russian billionaire who ran up a lunch tab (including tip) for nearly $19,000. His meal included three bottles of wine, totaling $8,600 for his small group of business acquaintances and himself.[17] Such extravagance truly exceeds the bounds of reason for anyone who struggles to make ends meet. It is comparable to the lavish living illustrated in the story of the rich man and the poor man, Lazarus, in the 16th chapter of the gospel of Luke. It further epitomizes what the epistle of James says:

> Come now, you rich, weep and howl for your miseries which are coming upon you. Your riches have rotted and your garments have become moth eaten. Your gold and your silver have rusted; and their rust will be a witness against you and will consume your flesh like fire. It is in the last days that you have stored up your treasure! (James 5:1-3)

The Bible has a number of things to say about wealthy people and how difficult it is for them to enter the kingdom of heaven (Matthew 19:23-24). However, it is also very easy to assume that we would be generous and giving with our wealth—if only we had it.

It's like the story of the two guys who got into a discussion one day about what they would do if they were wealthy. The first man asked the second man, "What would you do if you had two houses?" The second man replied that he would keep one for himself and his household, and then give the second one to a homeless family. Then the first man asked, "What would you do if you had two cows?" The second one responded, "If I had two cows, I would keep one for the milk and all the by-products it would provide, and I would give the other cow to an orphanage or to a charitable organization that could use it." Finally the first man inquired, "What would you do if you had two coats?" The second man thought for a minute and then said, "I would keep them." The first man questioned him as to why he would keep both coats since he was so generous with his imaginary house and cow. The second man reluctantly replied,

"Because I own two coats."

Like most of us, the second man could give away all day long what he didn't have. He could be generous to a fault when providing others with possessions he only dreamed of owning. It's the easiest thing in the world to be generous with someone else's money (just look how generous politicians are with other people's money!) or to give away money that we can only imagine. However, it's a totally different situation when one actually does have a lot of wealth. Instead of being truly generous, most people with money only think of ways to make more money, and then how to make even more with that money— and if they contribute any of their wealth to charities, worthwhile organizations, or political causes, it's almost always to receive something in return, whether it be recognition, influence, self-gratification, or simply a tax write-off.

There is a bottom line to this sad reality concerning human nature: What do we do with what we really have, not what would we do if we had more? Simply put, if we don't honor God with all He has given us, chances are that we, too, could frivolously blow $19,000 on a lunch (if money were not an issue), and we could refuse to give God the time of day, if it were truly going to cost us something.

Calder, Rich. "Nets Buyer & Pals Hoop It Up." *New York Post Online Edition*. NYP Holdings, Inc., 23 Oct. 2009. Web. 04 Dec. 2013.

The Last Taboo

Not a day goes by that the news media do not report a multitude of heinous crimes committed by various people. From suicide bombers to child molesters, the litany of man's inhumanity has no end. Monstrous and insane behavior has become the order of the day. When a demented soul shoots up a schoolyard or a crazed mother kills her children, one thing you and I will never, ever hear is even the remote suggestion that some people's wicked actions may very well be the result of "demon possession."

However, the Bible often addresses the reality of demon possession and how Jesus Christ and His apostles exorcised evil spirits from people. In one Biblical episode, two men were possessed by *thousands* of demons as they ran naked throughout a graveyard and slept among the tombs. They were driven to extreme acts of violence and manifested supernatural strength as they tore apart the metal chains and iron shackles binding them. The demons not only drove these pitiful men mad, but they also drove them into the desert, in order to destroy them (Luke 8:26-39; Matthew 8:28-34).

Jesus, at one time, drove out seven demons from Mary Magdalene, and on another occasion, the disciples of Christ came to Jesus rejoicing in the fact that demons were subjected to them in His name (Luke 8:2, 10:20). In addition, the apostle Paul exorcised a devil out of a slave girl and he temporarily struck blind a man named Bar-Jesus who manifested supernatural powers as a magician (Acts 16:16-18; 13:6-11). This man was well versed in black magic, sorcery, and witchcraft, and Paul referred to him as a "son of the devil who was full of deceit and fraud" (v. 10).

There were also seven Jewish exorcists who attempted to use Jesus' name to drive out demons from a man, but because they did not have a personal relationship with Christ, they were powerless before the possessed man. Instead of casting out the evil spirits from him, the demonically driven individual leaped on the seven Jewish brothers and overpowered them with his supernatural strength. He tore off their clothes and chased them, wounded and bleeding, from the house (Acts 19:11-17).

The Scriptures make it abundantly clear that demons are real, having an eternal hatred toward God and an infernal malice towards all men. Consequently, they work feverishly to damn as many souls to hell as possible, in order to spite God and to ruin men who are made in His image and likeness. Evil spirits lash out at God by deceiving men into disbelieving what God has said, and they blaspheme Him by goading men to commit every form of evil and to disobey God in all that He has commanded.

It was the prophet Samuel who said in the face of King Saul's disobedience that "rebellion is as the sin of witchcraft and stubbornness is as idolatry" (1 Samuel 15:23, Amp). This is how people become possessed and why the powers of darkness can influence individuals to do some of the most abominable things imaginable. Rebellion and refusal to believe in and obey God open men up to the possibility of becoming possessed, and once an evil spirit possesses a man, that spirit can drive a person to engage in behavior so vile that it defies all logic to the natural mind.

However, in spite of this, how often is demon possession ever considered in the face of even the most shocking displays of wickedness today? Never! Regardless of how outrageous the crime or how heinous the act, demon possession is never mentioned as the possible cause of someone's demented behavior. We have become too sophisticated for our own good. We mock the reality of hell and scoff at the existence of a devil, and what better way for Satan to continue his stealing, killing, and destroying than to hide under the cloak of mankind denying his existence and demonic activity? Our modern-day enlightenment and intellectual refinement refuse to believe in evil spirits and ridicule the very idea of satanic beings.

Instead, every form of abnormal behavior and insane conduct is labeled as a mental disorder, a psychological problem, or some kind of psychosis or psychopathic condition. Never will the mainstream press, the media, the cultural elite, academia, or the mental health organizations consider the possibility of demon possession—regardless of how outrageous a person's actions might be. Demon possession is the forbidden subject today, even within some churches. It is the final prohibition. It is the last taboo!

However, there is an old saying, that "a problem well stated is a problem half solved." As long as we continue to deny the real cause of so much wickedness today, we will never be able to solve the true problem when dealing with it. Only by acknowledging the existence of evil spirits and realizing their intentions, will we know how to deal with and get victory over them. The power of God alone can drive out a demonic spirit, and only obedience to Jesus Christ can protect us from satanic influence and possession.

Having said all of this, it is also very important we not go to the other extreme when it comes to demonic possession. Some deliverance ministries today manage to see a devil in almost anything and everything. If a person smokes, they say he has a demon of nicotine; if a person is immoral, he has a demon of lust; if they drink, a demon of alcohol; if they use profanity, a demon of cursing; and so on and so forth. Some of these over-zealous exorcists even label various cancers and sicknesses as demons. The devil himself must find this type of fanaticism very humorous because it only cheapens and diminishes the reality of demon possession. If he can get men to believe in demons of nose picking, nail biting, head scratching, and ulcerating tumors, then he can reduce the terrible reality of satanic possession to pure foolishness and poppycock—another great cloak for him to hide behind.

God, however, wants people to be mature in their thinking and discerning in their spirits. He has never placed a premium on spiritual ignorance, especially when dealing with the reality of demons and their influences. As such, we can recognize demonic activity and begin wondering, "When are we going to admit what the real problem could be and deal with it the way it needs to be dealt with?

The Ultimate Freak Show

A freak is usually described as a person who is abnormal or odd; someone who exhibits peculiar behavior. Even today, in our politically correct push to promote diversity, there are still carnivals and circuses providing freak shows as part of their entertainment. Be it the fat lady in the circus, the two-headed man, the bearded lady, the sword swallower, the fire eater, or anyone who happens to exhibit characteristics that both shock and mystify, they automatically become objects of curiosity and interest.

To witness someone or something truly out of the ordinary is enough to make anyone pause and stare or become dumbfounded by what they see. In light of this fact, it's interesting to observe how the Bible describes what the world would view as the ultimate freak show. Dozens of scriptural passages describe certain people as being very peculiar. These people are so out of the ordinary that they are not only viewed as being strange and distinctive, but they are hated because of their uniqueness. They are even persecuted and murdered because of their refusal to be like everyone else around them.

One such person at the front of this lengthy parade of freaks was Abel. He was treated with utter contempt because he dared to worship and obey God in the way God required. His brother, Cain, on the other hand, insisted on worshipping and obeying God in his own way and was infuriated when God refused to accept his form of worship. Consequently, Cain loathed his brother to the point where he killed Abel because of his different style of approaching God. Six thousand years have come and gone, and this never-ending freak show continues. Generation after generation have risen up against God's chosen freaks and have hated them, maligned them, imprisoned them, tortured them, and killed them because they dared to be different.

Even Jesus referred to this fact when He said this of His generation:

> The wisdom of God said, "I will send to them prophets and
> apostles, and some of them they will kill and some they will
> persecute, so that the blood of all the prophets, shed since
> the foundation of the world, may be charged against this

generation, from the blood of Abel to the blood of Zechariah, who was killed between the altar and the house of God; yes, I tell you, it shall be charged against this generation." (Luke 11:49-51)

He also made it abundantly clear that we will not be regarded differently than He was:

If the world hates you, you know that it has hated Me before it hated you. If you were of the world, the world would love its own; but because you are not of the world, but I chose you out of the world, because of this the world hates you. Remember the word that I said to you: "A slave is not greater than his master." If they persecuted Me, they will also persecute you [...] because they do not know the One who sent Me. (John 15:18-21)

The apostle Paul wrote about this from personal experience:

God has exhibited us apostles last of all, as men condemned to death; because we have become a spectacle to the world, both to angels and to men. We are fools for Christ's sake. ... We are weak ... [and] we are without honor. ... We are both hungry and thirsty, and are poorly clothed, and are roughly treated, and are homeless; and we toil, working with our own hands; when we are reviled, we bless; when we are persecuted, we endure; when we are slandered, we try to conciliate; we have become as the scum of the world, the dregs of all things, even until now. (1 Corinthians 4:9-13)

In the Old Testament, God told His people that they were to be "a peculiar people" (Exodus 19:5; Deuteronomy 14:2; 26:18, Amp). He told them that they were to be set apart and to be holy because He is holy (Leviticus 11:44). In short, they were to be "freaks"—freaks of nature. They were to no longer lead lives of self-indulgence. They were no longer to be part of the world's values and participate in the deeds of darkness. Instead, they were commanded to deny themselves, pick up their crosses daily, and follow Christ (Matthew 10:38).

They are thus hated by both the "religious" and the irreligious, reviled by both the rich and the poor, and vilified by both the learned and the ignorant because these believers dare to turn from their sins and insist that others must do likewise if they want to be saved. They are considered freaks; anyone who believes in an eternal hell for unrepentant sinners is a freak, and anyone who professes to be a creationist rather than an evolutionist is a freak. Anyone who upholds the Bible as the infallible Word of God is a freak, as well.

Abel was the very first freak in the eyes of the world. Do we, too, have what it takes to be a member of God's ultimate freak show, or are we just going to be another nameless face among the mindless masses of humanity who insist that we all must look and think alike?

The Age of Recklessness

In 2 Timothy 3, the apostle Paul predicts that in the last days very difficult times will come. Although he predicts men will profess to believe in God, he gives 19 brief descriptions of just how ungodly people will actually be. He said men will be the following:

1. Lovers of self
2. Lovers of money
3. Boastful
4. Arrogant
5. Revilers
6. Disobedient to parents
7. Ungrateful
8. Unholy
9. Unloving
10. Irreconcilable
11. Malicious gossips

12. Without self-control
13. Brutal
14. Haters of good
15. Treacherous
16. Reckless
17. Conceited
18. Lovers of pleasure rather than of God
19. Holding to a form of godliness

One of the last adjectives Paul uses to portray men in the latter days is "reckless." Interesting word, isn't it? Essentially, it means to act irresponsibly or carelessly, throwing caution to the wind and giving little or no thought to any negative consequences or fatal outcomes. Unquestionably, there have always been people in society who fit the description of recklessness. To rob a bank is daring, to engage in extramarital affairs is risky, to steal from one's employer is careless, to abuse drugs is irresponsible, to drive while intoxicated is dangerous, and to engage in any number of illegal activities demonstrates poor judgment.

However, the recklessness the Bible predicts suggests a growing defiance and fearless contempt for rules and authority, characterized by an attitude of "Nothing matters" and "Life is pointless." It goes way beyond the realm of human weakness that may prompt some people to gratify their sexual desires with an extramarital affair or entice others to satisfy their monetary greed with ill-gotten gain. No, the recklessness the Scriptures predict defies all reason.

This fearless contempt can be seen in the growing phenomena of massacres in schoolyards, places of employment, crowded malls, and theaters. It can be seen in the escalating number of people trying to outrun pursuit from law enforcement officers, and in the increasing accounts of daredevils engaging in death-defying stunts. It can be seen in the explosion of sexually transmitted diseases, drug wars, gang violence, mass murders, serial killings and suicides.

This recklessness has been spawned out of a rejection of God and has grown out of hostility toward Him. It has been incubated in hell and hatched on earth and has now taken on a life of its own—because an increasing number of people refuse to give God honor or thanks. As a result, in this age of recklessness, "God has given [these defiant people] over to a depraved mind to do the things that are not proper" (see Romans 1) You can be sure that as long as more and more people continue to defy the God of heaven, their recklessness will produce more and more hell on earth.

Swines and Canines

Did you know that God Himself refers to some people as pigs and others as dogs? Sounds offensive, doesn't it? Thin-skinned people, those with delicate feelings, will undoubtedly be disturbed by such seemingly insulting comments. However, in the eyes of heaven, some people are like contemptible and disgusting swine in regards to what they spiritually feed their minds and souls, and how ungrateful they are by nature. Also in God's economy, other people resemble carnivorous jackals and vicious wolves with sharp teeth to attack and devour their opponents and their prey. In short, both pigs and dogs will stick their snouts in almost anything, and they will feed on garbage and filth that would make more-refined palates nauseated and ill. They manifest no discernment in regards to spiritual realities, either.

The Old Testament refers to both pigs and dogs as unclean animals that were not to be consumed as man's food (Leviticus 11:7, 27). However, in the New Testament, Jesus has made it abundantly clear that it doesn't matter what a man eats because it will not defile him spiritually (Matthew 15:17-20; Mark 7:14-23). Nevertheless, the spiritual significance of swine and canines is still very much applicable to today. Jesus said,

> Do not give what is holy to dogs, and do not throw your
> pearls before swine, or they will trample them under their
> feet, and turn and tear you to pieces. (Matthew 7:6)

People who are hostile toward God (and the things of God) will viciously attack those who take a stand for Him and for His moral laws, and people who have no appreciation for God's countless blessings will trample His graces under their feet as they devour the rubbish around them. The apostle Peter said men who come to a saving knowledge of God and then stray from Him are like dogs returning to their vomit (see 2 Peter 2:21-22). And Christ declared,

> Blessed are those who wash their robes, so that they may
> have the right to the tree of life, and may enter by the gates
> into the city. Outside are the dogs and the sorcerers and the

immoral persons and the murderers and the idolaters, and everyone who loves and practices lying. (Revelation 22:14-15)

It is the spiritual "dogs" leading God's list of Who's Who in hell. Dogs come before sorcerers, immoral people, murderers, idolaters, and liars. These are the atheists and moral progressives who sneer at the reality of God, revolt at His moral restraints, and are forever attacking God's people and assaulting God's Word. Yet their defiance of Almighty God and of His ethical laws will put them in the front of this parade to hell. The pigs and the swine will bring up the rear of this godless procession as they goose-step into eternal darkness and strut from the presence of Him whom they so foolishly despised, ignored and/or resisted. Their final strutting, though, will not be with their heads held high, but rather, as a march of shame and a parade of fools.

When God calls some people swine and others canines, we should not foolishly react with self-righteous indignation; instead, we should humbly step back and soberly evaluate ourselves. Are we going to be in the group that washes their robes in the blood of the Lamb and thereby enters the kingdom of God, or are we going to be among the swine and the canines who promenade right into the realm of the damned? No one will be a spectator in this eternal procession. Everyone will be marching to the drumbeat of one group or the other, with no exceptions!

Shouters and Doubters

"Praise the Lord! Hallelujah! Glory to God! Amen!"
"No way! Who said? I don't believe it! Prove it!"

The world is full of shouters and doubters—those who really don't know what it is they believe but loudly shout their enthusiasm or disdain for Almighty God anyway. There are also those whose faith in God is little more than sloppy sentimentality. People who believe without investigation are foolishly gullible, and people who disbelieve without investigation are willfully ignorant. Each group has their feet planted in midair because of their shallow understanding.

The apostle Paul had this to say when he preached in the synagogue at Berea:

> [The Bereans] were more noble-minded than those in Thessalonica, for they received the word with great eagerness, examining the Scriptures daily to see whether these things were so. Therefore many of them believed, along with a number of prominent Greek women and men. But when the Jews of Thessalonica found out that the word of God had been proclaimed by Paul in Berea also, they came there as well, agitating and stirring up the crowds. (Acts 17:11-13)

The Bereans were commended because they listened attentively to Paul, even though they had their doubts, and rather than arrogantly dismissing—or blindly accepting—what he taught, they took the time and made the effort to investigate and scrutinize his claims. Contrarily, many of the Thessalonian Jews furiously objected to Paul's preaching without bothering to intelligently examine his assertions. In a way, it was good to see a man like "Doubting Thomas," who absolutely refused to believe in the risen Christ without physical proof. He demanded to put his fingers into the nail prints of Jesus' hands and to put his own hand into the hole in Christ's side (see John 20:24-25).

Thomas, though, had every reason to believe "sight unseen," because of the many times Christ foretold of His death, burial, and resurrection (see Matthew

16:21; 20:18-19; Mark 8:31; 9:31; Luke 9:22, 44-45; 22:14-21; John 16:16-22). Even when a number of trustworthy men and women powerfully testified about seeing the resurrected Lord, Thomas still refused to believe.

Consequently, Jesus rebuked Thomas for his lack of faith because his skepticism was not grounded in sound knowledge but rooted in pure stubbornness. He obstinately would not believe; therefore, his unbelief became sin and not just foolishness. Jesus then presents Thomas with His irrefutable proof, and when he verifies His resurrection, Thomas falls on his knees and proclaims Christ to be His Lord and His God (John 20:28). Jesus reproves the skeptic for demanding such unreasonable evidence, and says that people are blessed if they believe without seeing.

However, their belief must still be based on true understanding and not on fanatical emotion or unfounded declarations. Far too many naïve people today believe almost anything without honestly knowing what they proclaim to be true. A multitude of people are simply pseudo-intellectuals and shallow individuals who "know not of what they speak" because their sentiments are based on emotion and what they have heard, not in objective investigation. The apostle Peter says we are to be very diligent in building our faith up in knowledge (2 Peter 1:5) and to be prepared to give an answer to all men for the faith we have within us (1 Peter 3:15). The apostle Paul tells us to be "diligent to present yourself approved to God as a workman who does not need to be ashamed, accurately handling the word of truth" (2 Timothy 2:15).

Heaven has little respect for either shouters or doubters if they do not really know what it is they are shouting or doubting. God has nothing against doubters if their doubt motivates them to earnestly seek the truth; likewise, God does not commend believers who never bother to investigate what it is they proclaim to believe.

So the next time someone shouts, "Praise the Lord," let's hope they genuinely know the Lord about whom they are shouting. Also, when a doubter says, "I don't believe," he ought to ask himself if his disbelief is rooted in intelligent arguments or merely planted in ridiculous assumptions. Either way, God does not put a premium on ignorance nor a value on stupidity. So start shouting, "Praise the Lord Jesus Christ!" Just make sure your feet are firmly planted on the ground and not in midair.

Holy Cows and Sacred Calves

The Bible says very clearly that God made man in His own image and likeness—male and female He created them (see Genesis 1:26-27). What God is, in an infinite way, man is in a finite one. Men and women reflect the image of God in their spirit, intellect, and consciousness. Both God and man can experience a gamut of emotions, including mercy and compassion, as well as wrath and vengeance.

In addition, three distinct personalities exist in the triune Godhead: the Father, Son, and Holy Spirit. Man has three distinct personages in him as well: a body, a spirit, and a soul (which encompasses his personality, intellect, and emotions). The three entities are one and the same; God, too, is three in one.

God designed men and women to enjoy eternal fellowship and intimate communion with Him, but sadly, man revolted against his Creator and shattered that glorious union, creating a void he has desperately tried to fill. In his attempts to reconnect with God, man has endeavored many times over to re-create God in man's own fallen image. Man wants a god who is more to his own liking: more comfortable to be around; a god who puts little or no demands upon him; and a god who will bless and prosper him in all of his sins, false beliefs, and immoral lifestyles.

Therefore, men throughout every age have fashioned and molded gold, silver, wood, and stones into countless idols they feel most comfortable being around—gods of pleasure, power, money, and fame; gods of magic, divination, sorcery, and spells; gods of humanism, materialism, and merrymaking. Of course, men and women here in the West have become too sophisticated to worship inanimate objects. Instead, we have erected holy cows and sacred calves that no one dares blaspheme or challenge.

Evolution is one such holy cow that no one dares oppose. It must never be challenged or defied—especially by anyone in education or the scientific community. To do so would surely result in losing one's job or having one's career destroyed by the "thought police" of evolution. All creationists (regardless of their educational achievements) would be branded as heretical apostates by the clergy of Darwin's zealous legions.

Another holy cow is the "separation of church and state." The convoluted claims of this sacred calf cannot be touched. Public prayer to the God of heaven will not be tolerated; anyone refusing to bow down to this four-legged animal will be immediately punished by the powers that be.

Abortion, also, is an idol people dare not touch and is here to stay. No political leader or religious community, and no amount of protests, will ever remove this bovine from its pedestal. Its priests are too powerful and its worshipers too numerous to resist. This wholesale murder of innocent human beings has become a sacrament, and any blasphemer who withstands this cow will be viciously attacked. He will be denounced by its priestly leaders in the media, the schools, the courts, and the entertainment industry, as well as by its countless worshipers.

The entire homosexual agenda is another consecrated bull that must be worshipped and adored without question or hesitation. Failure to do so will immediately incur the wrath of the politically correct "thought enforcers" who will label any heretics as "hateful," "intolerant," "homophobic," "fanatical," and "dangerous." Their vocal onslaughts are taken right out of the Stalinist playbook: "Accuse! Accuse! Accuse! Whenever possible, use the words 'bigot' and 'racist.'" Such communist tactics are sure to silence!

The priests and priestesses, along with the staunch supporters of this gay religion, are far too many and far too mighty to stand against. Men everywhere must kiss this consecrated calf and stand in reverent silence before it. If not, they will suffer immensely in their classrooms, on their jobs, and as political candidates (and in some cases, even within their churches).

From the "free speech" of pornography to the inclusiveness of every belief, there are many smaller exalted cows, comprising the entire pantheon of "political correctness" to which people feel pressured and compelled to pay homage. The truth of the matter is that everyone, without exception, worships something. The agnostics and atheists pay homage to themselves and to their agendas; the false religions and cults idolize their imaginary, twisted deities; the materialists revere "things"; the covetous idolize money; the promiscuous glorify pleasure; and the politicians enshrine power. One can even idolize one's spouse or children. The bottom line is, whatever we put before God becomes our god; it is our sacred calf and our holy cow. Jesus said,

No one can serve two masters, for either he will hate the one and love the other, or he will be devoted to one and despise the other. (Matthew 6:24)

Who truly is your master? The God of heaven, who created you in His image and likeness, or is it a god you have fashioned and molded into your own likeness and image? If it is the latter, then rest assured that it is a consecrated bull, and the God of heaven will never tolerate a rival. He is a jealous God, and all sacred calves, holy cows, and hallowed bulls will someday become dust beneath His feet.

Lord of the Flies

Without question, flies can be extremely annoying and repulsive. Not only can they instantly ruin an outside barbeque or a fun family picnic, but they can spread a multitude of germs while they're at it, generating a host of diseases. In short, flies are disgusting.

It was the wisest of wise men who said, "Dead flies make a perfumer's oil stink, so a little foolishness is weightier than wisdom and honor" (Ecclesiastes 10:1).

Let's face it, flies are never equated with anything wholesome or edifying; yet the ancient Philistine city of Ekron actually had a god in their pantheon of gods called "Baal-zebub" (otherwise known as "Beelzebul") and was known as "Lord of the dung heap" or more commonly referred to as "Lord of the flies" (see 2 Kings 1). Jesus Christ identified him in no uncertain terms as being Satan, "the ruler of the demons" (Matthew 12:22-29; Luke 11:14-20).

Demons are infernal pests that feed on human misery and delight in every form of sin and wickedness. The more vile a person's sin, the more these satanic flies try to stimulate and reproduce more of the same. They have an insatiable lust for murder and depravity. They inspire every type of immorality and rejoice in instigating conflicts and wars. Man is truly no match for this Lord of the flies with his countless minions. They are fierce, they are powerful and relentless, and they are everywhere.

Their driving ambition is to spite God and curse Him day and night. These demons are fallen angels, filled with infernal rage over their forfeited high position and that which God will bestow upon man. Frankly, it is very likely that God's plan to create man and to eventually exalt him above the angels is what prompted Satan's proud revolt and incited so many angels to throw their lot in with him.

They have absolutely no love for man; when they entice men to worship them as the Philistines did in Ekron, it is only to spite God—not out of any love for human beings. They delight in the ruination of every man's spirit and rejoice in their eternal damnation. If they are unable to damn a soul, they will at least try desperately to wreak havoc in his earthly existence as much as possible. They know full well the admonition of Solomon when he said, "A little foolishness is weightier than wisdom and honor."

Foolishness can ruin a reputation, a career, a church, an individual, and a country in a heartbeat—and Satan knows this very well! No doubt, hell has a wretched slogan that says, "If you can't damn a soul, then ruin it!" The Lord of the flies understands how "foolishness" will debase a man and a ministry almost as quickly as gross, flagrant sin will, so he promotes foolishness to the point where it can cripple any opposition to him and his kingdom. How many evangelists, missionaries, and church leaders have had their ministries paralyzed or destroyed with immoral behavior and unethical practices, and with petty, self-serving doctrines? Though people can be forgiven for their foolish behavior, in the end, their misconduct will usually far outweigh their wise deeds in the eyes of the world.

An American president's adulterous activities in the Oval Office will be what most people remember about him, regardless of how much good he may have done. Godly Catholic priests will always have a dark cloud hanging over their heads because of the deplorable behavior of a few pedophiliac priests. Televangelists who misuse the hard-earned money of their contributors will be remembered most for their dishonesty. Missionaries who engage in Christ-dishonoring activities bring scandal on other Christ-honoring outreaches. Christians who publicly profess the name of Jesus become hamstrung in their attempts to lead others to Christ, if the unsaved perceive them as hypocrites.

The Lord of the dung heap delights in foolishness because it is such a powerful weapon in blaspheming the God of heaven. He tells his demonic flies to never cease offending the Lord of Hosts by damning men who are made in His image, and if they are unable to drag men to hell, to then drag them through the mud so their dirty faces will mock the image of the God who made them! If he cannot damn us with his sinful diseases, he will try to defile us with his foolishness. Satan knows it is extremely easy to spoil men's lives with foolishness because foolishness is bound up in their very natures. It was Jesus who said,

> From within, out of the heart of men, proceed the evil
> thoughts, fornications, thefts, murders, adulteries, deeds of
> coveting and wickedness, as well as deceit, sensuality, envy,

slander, pride and foolishness. All these evil things proceed
from within and defile the man. (Mark 7:21-23)

Did you notice the last thing described on this list of things coming from the human heart? Foolishness. Foolish acts and thoughts don't necessarily need to be flagrant sins. They can simply be beliefs or behaviors that are senseless, asinine, irrational, or preposterous. No matter how we may define "foolishness," it can truly ruin our earthly lives and our eternal souls. Its offensive odor can overpower the fragrance of many righteous deeds for years to come.

The only effective repellent against the hordes of demonic six-winged insects is the blood of Christ and the wisdom of God, which will keep our foolish hearts from engaging in activities or promoting beliefs that will dishonor Him and defile our witness of Him. The bottom line is that the wisdom of the King of Kings is the only true antidote for the influencing foolishness of the Lord of the flies.

Hearing Aids for the Blind

Have you ever tried to listen to two conversations at the same time? It is physically impossible. Sure, we can simultaneously hear the sounds of a dozen people chatting around us at a single moment, but we can only truly listen to one person talking to us at a time. We are just not constructed to multi-task in any other way when it comes to listening. We will always have to tune out one thing in order to tune in another if we really want to concentrate on what is being spoken.

If this is true on a physical level, it is even more real on the spiritual plane. God is always speaking to men—always! However, Satan continuously has 100,000 different sirens beckoning for our attention in order to drown out anything and everything God may be saying to us. The devil knows that if he can distract us from listening to the voice of God, we are never going to be able to clearly see spiritual realities. Spiritual blindness can never be corrected if we are too deaf to hear God's voice.

The apostle Paul tells us in his epistle to the Romans that believing comes through hearing the Word of God (Romans 10:17). People who are spiritually blind must hear before they can see. Even committed Christians must listen attentively if they are going to see with clarity. Mary Magdalene was a classic example of a believer who needed hearing aids before she could focus clearly. She was the very first person to whom the resurrected Christ appeared after He came out of the grave. Mary was so distraught and heartbroken over the death of Jesus that she was blinded in His presence. She was looking right at Him and didn't recognize Him. She thought He was the graveyard gardener! Imagine that! The Lord was standing right in front of her, but she was so blinded with grief that she didn't recognize Him. It was not until she *heard* Him call her name that her eyes opened and she saw to whom she was listening (John 20:14-17).

Likewise, in Luke 24:13-35, we're told of two disciples on the road to Emmaus who were looking right at the resurrected Jesus as He began to walk beside them. Then when the Lord asked them what they were discussing together as they journeyed to their village, Cleopas stared incredulously at Christ, asking if He were the only one in Jerusalem who didn't know what took place over the past few days; i.e., the crucifixion of Jesus who was hoped to be Israel's redeemer. Jesus pretended not to know what things they were talking about, and then mildly rebuked them for their slowness of heart when it came to listening to the words of God that were spoken through His prophets.

Christ then proceeded to explain to them all of the scriptural prophecies regarding His death, burial, and resurrection. While listening to Jesus, the disciples' hearts began to burn with hope and excitement as the Lord continued to speak about God's Word. Later, at dinner, their eyes were opened and they recognized Him when He broke the bread and then vanished before their eyes. Like Mary, these disciples needed hearing aids before they could see and understand what Jesus was saying.

God also spoke in a like manner to His spiritually blind people during the days of Isaiah the prophet when He said,

> Hear, you deaf! And look, you blind, that you may see. Who among you will give ear to this? Who will give heed and listen hereafter? (Isaiah 42:18, 23)

God said "hear, you deaf" before He said "look, you blind." The Lord's stubborn people needed to listen closely to Him if they were going to see what He was saying. Thousands of years have come and gone and nothing has changed, because human nature has not changed. When people dismiss the Bible as being the literal words of God, they foolishly stop up their ears from listening to Him and continue to grope in darkness. When Christians fail to regularly and sincerely read the Scriptures, they, too, grow hard-of-hearing and therefore their vision becomes clouded.

Oftentimes, people look for God only in great or exciting experiences, but they need to listen carefully in order to see. For instance, when Elijah the prophet went to meet God on Mount Horeb, he stood inside a dark cave, waiting for the Lord. There came a great and powerful wind that was so strong the rocks on the mountain were shattering to pieces from the force of the wind, but the Lord was not in the wind. Then there was a terrible earthquake, followed by a blazing fire that consumed the mountain, but God was not in either one of these great and mighty things. Then there was the sound of a gentle breeze, and in it was the quiet voice of the Lord. In that soft blowing, Elijah could hear the voice of God because he was listening for it (see 1 Kings 19:9-13).

If we are to see clearly what God wants us to do, we must listen for His whisper. Jesus said, "My sheep hear My voice, and I know them, and they follow Me" (John 10:27). He also said,

> Truly, truly, I say to you, he who hears My word, and believes Him who sent me, has eternal life, and does not come into judgment, but has passed out of death into life. (5:24)

Furthermore, He warned if people do not listen attentively with a determination to act upon what God says, then they will eventually lose their sight as well. Quoting from Isaiah, he said,

> You will keep on hearing, but will not understand; you will keep on seeing, but will not perceive; for the heart of this people has become dull, with their ears they scarcely hear, and they have closed their eyes, otherwise they would see with their eyes, hear with their ears, and understand with their heart and return, and I would heal them. (Matthew 13:14-15)

When Jesus said these things, He was explaining His parable of the sower and the seed; because people don't listen to God with a resolve to obey Him, Satan snatches away the "seed," or "the Word of God," from them (Matthew 13:19). The author of Hebrews also commented on this fact when he said, "Concerning [Christ] we have much to say, and it is hard to explain, since you have become dull of hearing" (Hebrews 5:11).

When Jesus healed a man who was born blind, the religious leaders accused Christ of breaking the Sabbath. Jesus responded, "For judgment I came into this world, so that those who do not see may see, and those who see may become blind" (John 9:39). These self-righteous preachers would not listen to Jesus. Therefore they became blind, spiritually. If we fail to clearly see the things of God, we need to put on the hearing aids of the Holy Spirit and listen closely to what God is saying to us. If we do, we will be amazed at how clearly we will see with our ears.

Hazardous Area—Hard Hats Required

War can be very hazardous to one's health. The dangers of military conflicts are numerous, from bullet holes and burning shrapnel to land mines and exploding grenades—the perils of a firefight and the threat of an ambush can be lethal. In short, combat is scary and war is hell; however, no armed conflict on earth compares to the dangers of the battle between men and demons. The arsenals and strategies of the Evil One are limitless. If Lucifer cannot destroy a man one way, he will attempt to wound and cripple him with a different method. Apart from the power of Christ and the grace of God, man is no match for such an infernal enemy.

In the midst of such spiritual dangers, a hard hat is essential for survival. In Ephesians 6, the apostle Paul lists all of the military gear necessary in this eternal conflict: the trousers/belt of truth, the flak jacket of righteousness, the boots of the gospel, the helmet of salvation, and the weapon of God's Word.

Did you notice what came just before the Word of God? It was the helmet of salvation, or to put it differently, a believer's hard hat. The helmet of salvation is the knowledge of what a Christian professes to believe. Without a clear understanding of our salvation in Christ, our weapon of war becomes useless. What good is a rifle if we don't know how to use it, and what good is the Word of God if we don't know how to handle it?

Peter tells us to

> [apply] all diligence, in your faith supply moral excellence, and in your moral excellence, knowledge, and in your knowledge, self-control and in your self-control, perseverance, and in your perseverance, godliness, and in your godliness, brotherly kindness, and in your brotherly kindness, love. For if these qualities are yours and are increasing, they render you neither useless nor unfruitful in the true knowledge of our Lord Jesus Christ. (2 Peter 1:5-8)

The importance of knowledge is listed right up there with diligence and moral excellence. Peter admonishes believers to know what it is they profess to believe (2 Peter 3:17-18). I am not in any way trying to sound self-righteous or judgmental, but I believe it is truly appalling how ignorant many Christians are in their knowledge of Jesus and of the Bible. One great theologian put it as follows: "Ignorance of Scripture is ignorance of Christ."[18] Many church members today cannot recite the Ten Commandments or state what the greatest commandment is, let alone say with absolute certainty who Jesus is or why He had to suffer and die on a cross.

That is why the minds of Christians are always in the devil's crosshairs. He continuously aims at their thought life and zeroes in on their understanding. The more he can render believers' knowledge worthless, the less of a threat they become to his relentless attacks and to his diabolical agenda, especially if they do not follow Paul's advice to dwell upon things that are honorable, right, pure, lovely, good, excellent, and praiseworthy (see Philippians 4:8).

We are to diligently study the Scriptures if we are going to be able to handle the sword of God's Word correctly and be approved by Him (2 Timothy 2:15). Paul tells us,

> All Scripture is inspired by God and profitable for teaching, for reproof, for correction, for training in righteousness; so that the man of God may be adequate, equipped for every good work. (2 Timothy 3:16-17)

Many foolish individuals assume when a person becomes a Christian, he is required to put his head in a bucket and dismiss his brain with a shotgun, and they accuse Bible believers of leaving their reasoning at the door in order to "live by faith." However, the archenemy of God knows that an ignorant believer is an easy target for his deceptions and a pushover for his lies. Therefore, just as a person wears a hard hat for protection against hazards, you can be sure the "helmet of salvation" is the spiritual knowledge protecting us from the dangers of an enemy who always aims his weapons at a man's mind.

D'Ambrosio, Marcellino. "Ignorance of Scripture Is Ignorance of Christ." *The Crossroads Initiative*. Crossroads Productions, Inc., n.d. Web. 04 Dec. 2013.

Afterbirths and Afterthoughts

An afterthought is an idea that occurs after an occasion takes place; it is not expected or planned ahead of time. On the other hand, afterbirth is something totally expected when a human birth takes place. It is the placenta and fetal membranes that are expelled from a woman's uterus after delivery and are discarded. Until medical research came along, afterbirth was just an inconvenient blob of matter with no purpose or significance whatsoever.

Well, God has no afterthoughts, especially when it comes to each and every human being conceived in the womb. An unborn child is not a meaningless lump of protoplasm, nor is it the equivalent of afterbirth to be discarded. It is a child that has been known by God for all eternity. God said of the prophet Jeremiah, "Before I formed you in the womb I knew you, and before you were born I consecrated you; I have appointed you a prophet to the nations" (Jeremiah 1:5). The Lord also mentions the Persian king, Cyrus, *by name,* over 200 years before he was born! God predicted how he would use this gentile king to release the Jews from their captivity and allow them to return to their homeland (Isaiah 45:1-7).

In addition, God foretold of a coming king of Judah by the name of Josiah more than 300 years before Josiah came upon the scene (1 Kings 13:2; 2 Kings 23:4-20). The Creator of all mankind also predicted the coming births of Isaac, Samson, the son of a Shunammite woman, John the Baptist, and even Jesus Christ Himself before they were conceived in their mothers' wombs (see Genesis 18:1-15, Judges 13, 2 Kings 4:8-17, Luke 1:5-20, 26-38)!

Of unborn children, David wrote,

> Even the darkness is not dark to You, and the night is as bright as the day. Darkness and light are alike to You. For You formed my inward parts; You wove me in my mother's womb. I will give thanks to You, for I am fearfully and wonderfully made; wonderful are Your works, and my soul knows it very well. My frame was not hidden from You, when I was made in secret, and skillfully wrought in the

depths of the earth [womb]; Your eyes have seen my unformed substance; and in Your book were all written the days that were ordained for me, when as yet there was not one of them. How precious also are Your thoughts to me, O God! How vast is the sum of them! If I should count them, they would outnumber the sand. When I awake, I am still with You. (Psalm 139:12-18)

In Exodus 21:22-25 we see that God places the same intrinsic value upon an unborn child as he does a full-grown man. Regardless of what the politically correct crowd tells us, an unborn child is a human being that has every right to live, just as the rest of mankind does, and must not be murdered in the name of "choice." God said,

Deliver those who are being taken away to death, and those who are staggering to slaughter, oh hold them back. If you say, "See, we did not know this," does He not consider it who weighs the hearts? And does He not know it who keeps your soul? (Proverbs 24:11-12)

We live in a society that demands respect for animals but not for unborn children. The campaign of political correctness is to save the whales, be kind to the penguins, pet the buffalo, and revere the spotted owl, but it is open season on unborn babies, which have been reduced to subhuman blobs by those who refuse to acknowledge the stamp of God's image upon the developing fetus. The Department of Fish and Game has more power than the F.B.I. and more authority than our nation's police departments; its employees can search homes without warrants and fine and jail poachers without mercy when it comes to protecting the wildlife, but where is the same concern for the most helpless of mankind?

The truth of the matter is when unborn children are treated as afterbirths, the value of all mankind is greatly reduced. No man is safe as long as unborn children are endangered. It was Darwin's survival-of-the-fittest theories that inspired men like Hitler, Stalin, Castro, Kim Jong Il, and many other heartless dictators to believe that the "right" of the state was supreme. The "right" of the state devalued human life to the point where human beings became "property" of the government. Should the state decide to execute anyone for any reason, it is the state's "choice"; it is the state's "right" because as far as their courts were concerned, the state is the final authority.

Let's make no mistake about it; no human life is sacred if we view preborn children as afterthoughts and treat them as afterbirths. Should we do so, we will not escape the wrath of Him who has no afterthoughts and views no child as afterbirth.

Fountains and Cisterns

It doesn't take a guttersnipe to come up with at least a half-dozen crude euphemisms to describe a man or woman's sexual organs. From stand-up comedians and foulmouthed entertainers to hardened prisoners and callous military personnel, the male and female anatomies have been depicted with a multitude of vulgar terms and in many unflattering ways. However, do you know what labels God uses? God calls a man's sexual apparatus a "fountain" and woman's, a "cistern" or a "well":

> My son, … drink water from your own cistern and fresh water from your own well. Should your springs be dispersed abroad, streams of water in the streets? Let them be yours alone and not for strangers with you. Let your fountain be blessed, and rejoice in the wife of your youth. As a loving hind and a graceful doe, let her breasts satisfy you at all times; be exhilarated always with her love. For why should you, my son, be exhilarated with an adulteress and embrace the bosom of a foreigner? (Proverbs 5:1, 14-20)

It is very interesting how God describes His design and intention for sexual activity. It's like a fountain continuously shooting water into the air, and then the water nourishes the basin or cistern, which in turn is constantly feeding the fountain. It is a perpetual motion that does not grow stagnant; rather, it ceaselessly refreshes, intoxicates, and invigorates.

Of course, God intends the by-product of this stimulating union to produce the fruit of children. However, the sexual fusion of two people becoming one flesh was primarily to draw two people together in an exclusive and continuous bond that was to reflect the spiritual oneness between God and the individual soul, or God and His people, or Christ and His church. That is why God is a jealous God and will not tolerate a rival. Anyone who claims to belong to Christ, and yet has other gods before Him, becomes an "adulteress" (James 4:4). The apostle Paul said,

Do you not know that your bodies are members of Christ? Shall I then take away the members of Christ and make them members of a prostitute? May it never be! Or do you not know that the one who joins himself to a prostitute is one body with her? For [God] says, "The two shall become one flesh." But the one who joins himself to the Lord is one spirit with Him. (1 Corinthians 6:15-17)

What Paul says here is so profound and mysterious that the greatest of theologians cannot fully explain it. The sexual union and committed bond between a husband and wife (male and female) best represent a living reproduction of Christ and His bride (the church) or God and His people (Israel).

That is why immediately following that insight, Paul says,

Flee immorality. Every other sin that a man commits is outside the body, but the immoral man sins against his own body. Or do you not know that your body is a temple of the Holy Spirit who is in you, whom you have from God, and that you are not your own? For you have been bought with a price: therefore glorify God in your body. (1 Corinthians 6:18-20)

And subsequently he writes,

Because of immoralities, each man is to have his own wife, and each woman is to have her own husband. The husband must fulfill his duty to his wife, and likewise also the wife to her husband. The wife does not have authority over her own body, but the husband does; and likewise also the husband does not have authority over his own body, but the wife does. Stop depriving one another, except by agreement for a time, so that you may devote yourselves to prayer, and come together again so that Satan will not tempt you because of your lack of self-control. (1 Corinthians 7:2-5)

God has made this marriage bond, this one-flesh union, so exclusive that no one but the married couples themselves can decide what is best for them and what is most fulfilling in regards to their sexual needs or desires. This is because

God has made each and every soul so unique and so different that no one touches God (or is touched by God) in the exact same way and to the exact same degree. The bond is exclusive, holy, and wonderful, and the union is spiritual, individual, and matchless.

Since Satan absolutely hates this bonding mystery between God and a soul, he never stops inspiring men to treat the organs of sexuality as something crass and tasteless. The devil loves to prompt people to debase the sexuality of male and female because it mocks the one-spirit union between God and man and between Christ and His people.

Now whenever you hear someone refer to reproductive anatomy in a crude or vulgar manner, remember that God calls one a "fountain" and the other a "cistern," and that their design was intended to reflect a union that is anything but indecent or obscene.

Smoking Section

Some people may not share my sympathy for smokers. Perhaps I sympathize with them since I used to be a smoker myself, and I know firsthand just how difficult it is to break loose from the addiction of nicotine. I also feel bad for smokers because they have been so ostracized and marginalized from mainstream society that they are forced to shiver alone in the freezing outdoors or compelled to huddle together outside in order to suck on their cherished cancer sticks. To put it bluntly, they are disparaged in their desperate attempts to simply enjoy fleeting puffs of noxious gas.

The assault on smokers began with the airline industry and then invaded hotels, theaters, restaurants, retail outlets, office buildings, coffee shops, schools, bars, and now has even infiltrated public parks and other outdoor recreational spaces; secondhand smoke has become public enemy number one. Tobacco companies have lost billions of dollars to salivating attorneys and unethical lawyers, and have been utterly demonized by the health-care industry. They have been prohibited from advertising their (legal) product in virtually every way (except in casinos due to their lobbyist influence over state lawmakers). In essence, our politically correct society will not tolerate the offensive smell of secondhand smoke—period! It is truly amazing how quickly the nasty habit of smoking has been put on life support with virtually no chance of being resurrected.

It might be well to ask, "Just what does God think of smokers and their secondhand smoke?" Men have become obsessed with it, but it appears God is far more concerned about matters with eternal consequences, and He is much more disturbed about things that are spiritually detrimental to one's health. It would be utterly hilarious (if it were not so tragic) to observe how diligent a man can be when it comes to stamping out microscopic particles of carbon, while at the same time enjoying, tolerating, or even promoting so many incredibly devastating habits morally and spiritually—things that will surely damn him for all eternity!

AIDS, for example, has killed and destroyed more people in the past 30 years than secondhand smoke has ever done or will ever do.[19],[20] However, the promiscuous lifestyles that often cause this terrible disease are protected and promoted with a zeal and determination that can only be described as fanatical and obsessive. Pornography, too, is a spiritually damning industry that is diligently fostered and viciously defended (with all the fury of a mother bear robbed of her cubs) by many of the same people who condemn secondhand smoke.

From premarital sex to violent video games and from abortions to occult practices, many of these morally lethal activities are viewed as harmless and insignificant in the eyes of most people, while secondhand smoke is vilified with extreme passion. Nevertheless, the apostle Paul said,

> Do you not know that the unrighteous will not inherit the kingdom of God? Do not be deceived; neither fornicators, nor idolaters, nor adulterers, nor effeminate, nor homosexuals, nor thieves, nor the covetous, nor drunkards, nor revilers, nor swindlers, will inherit the kingdom of God. (1 Corinthians 6:9-10)

I do not see "smokers" on this list, nor do I recognize secondhand smoke as being one of God's greatest concerns. Instead, smoke is what God uses to warn men, the same way Native Americans used to communicate with smoke signals. For example, when God destroyed the cities of Sodom and Gomorrah for their homosexual practices and legalized sodomy, the Bible says the smoke of these burning cities "ascended like the smoke of a furnace," which was a solemn admonition to all who practiced the same lifestyles (Genesis 19:28).

God uses smoke as a smoldering warning of impending doom to men if they refuse to repent of their wickedness. For example, during the coming "great tribulation" the Lord will unleash a judgment on mankind that can hardly be imagined. The Scriptures tell us,

> [Satan] opened the bottomless pit, and smoke went up out of the pit like the smoke of a great furnace; and the sun and the air were darkened by the smoke of the pit. Then out of the smoke came locusts upon the earth, and power was given them, as the scorpions of the earth have power. (Revelation 9:2-3)

Furthermore, the psalmist tells us the fate of all those who are in rebellion against God: "The wicked will perish; and the enemies of the Lord will be like the glory of the pastures, they vanish—like smoke they vanish away" (Psalm 37:20).

God also foretells of the coming destruction of all false religious systems by saying, "Her smoke rises up forever and ever" (Revelation 19:3). He also says of rebellious nations that their burning "will not be quenched night or day; [their] smoke will go up forever" (Isaiah 34:10).

Lastly, regarding all those who worship a coming world leader, or in the case of all those who take his mark, the apostle John warned,

> He also will drink of the wine of the wrath of God, which is mixed in full strength in the cup of His anger; and he will be tormented with fire and brimstone in the presence of the holy angels and in the presence of the Lamb. And the smoke of their torment goes up forever and ever; they have no rest day and night, those who worship the beast and his image, and whoever receives the mark of his name. (Revelation 14:10-11)

This is the smoke about which we need to truly be concerned because God is not going to judge us on the basis of how immaculate our lungs may look; rather, He will judge us by how spotless our souls appear. Consequently, for all those who abhor secondhand smoke, they need to realize hell is one vast "smoking section," and to be more concerned about one's lungs than one's soul is terribly foolish.

"Global AIDS Overview." *AIDS.gov.* U.S. Department of Health & Human Services, 2 Dec. 2013. Web. 04 Dec. 2013.

Falco, Miriam. "Secondhand Smoke Kills 600,000 Worldwide Annually." Web log post. *CNN Health - The Chart.* Cable News Network, 26 Nov. 2010. Web. 01 Dec. 2013.

The Color of Cowards

The dictionary has two basic definitions for the word "yellow." The first is simply the color yellow, referring to the pigment or dye that lies between orange and green in the color spectrum. The second definition refers to being cowardly, craven, or spineless. This characterization possibly came from the fearful nature of the Yellow-Bellied Sapsucker (the popular North American woodpecker with a red head and yellowish underpart). Consequently, if someone is referred to as a "Yellow-Bellied Sapsucker," it is merely a slang term for "coward."

Well in my opinion, the color of a spiritual coward is not yellow, but red—because a spiritual coward is essentially ashamed of his faith, and when someone is ashamed or embarrassed, his face innately blushes red or rosy. Jesus said,

> Whoever is ashamed of Me and My words in this adulterous and sinful generation, the Son of Man will also be ashamed of him when He comes in the glory of His Father with the holy angels. (Mark 8:38)

And,

> Everyone who confesses Me before men, the Son of Man will confess him also before the angels of God; but he who denies Me before men will be denied before the angels of God. (Luke 12:8-10)

Unfortunately, today it has been estimated that over ninety percent of church members never lead another soul to Christ.[21],[22] Very often when professing Christians are asked why they do not share their faith with others, their response is usually cloaked in pious words like, "My religion is a very personal thing between God and me and therefore it is no one else's business" or "I am a spiritual person and I worship God in my own way."

If these responses were decoded in heaven, they would likely translate as, "Belief in the Biblical Christ would make me look narrowminded and foolish in the minds of our adulterous and sinful generation; therefore, I find it embarrassing to talk about the God of the Bible in front of people who might belittle me." In short, they blush pink with embarrassment at the thought of publicly professing Christ because they are ashamed of His message of repentance, dying to self, judgment, and hell; yet they lay claim to having a "form of godliness" by declaring to be "spiritual" (2 Timothy 3:5-7).

Perhaps there are other rationalizations why many people do not publicize their faith in Jesus and the Bible, but God sees clearly what the true reasons are, and they frequently have more to do with pure embarrassment and a lack of courage than any self-proclaimed "personal" religious beliefs. For example, when God commanded Joshua to lead His people into battle, He clearly commanded,

> Be strong and courageous, for you shall give this people possession of the land which I swore to their fathers to give them. Only be strong and very courageous; be careful to do according to all the law which Moses My servant commanded you; do not turn from it to the right or to the left, so that you may have success wherever you go. ... Have I not commanded you? Be strong and courageous! Do not tremble or be dismayed, for the Lord your God is with you wherever you go. (Joshua 1:6-9)

God does not put a premium on being cowardly in our relationship with Him; instead, He tells us over and over again to be strong and courageous when faced with a world that hates us and a society that mocks the things of God. It was the apostle Paul who said "I am not ashamed of the gospel, for it is the power of God for salvation to everyone who believes" (Romans 1:16). Even Jesus Himself declared,

> He who overcomes will inherit these things, and I will be his God and he will be My son. But for the cowardly and unbelieving and abominable and murderers and immoral persons and sorcerers and idolaters and all liars, their part will be in the lake that burns with fire and brimstone, which is the second death. (Revelation 21:7-8)

Did you notice *cowards* lead this litany of the damned and the "Who's

Who" in hell? We would think they would be way down on the bottom of anyone's list when ranking the unfortunate occupants in the realm of the unsaved, wouldn't we? However, to Christ, cowards are detestable for their faintheartedness, excessive fear, and lack of trust. It is interesting to note that when God foretold of the impending destruction of Jerusalem for His people's wickedness and immoral lifestyles, He said,

> Were they ashamed because of the abomination they have done? They were not even ashamed at all; they did not even know how to blush. Therefore they shall fall among those who fall … because they have not listened to My words, and as for My law, they have rejected it also. (Jeremiah 6:15, 19; 8:12)

Our society has become like Israel of old just before their Babylonian captivity. They blushed when it came to proclaiming the things of God and His holiness; but they never turned red faced when it came to breaking God's moral laws, yet were fearfully embarrassed at committing to and wholeheartedly following Him. They weren't yellow. These cowards who merely hide behind church doors and then duck and run when in public to avoid professing Jesus manifest instead many different shades of red. On judgment day, however, the people who are ashamed of Christ in this world, and who blush at the thought of professing Him, are truly going to have something to be embarrassed about. One glimpse at the glory of God is going to make every spiritual coward wish they had been as bold as fearless lions and as determined as valiant warriors for His name's sake.

Thus, it's not the color yellow I fear most in this life, but the blush of red in the world to come. Christ was not ashamed to call us sinful men and women His brothers and sisters; likewise, we by God's grace ought not to be ashamed to call Jesus our Lord in this present age. Professing Christians everywhere need to boldly proclaim Him in this world that utterly despises Him, and within a church where many have unfortunately lost sight of Him.

Olson, David T. *The American Church in Crisis: Groundbreaking Research Based on a National Database of Over 200,000 Churches*. Grand Rapids, MI: Zondervan, 2008. Print.

Rainer, Thom S. *The Unchurched Next Door: Understanding Faith Stages as Keys to Sharing Your Faith*. Grand Rapids, MI: Zondervan, 2003. Print.

Slop on the Wall and Soup on the Ceiling

Almost without exception, any parent who has tried to feed an infant sitting in a high chair knows firsthand how messy it can be. By the time the task is finished, the room often looks like the aftermath of a sophomore food fight. Leave a two-year-old alone for three minutes to feed himself, and upon your return you would be tempted to ask, "Did you get any of that slop in your mouth, or did that bowl of spaghetti just explode in your face?"

In spite of the exasperation a parent may experience in attempting to feed a baby, no loving mother or father would ever consider not doing so (however, if I were to be totally honest, the thought had crossed my mind on occasion). If it is a mother and father's responsibility to make sure their children are physically fed, we can rest assured that it is the parents' God-given duty to feed their children spiritually. The Bible emphasizes how extremely important it is for mothers and fathers to teach their offspring about God and about His laws and His ways:

> These words, which I am commanding you today, shall be on your heart. You shall teach them diligently to your sons and shall talk of them when you sit in your house and when you walk by the way and when you lie down and when you rise up. … You shall write them on the doorposts of your house and on your gates. (Deuteronomy 6:6-9)

The Lord later goes on to say,

> You shall therefore impress these words of mine on your heart and on your soul; and you shall bind them as a sign on your hand, and they shall be as frontals on your forehead. You shall teach them to your sons, talking of them when you sit in your house and when you walk along the road and when you lie down and when you rise up. You shall write

them on the doorposts of your house and on your gates, so that your days and the days of your sons may be multiplied. (Deuteronomy 11:18-21)

In Proverbs, God says much about disciplining children:

Train up a child in the way he should go, even when he is old he will not depart from it. (22:6)

Foolishness is bound up in the heart of a child; the rod of discipline will remove it far from him. (22:15)

Do not hold back discipline from the child, although you strike him with a rod, he will not die. You shall strike him with the rod and rescue his soul from Sheol [an early grave and hell]. (23:13-14)

The rod and reproof give wisdom, but a child who gets his own way brings shame to his mother. (29:15)

The apostles Peter and Paul and the author of the book of Hebrews all stress the importance of feeding spiritual infants "the sincere milk of the word" because they know how critical it is to effectively pass the baton of God's Word from one generation to the next (1 Peter 2:2, KJV; 1 Corinthians 3:1-2; Hebrews 5:12).

God's people are just one generation away from apostasy and moral corruption if parents do not properly feed their children's spirits on His Word. The spiritual development of children is essential if they are to become strong and mature adults in God's army and His church. Helping a child learn about God is easy because, as Paul tells us, each and every human being has a built-in knowledge of God that needs to be cultivated and developed (Romans 1:19). The cynic and the God-haters could argue that children will believe in Santa Claus, the Easter Bunny, and any other fairy tale fed to them because they are naïve and gullible. Their arguments may sound plausible, but when closely examined, one can see it is not really comparing apples to apples or oranges to oranges; God connects with a child's soul and spirit, while fairy tales only excite a child's imagination.

Vladimir Lenin, the godless leader of the Russian revolution, once said,

"Give me four years to teach the children and the seed I have sown will never be uprooted." This God-hating atheist was not totally correct, but what he said has a great deal of truth to it. His words ring true because children are so impressionable that they can easily be swayed by either righteous influences or corrupt ones.

Unfortunately, the truth about God is being systematically beaten out of kids today by prohibiting them from praying in schools, reading the Bible in a classroom, or even so much as mentioning His name at a graduation ceremony. After all, if the devil can prevent the seeds about God planted in a child's heart from being watered and cultivated, then these spiritual seeds will surely shrivel up and die.

This is why it is so important to feed the innocent spirit of a child the Word of God and to nurture them on the truths of His Word. Sure, in children's naïvety, their understanding may appear to be sloppy and unrefined, but they will surely grow spiritually if they are lovingly fed by their parents. No mother or father in their right mind would be so foolish as to say they are going to wait until their children are old enough to feed themselves before they give them food to eat. Yet many parents have foolishly assumed they can adopt this strategy when it comes to spiritually feeding their offspring.

A baby in a high chair is apt to throw slop on the wall and splash soup on the ceiling, but be encouraged—know that his constant feeding will eventually lead to refinement and maturity, and perhaps even a few manners.

The Sons of Ebenezer

One of the most popular stories ever written was Charles Dickens' "A Christmas Carol." The famous tale of Ebenezer Scrooge and his ghostly visitors has truly become a timeless classic. Scrooge, a notorious miser who takes no joy in anything in life except being rich and hoarding every penny he possibly can, focuses entirely on money. He lives for money, he multiplies money, and he dreams of money. Money is absolutely everything to him, while both God and man mean virtually nothing (I might add in passing that there is no inkling in this classic story that Ebenezer Scrooge got any of his income by theft, swindles, or dishonest gain. He merely defrauded others by failing to pay them an honest day's wage and by neglecting the needs of those around him).

Ultimately, divine fate takes pity on this stingy old man and gives him one last chance to change his ways before being eternally damned for his wicked idolization of riches. It is a great story line with a powerful message, which in my opinion, is aimed primarily at the very rich of this world and therefore, can easily go right over the heads of the toiling masses of society. The Bible does speak of a coming judgment against the world's modern-day scrooges and their obsessions with wealth:

> Come now, you rich, weep and howl for your miseries which are coming upon you. Your riches have rotted and your garments have become moth-eaten. Your gold and your silver have rusted; and their rust will be a witness against you and will consume your flesh like fire. It is in the last days that you have stored up your treasure! Behold, the pay of the laborers who mowed your fields, and which has been withheld by you, cries out against you; and the outcry of those who did the harvesting has reached the ears of the Lord of [the Sabbath]. You have lived luxuriously on the earth and led a life of wanton pleasure; you have fattened your hearts in a day of slaughter. (James 5:1-5)

Also, at the very end of the world, Christ will return, and according to

Isaiah, today's scrooges are going to

> enter the rock and hide in the dust from the terror of the Lord
> and from the splendor of His majesty. ... The idols will
> completely vanish. Men will go into caves of the rocks and
> into holes of the ground before the terror of the Lord and the
> splendor of His majesty, when He arises to make the earth
> tremble. In that day men will cast away to the moles and the
> bats their idols of silver and their idols of gold, which they
> made for themselves to worship, in order to go into the
> caverns of the rocks and the clefts of the cliffs before the
> terror of the Lord and the splendor of His majesty, when He
> arises to make the earth tremble. (Isaiah 2:10, 18-21)

The filthy-rich money worshippers (like the rich man in Jesus' story recorded in Luke 16) have a special judgment in store for them, but what about the sons of Ebenezer? What about those who can so easily condemn today's multimillion- and billion-dollar CEOs, bankers, investors, and fat cats, while at the same time failing to see the "plank" in their own eye—their own lust for money (see Matthew 7:1-5)?

All around us the love of Christ is growing colder, and fewer people today are finding their joy in God and the things of God. You may recall the example I gave in a previous chapter where people who were reluctant to attend a Bible study or church service, suddenly found no excuses when they were promised $1,000 for showing up. A person's motive in this situation determines whether or not he/she is a son/daughter of Ebenezer. Are people going because Jesus Christ is there or because their real god showed up? If they arrive for the money, indeed they are the sons and daughters of Ebenezer; yet they would never consider themselves to be an offspring of old Scrooge. Nonetheless, they worship the same idol in their hearts that he did. Jesus explains,

> No one can serve two masters; for either he will hate the one
> and love the other, or he will be devoted to one and despise
> the other. You cannot serve God and wealth. (Matthew 6:24)

What makes anything valuable? Value is simply how much we are willing to pay or sacrifice for something. If we are not willing to tear ourselves away from our TVs, computers, cell phones, or beds to participate in a Christ-honoring event, then He is just not that important to us, ergo, not that valued by us—especially if we would be willing to make these sacrifices if promised a large sum of money for doing so—and the spirit of old money-worshipping Scrooge is still very much alive and well. "Like father, like son," and without a doubt, Ebenezer has a multitude of sons and daughters today who are unwittingly trying to serve two masters.

The Outrageous Crime of Trespassing

There once was a man who for over ten years didn't sleep well at night, and often experienced a lack of peace throughout the day. So one night, he decided to go to confession to a Catholic priest in the hope of clearing his conscience with God and thereby eliminating his insomnia and enabling him to enjoy serenity during the daytime hours.

When he knelt down in the confessional, he said, "Bless me, father, for I have sinned, and it has been many years since I have been to confession, even though I attend church at Christmas and Easter and the few other times I feel like it." The priest said, "Well, my son, it's good that you are here to make your peace with God. So what is it you have done to offend Him, for which you need to ask His forgiveness?"

The man replied, "Well, father, about ten years ago, I was walking through a field and I noticed a sign that said, "Private Property—No Trespassing," and even though I knew I should have turned back, I nevertheless climbed over the wire fence and trespassed over the rancher's farm. The priest exclaimed, "My goodness, son, you must have a very delicate and sensitive conscience! Look, God is very loving, compassionate, and forgiving; such a trivial thing to God is not worth losing sleep over. Go in peace and be well. Now, is there anything else you need to seek God's forgiveness for before you leave?"

The man thought for a brief moment and then responded, "Well, father, now that you ask, when I was trespassing through the farmer's field, I stole one of his ropes." The priest kindly said to the man, "Since it was just one rope, the farmer probably never even knew it was missing, so tell God that you are sorry and before you leave, say a prayer for the farmer's well-being as your penance. Is that everything now, my son?"

The man thought a little while and answered, "Well, father, now that you ask, when I trespassed through the farmer's field, there happened to be a horse's bridle at the end of the rope I stole." The priest then sighed and replied, "Well, look, it was a long time ago and the horse's bridle has probably been replaced by now, so for your penance, estimate how much it was worth and give that amount to the church this Sunday or as alms to the poor, and God will forgive your indiscretion. Now is that everything, my son?"

The man thought even harder and then remarked, "Well now that you ask, there was actually a horse in the bridle of the rope I stole when I trespassed over that farmer's ranch." The priest then raised his voice and yelled, "You stole that farmer's horse? Why didn't you say so when you first came in here? Look, son, you need to return or replace that farmer's horse and tell God you are sorry, and He will forgive you of your theft. Now is that finally everything?"

The man pondered for a moment and then his eyes widened and he said, "Gosh, father, now that you ask, I actually took the farmer's life savings that were in the saddle bags on the horse that was in the bridle on the rope I stole when I trespassed on his ranch." The priest bellowed, "You stole that poor man's life savings? What is wrong with you?! You need to go to that farmer and return every penny you took, plus interest, and ask him to forgive you, and God will then forgive you as well. Now go, do so immediately, and God will be merciful to you."

The man countered, "Well, father, I can't return the money because I blew it all on drugs, prostitutes, and horse races." The priest was almost beyond himself with frustration and shouted, "Then you need to go to that farmer right now and tell him all you have done, beg for his forgiveness, and ask him if you can repay him every cent by working for him as long as it takes to pay off your debt. Then God, in His great mercy, will forgive you of your terrible crimes."

The man then told the priest he couldn't do that, either. "Why not?" asked the priest. The man explained, "Because the farmer is dead! I shot him five times in the chest while he was sitting on top of the horse that was carrying the bags with his life savings at the time when I was trespassing on his farm and stealing his rope with the horse's bridle that his horse was in."

The priest then exploded in total rage, screaming at the top of his lungs, "You spoke of the many minor acts of your misconduct before even mentioning the biggest one of all. No wonder you had no peace and couldn't sleep at night; you will never have any peace as long as you trivialize your great crimes and continue to make big issues out of matters that mean nothing to God!"

If there is a lesson to be learned in this ridiculous fable, it lies in the fact that some things never change. Jesus got into the face of the religious leaders of His day, accusing them of "straining out gnats and swallowing camels," because they were notorious for making huge issues out of nothing and minimizing that which is most important to God (see Matthew 23:24).

Today, we think nothing of murdering millions of unborn children while passing laws to protect pets and other animals. We obsess over people getting fat on french fries, while filling our minds with pornography and godless entertainment. We are outraged over secondhand smoke but laugh at the blasphemies that constantly insult God. We have become masters at calling "evil good and good evil; [we] substitute darkness for light and light for dark; [and we] substitute bitter for sweet and sweet for bitter" (Isaiah 5:20). Not to worry, though, as long as our sensitive hearts don't trespass on someone's property, we can always assure ourselves we are basically "good people," in spite of the fact that peace is nowhere to be found today.

Horseshoes and Hand Grenades

There is an old adage in the world of sports and competition that says, "'Close' only counts in horseshoes and hand grenades." Well, I am sure there are many things in life where being "close" can matter greatly, but it counts for nothing when it comes to a person's salvation and eternal life. In reality, a person is either male or female; a woman is either pregnant or she isn't; an animal is either alive or dead; and a soul is either saved or lost. In short, being "close" can be a positive thing in some earthly circumstances, but it definitely doesn't count in the final analysis pertaining to spiritual things.

In the gospel of Mark, we read about a scribe who asked Jesus Christ which is the greatest commandment in the eyes of God. The Lord then recites from Deuteronomy 6:5, saying that men are to "love the Lord [their] God with all of [their] heart, and all of their soul, [and all of [their] mind and all of [their] strength" (Mark 12:30). The scribe saw the wisdom of Christ's words and agreed with Jesus by saying that to keep the greatest commandment would be better than all of the burnt offerings and sacrifices a person could offer to the God of heaven.

When the Lord saw how intelligently the man answered, He said to him, "You are not far from the kingdom of God" (Mark 12:28-34). Did you notice Jesus did not say the man was saved, but that he was "not far" from the kingdom of God? In other words, he was "close," so very, very close. Have you ever wondered if this intelligent-sounding man ever made it to heaven? The answer cannot be known for sure in this world; however, if that religious man who answered Christ "intelligently" missed getting into the kingdom, then what good did it do him by being so close, or as Jesus put it, "not far" from entering heaven? If a person misses the kingdom of God by centimeters or by lightyears, what difference does it make? In the end they are damned, regardless of how "close" they may have come to possessing eternal life.

Look at the two condemned thieves flanking the crucified Christ. Both of these criminals were under the exact same sentence of death by crucifixion; both were suffering in the exact same way; and both of them were so "close" to their redeemer, they could have almost touched Jesus. Regardless, only one of the dying sinners beside Christ (tradition says, the thief at Christ's right hand) reached out from his deathbed and implored Jesus to remember him when the Lord entered into His kingdom (Luke 23:41-43). The Savior of the world assured the wicked man that, because of his repentant heart and subsequent trust in Him, the thief would now steal heaven with his dying breath.

On the other hand, the thief on Christ's other side is so close, so near to Jesus, that heaven is just a breath away from him, but the wretched man appears to have died blaspheming and is, no doubt, still blaspheming. He just missed eternal life by inches! He might as well have missed heaven by light-years because being "close" does not count for anything when it comes to the final destination of men and women, and being *not far* from the kingdom of God does not mean being *in* the kingdom of God.

The truth of the matter is that being "close" will only add to a condemned soul's torment when he (or she) clearly sees his opportunity for salvation had just been a heartbeat away. In the gospel of John, Jesus clearly tells us He didn't come into the world to condemn it, but to save it, and that anyone who puts their trust in Him will not be condemned, while everyone else is already condemned (see John 3:17-18).

The two outlaws to the right and left of Jesus were not the only ones who were "close" to the Savior that fateful Good Friday. So were those who were passing by and "hurling abuse at Him, wagging their heads and saying, 'You who are going to destroy the temple and rebuild it in three days, save Yourself! If you are the Son of God, come down from the cross'" (Matthew 27:39-40). They were so close to Christ that they, too, could have reached out to touch Him. Instead, they knew only enough about what Jesus said and did to distort it, and then they walked away in a self-righteous huff, failing miserably to be absorbed by God's mercy at the foot of Christ's cross.

The "religious" leaders also stood at an arm's distance from the Savior of the world, yet they mocked Him and challenged Him to come off that cursed cross; then, and only then, would they believe in Him. The Roman soldiers ridiculed Jesus, as well, casting lots for the only thing Christ owned in this world —His clothing. They, too, more than anyone, could have reached out and touched their Creator, but it was only the soldier who pierced Christ's side with a spear that came to recognize Him and repented before Him (Mark 15:39).

Each one of these people could have extended their arm and touched Jesus Christ and entered heaven with just one sorrowful finger, but they missed God's eternal kingdom by a hairbreadth. Most assuredly, every human being who misses heaven by a mere touch will eternally regret their foolish negligence because they will discover too late that being "close" only counts in horseshoes and hand grenades, not in eternal salvation.

The Great Apostasy

The apostle Paul foretold that, at the close of the church age, a major sign to look for signaling the end of the world and the return of Christ would be a global apostasy (see 2 Thessalonians 2). "Apostasy" is defined as falling away from the faith; it is a departure from biblical beliefs and a forsaking of sound doctrine and religious tradition. It does *not* mean a rejection of belief in God or a dismissal of religion altogether. On the contrary, apostasy implies a substitution of the truth with what is false; it exchanges what is right for what is wrong and calls what is good, evil and what is evil, good. It cultivates the security and comfort of acknowledging God without the self-denial that comes from obeying Him.

In Matthew 24, Jesus predicted a number of events that would transpire before the nearly complete destruction of this planet. What leads the list is an explosion of false teachers, pastors, priests, and gurus who would be claiming to speak for God, and yet mislead multitudes of gullible and undiscerning people into believing a lie (vv. 4-5).

Anyone with spiritual discernment can see that this sign Jesus gave, and the apostle Paul said must take place, is happening right before our eyes. Granted, false prophets, religions, and beliefs have been around since the dawn of mankind, but today their numbers are exploding exponentially. The demonically inspired doctrines have become rampant, and the deceptions of the evil one have become ubiquitous. The reason why there is so much deception today is because people would rather be deceived than adhere to the truth. Paul says,

> For this reason God will send upon them a deluding influence so that they will believe what is false, in order that they all may be judged who did not believe the truth, but took pleasure in wickedness. (2 Thessalonians 2:11-12)

Paul further states in 2 Timothy 4:3-4,

> The time will come when they will not endure sound doctrine; but wanting to have their ears tickled, they will accumulate for themselves teachers in accordance to their

own desires, and will turn away their ears from the truth and will turn aside to myths.

Like never before, people want to believe a lie because they love their sins. They have no intention of turning to God in repentance, so they seek out teachers who will "tickle their ears" with untruths, and who encourage them in their sin and promote their lifestyles that are offensive to God. Paul proclaims that man's only hope of not being carried away with the deluge of lies and the flood of deceptions in the last days is to preach and believe God's Word. He exhorts,

> I solemnly charge you in the presence of God and of Christ Jesus, who is to judge the living [saved] and the dead [lost], and by His appearing and His kingdom; preach the word; be ready in season and out of season; reprove, rebuke, exhort, with great patience and instruction. (2 Timothy 4:1-2)

Belief in God's Word and obedience to His commands are the only foolproof measures that will keep a person who professes to believe in God from becoming an apostate.

Therefore, the next time people attempt to persuade us into disbelieving what God has said on an issue, we need to sincerely ask ourselves, *Is this truly what God has said, or is this simply what I want to believe?* If the answer is the latter, then we have unwittingly become part of the great apostasy the Bible predicted would come. It is important to note that the tiny seeds of today's global apostasy were planted over six thousand years ago when Satan whispered his first words to mankind: "Indeed, has God [really] said…?" The father of lies never tires of posing this diabolical question to mankind because He knows how gullible people everywhere love to "have their ears tickled"— especially when they don't like what God has said on any particular matter.

The Vanishing Point

Have you ever looked down a straight road or a set of railroad tracks and noticed that the highway or the parallel train tracks eventually come to a point and then vanish from sight? Well, when the prophet Micah predicted the birth place of Jesus Christ, he said,

> But as for you, Bethlehem Ephrathah, too little to be among the clans of Judah, from you One will go forth for Me to be ruler in Israel. His goings forth are from long ago, from the days of eternity. (Micah 5:2)

The word Micah uses to denote "eternity" literally means "from everlasting to everlasting" and implies "from beyond the vanishing point." What the prophet means by this is that if a person thinks as far back in his mind as he can possibly go in regards to time and space, there comes a place where his thoughts mysteriously vanish. In other words, he cannot think beyond a certain point. If we think back to a time when God created the heavens and the earth and then the angels, and back to a time when God alone existed, that is just about as far back as our minds can take us before our thoughts reach a point where they just evaporate; we simply cannot imagine beyond that distant point.

The same holds true if we go the other direction in our minds, thinking as far into the future as our minds can take us—whether to the end of the world, or Christ's thousand-year reign, or to the eternal kingdom and beyond—there comes a point where our thinking can go no further. This too is a vanishing point, only it is in the opposite direction of the past.

Micah tells us that Jesus Christ is from "everlasting to everlasting"; He goes beyond the vanishing point in both directions. In Revelation, Jesus said, "I am the Alpha and the Omega ... who is and who was and who is to come, the Almighty"; and later, "I am the Alpha and the Omega, the first and the last, the beginning and the end" (1:8; 22:13). Christ is the A to Z, the First and the Last, the Beginning and the End. There is no one before Him or after Him. He is from "everlasting to everlasting," going beyond the vanishing point in both the past and the future! While, like Christ, we have no end, unlike Christ, we do have a beginning. Just a few short years ago we had never even existed, but now our existence will extend way beyond the future vanishing point. Is this not a heavy thought? We are now immortal, eternal. We cannot change this fact because as wise King Solomon said, "Everything God does will remain forever. … For God has so worked [in such a way] that men should fear Him" (Ecclesiastes 3:14).

Man can deny the afterlife as much as he chooses, but his wishful thinking will not change the fact that he will live forever beyond the grave. So the ultimate question is not, "Am I going to live forever?" but rather, "Where am I going to eternally exist?" It is either going to be in God's eternal kingdom or in the everlasting lake of fire. There are no other destinations, and we are all heading for one place or the other. There are no other options!

The atheists are hoping beyond hope that when they die, their bodies will simply be dumped into a hole and that will be the end of them. Those who believe in reincarnation delude themselves into believing they will be given endless rebirths after they die. The mind sciences teach that death and dying are merely concepts of the mind and that heaven and hell do not exist. What wishful thinking!

But God says, "It is appointed for [every man] to die once and after this comes judgment" (Hebrews 9:27).

The Bible uses the word "sleep" over 130 different times and often associates the word "sleep" with death. Almost every time a king of Israel died, the Scriptures tell us that he "slept with his fathers." Also, just before Jesus raised Jairus' daughter and Lazarus from the dead, He said they were just "asleep" (John 11:11; Luke 8:52). Furthermore, the apostle Paul says that all those who have "fallen asleep" in Christ will arise (1 Corinthians 15:12-18). Peter, too, uses the word "sleep" to denote death (2 Peter 3:4).

When we go to sleep at night, we expect to wake up in the morning. Similarly, when we die, our lifeless bodies will awake as well because the Word of God emphatically insists our decaying corpses are merely asleep. Our spirits do not sleep; only our bodies slumber after death. The writer of Ecclesiastes emphasized this best when he wrote, "The dust [out of which God made man's body] will return to the earth as it was, and the spirit will return to God who gave it" (12:7).

Unfortunately, we live in a world that is filled with shallow and fuzzy thinkers who never seriously contemplate the "vanishing point" of their immortal existence. To realize we will still be conscious way beyond that point of imagining is truly something a deep thinker cannot wrap his mind around, let alone the misguided thinking of a philosopher. It is only the thoughts of a truly reflective person that will lead him to make the best choice as to which location he will spend his eternity. I once heard a very wise saying: "Man must know where he came from, where he is going, and to Whom he must someday give strict account."

The thoughts of a shallow thinker will barely lift him beyond the present and fleeting preoccupations in this world and all it has to offer; whereas, the truly wise person will look all the way down the highway of life and know for certain there is an eternity beyond the vanishing point. Which type of person are you going to be in the face of eternity, a sage or a fool?

The Taste of Humble Pie

For a guy who doesn't like pie, I have sure eaten a lot of it in my Christian walk—humble pie, that is. Humble pie is truly one of the most distasteful desserts to digest. Every time I am forced to eat it, I've had to hold my nose, shut my eyes tight, and swallow hard. It is like horrible-tasting medicine, but it is essential for spiritual health and Christian growth. As a matter of fact, I just ate some recently and have discovered I still have not developed a liking for it after all these years.

I was waiting in a long line at the post office in order to mail a Christmas present to my son in the mission field overseas. I had mailed him several packages previously without difficulty, but this time the post office clerk said that he would not accept my package because the forms were not filled out properly. I insisted that I had always completed the paperwork the exact same way in the past, but he seemed intoxicated with his sense of authority as he informed me that the new regulations of "Homeland Security" demanded that I do things differently; therefore, he would not mail the package. I picked up my unmailed box, and as I turned on my heel to leave I said in exasperation, "If I were a Middle Eastern terrorist you would mail this Christmas present in a heartbeat!"

Needless to say, the Holy Spirit nudged me and said, *"Hey John, have you had any humble pie lately? I think it's time to have another piece."* I thought, *Oh Lord, not again; I hate that stuff!* And then I conceded that there is only one thing I hate worse than humble pie and that's anything that disturbs my peace with God. So I took a deep breath, held my nose, and got at the end of another long line. I even had to let someone go ahead of me, in order to be matched up with the specific postal clerk whom I had just insulted. When I got up to his station, I said that I wanted to buy stamps and that I also wanted to apologize to him for saying what I did. He graciously accepted my apology, and I left with a sense of peace in my heart, even though the medicine tasted awful. To tell you the truth, I have eaten enough humble pie in my Christian life to gag a horse and clog the arteries of a gorilla.

As a new believer I remember sitting before a picture of Christ one night and praying. I had turned off all the lights in the house, and my only means of illumination was a lone, lit candle that I had placed before a portrait of Jesus. I often prayed in the dark like this because it helped me focus and concentrate while talking to God.

Well, I had some neighbors who owned a worthless (in my opinion) dog named Spiro. This mutt was an annoying barker who just drove me crazy with its ceaseless yapping. It didn't help that, having recently returned from Vietnam where dogs were used by the enemy to locate "intruders," the sound of barking often caused me to break out in a sweat. So here I am sitting in the dark before my candle-lit painting of Christ when this mangy fool starts barking. I just saw red! I stood, walked out the door, picked up the first rock I could find and threw it as hard as I could at this irritating buffoon, hoping to smack him right between the eyes. But as soon as I let loose of that stone, the dog's owner opened the door. The stone went zooming past the dog's head and hit the side of their house right next to the open door. I then yelled at the mongrel's master to get that ignorant dog in the house before I knocked some sense into him and ripped his lungs out!

Then I returned to the picture of Christ and said, *"Now where were we, Lord?"* As one might expect, the Spirit of the Lord spoke to my heart and said, *"Now that wasn't too swift, was it John? You need to go over to your neighbors' house and tell them that you are sorry."* Of course my own spirit was saying, *"Oh Lord, give me a break; that annoying animal is just a curse and You know it!"* The Lord said, *"I don't care; go."*

Boy, talk about humble pie! I knocked on my neighbor's door and while I am apologizing for what I said and did, that stupid beast just kept barking in my face. I was really tempted to kick his front teeth out, but I figured the Lord had probably told him to bark at me, so I swallowed the whole bitter pie with one gulp and then went home with my own tail between my legs. When I resumed my praying I truly felt humbled, but I had a restored peace with God—a peace that not even that four-legged devil could rob me of. I'm reminded now of what Jesus said:

> You have heard that the ancients were told, "You shall not commit murder" and "Whoever commits murder shall be liable to the court." But I say to you that everyone who is angry with his brother shall be guilty before the court; and

whoever says to his brother, "You good-for-nothing," shall be guilty before the supreme court; and whoever says, "You fool," shall be guilty enough to go into the fiery hell. Therefore if you are presenting your offering at the altar, and there remember that your brother has something against you, leave your offering there before the altar and go; first be reconciled to your brother, and then come and present your offering. Make friends quickly with your opponent at law while you are with him on the way, so that your opponent may not hand you over to the judge, and the judge to the officer, and you be thrown into prison. Truly I say to you, you will not come out of there until you have paid up the last cent. (Matthew 5:21-26)

Let's face it, pride is what keeps us from reconciling with others, and it is what keeps us from having that inner joy of peace with God. In our marriages, churches, classrooms, work places, neighborhoods, and, indeed, world, "humble pie" can be just the distasteful medicine we need to chew on, in order to enjoy a strong and healthy relationship with our Creator and be at peace with others.

Songs and Dirges

Have you ever had someone in your life who, regardless of what you said or did, invariably managed to find fault and thereby criticized and complained a lot? There just seems to be no pleasing some people, no matter how hard you may try to connect with their spirit.

I have been employed in the grocery industry for many years and have run across a number of people who cannot be pleased, in spite of all attempts to satisfy their every whim. The sad reality is that anyone who has worked with the public for any length of time has probably experienced this same kind of frustration. However, no one has encountered this kind of exasperation more than the God of heaven when it comes to dealing with faultfinders, grumblers and complainers. Jesus expressed this annoyance when He said,

> To what shall I compare this generation? It is like children sitting in the market places, who call out to the other children, and say, "We played the flute for you, and you did not dance; we sang a dirge, and you did not mourn." For John [the Baptist] came neither eating nor drinking, and they say, "He has a demon!" The Son of Man came eating and drinking, and they say, "Behold, a gluttonous man and a drunkard, a friend of tax collectors and sinners!" Yet wisdom is vindicated by her deeds. (Matthew 11:16-19)

Let's be clear, John the Baptist was a no-nonsense prophet whose words were a constant-drumbeat message of repentance, hell, and eternal fire and brimstone. He wore rough clothing, fed on insects, and essentially told people to "turn or burn." The very first words in John's public ministry were, "Repent, for the kingdom of heaven is at hand" (Matthew 3:2).

The self-righteous leaders and "sensitive" people of John's day scornfully accused him of being insane and even of being demon possessed. His message seemed so unrefined and uncultured to the delicate ears of the "religious" and the enlightened minds of the "educated" that they wrote John off as just an old coot who would be better off locked up in prison. Then Jesus Christ came along with the exact same message of "Repent, for the kingdom of heaven is at hand"; however, His approach was entirely different from John's (Matthew 4:17). Jesus lovingly and compassionately reached out to sinful men as He ate and drank with the lowly, socialized with the unsaved, and tried desperately to show all men the love of God.

The same people who condemned John the Baptist of being a lunatic turned right around and accused Jesus of being a glutton and a drunkard. Two thousand years have come and gone, and people have not changed because the human heart has not changed. There are still some preachers and teachers like John the Baptist today, and even though they are few, they are not totally extinct. As a matter of fact, I personally have been accused of being a hard-nosed guy when it comes to teaching or preaching God's Word, and people dislike me for it. Their delicate palates cannot stomach my approach, and with my U.S. Marine background, I can fully understand why.

However, many of these same fickle individuals can remain just as spiritually unmoved when they hear a teacher or preacher emphasize the love and compassion of God and about our need to repent of our sins and follow Jesus Christ in obedience. Surely the words "repentance," "commitment," "obedience," and "dying to oneself" turn people off and prompt them to find fault with the messenger—because they cannot tolerate the message. Jesus reproved His "religious" generation for hating, stoning, and killing the prophets God would send to them in order to turn them from their wicked ways (Matthew 23:37). Christ also commended His followers by saying,

> Blessed are you when people insult you and persecute you,
> and falsely say all kinds of evil against you because of Me.
> Rejoice and be glad, for your reward in heaven is great; for
> in the same way they persecuted the prophets who were
> before you. (Matthew 5:11-12)

John the Baptist sang a dirge while Jesus played a flute, and these same self-righteous people found fault with both of these men of God. The methods of the baptizer and the Lord of heaven were different, but their announcements were the same, so they were despised and vilified by the same politically correct people who could not stomach their message of repentance. In short, men and women put their hands over their ears and blinders on their eyes while doing everything in their power to shut these men up and to silence their uncompromising demands of turning from sin, and in the end, John was decapitated for his message and Jesus was tortured to death for His.

Whether we attend a celebration where people are dancing or we observe a funeral where people are mourning, we need to remember that God is speaking to us in both of these situations. Furthermore, if we remain unmoved by God's dirge or untouched by His song, we should know for certain that we will not escape His message of judgment, regardless of how much we find fault with His messengers.

Potholes and Manure Piles

Jesus used a number of different metaphors when it came to preaching and teaching. He told His disciples they were to be the light of the world, the salt of the earth, and the leaven for society. He referred to Himself as being The Living Water, The Door, The Vine, The Bread of Life, The Good Shepherd, The Lord of the Sabbath, The Way, The Truth, and The Life. He compared the kingdom of God to a banquet, a fishing net, and a mustard seed. He called Herod a fox and the religious hypocrites snakes, vipers, and blind guides.

Christ was a master of metaphors and a skilled craftsman in the use of similes. On one occasion recorded in the gospel of Matthew, He taught,

> You are the salt of the earth; but if the salt has become tasteless, how can it be made salty again? It is no longer good for anything, except to be thrown out and trampled under foot by men. (Matthew 5:13)

He also instructed in the gospel of Mark,

> Salt is good; but if the salt becomes unsalty, with what will you make it salty again? Have salt in yourselves, and be at peace with one another. (Mark 9:50)

Even Job once said, "Can something tasteless be eaten without salt, or is there any taste in the white of an egg?" (Job 6:6).

Salt is a crystalline substance that arrests decay and acts as a preservative, gives flavor, seasons food, and possesses healing properties and restoration qualities. It is also a pungent material that can sting. Unquestionably, salt is a valuable and necessary substance for so many reasons, but according to Jesus, salt can also become useless. He warned that if salt loses its saltiness, it becomes so unusable that not even holes in the ground, or manure piles on a hill, can benefit from it. He also points out that if salt becomes tasteless, nothing can bring back its flavor. Of course, too much salt on something can ruin it or make it intensely unpleasant, but it appears Christ is far more concerned with the condition of *saltlessness* than He is with the misuse of salt. In God's economy, tasteless salt is nauseating.

Consider what Jesus said to the church members in the city of Laodicea:

> I know your deeds, that you are neither cold nor hot; I wish that you were cold or hot. So because you are lukewarm, and neither hot nor cold, I will spit you out of My mouth. Because you say, "I am rich, and have become wealthy, and have need of nothing," and you do not know that you are wretched and miserable and poor and blind and naked, I advise you to buy from Me gold refined by fire so that you may become rich, and white garments so that you may clothe yourself, and that the shame of your nakedness will not be revealed; and eye salve to anoint your eyes so that you may see. (Revelation 3:15-18)

The only cure for lukewarmness is repentance and fiery discipline, and though there may very well be no earthly remedy for tasteless salt, God can salvage almost anything with fire—if we just let Him. What makes saltless Christians and lukewarm believers so nauseous to God is not only their uselessness, but their blindness to their tasteless condition. Saltless church members are inoculated with just enough religious dope to make them feel comfortable in their sins and blind to their tastelessness. When we lose our saltiness, we become ineffectual for righteousness because we no longer get upset with unrighteousness; we fail to confront wickedness, so our "goodness" becomes flavorless, and our "spirituality" becomes pointless, as it has no zeal or passion for God and the things of God.

Jesus used a parable to demonstrate how our spiritual light can go out (or be greatly diminished) by the measuring bowl of commerce and the slothfulness and sensuality of a bed (see Mark 4:21). Likewise, our spiritual saltiness can lose its ability to season, preserve, and heal if it loses its taste by lukewarm spirituality. Christ finds both lukewarmness and saltlessness to be so useless to Him that we can't even be used for the most mundane things, let alone great endeavors.

If we refuse to become flavorful salt for Christ, our doublemindedness and/or lack of enthusiasm for Him may make us as useless as Lot's wife, whose disobedience turned her into a lifeless pillar of salt (see Genesis 19:26). Her crystallized corpse had no other practical value but to stand as a mute testimony to others of what not to become—a tasteless statue of salt in the middle of nowhere.

How salty are we in the eyes of God, in comparison to the white granules with which we flavor our meals? If the salt in our own salt shaker is tasteless, it is of no use to us, and if our lives are flavorless in the eyes of God, what good are we to His desires? We cannot be used for even the most lowly purposes, as far as He is concerned—not even to fill holes or disinfect manure piles.

Tombstones and Epitaphs

What would you like written on your gravestone? This is not something most people even briefly consider, let alone seriously reflect upon. However, when we solemnly contemplate this question, we realize there are multitudes of different ways people can be eulogized on their headstones. Here are some examples:

> "Here lies so-and-so; he accumulated great wealth but was bankrupt in heaven's economy."

> "Here lies what's-her-name; she won 7 Oscars but was unknown in the kingdom of God."

> "Here lies Bubba; he watched 58 hours of TV a week but knew nothing about God's Word."

> "Here lies Miss Universe; she was incredibly beautiful in the eyes of the world, but her soul was marred beyond recognition."

> "Here lies an Olympic gold medalist who was unfit for spiritual greatness."

> "Here lies Jane-do-Little and here lies John-do-Nothing; they were greatly successful in their careers, but they did little or nothing for Christ's name's sake."

Believe it or not, everyone has an epitaph in heaven, even if their earthly headstone simply reads "Unknown," and only the inscription in the kingdom of God will truly matter in the end. Unfortunately, vast numbers of humanity are far more concerned about leaving a temporary legacy rather than an eternal one.

King David's rebellious and self-absorbed son, Absalom, wanted so badly to be remembered that he vainly erected a monument to himself so his memory would live on after his death. In the end, though, he was buried under a pile of rocks for his wickedness (see 2 Samuel 18:17-18). The same thing can be said of Achan and his family. Material things meant so much to them that they defied God's command in order to become rich, but in the end, they also perished in disgrace under a mountain of stones (see Joshua 7:16-26).

In the books of Kings and Chronicles, we read of 45 different rulers of Israel and Judah; of them, less than 10 were righteous in the eyes of God. All the rest had epitaphs that read: "He did evil in the sight of the Lord." Everyone will someday have an epitaph. Even Christ had one above his head declaring, "This is Jesus, the King of the Jews," but His ultimate tribute will say, "KING OF KINGS, AND LORD OF LORDS" (Matthew 27:37, Amp; Revelation 19:16, KJV).

Apart from Christ, the apostle Paul appears to have earned the most coveted tombstone of all. His "final inscription" reads:

> The time of my departure has come. I have fought the good fight, I have finished the course, I have kept the faith; in the future there is laid up for me the crown of righteousness, which the Lord, the righteous Judge, will award to me on that day. (2 Timothy 4:6-8)

It was Solomon who said of men like Paul, "A good name is better than a good ointment, and the day of one's death is better than the day of one's birth" (Ecclesiastes 7:1).

If a person develops a good name toward heaven in this life, the day of their death will truly be better than the day of their birth—better because their praiseworthy inscription will be forever etched in the kingdom of God. On the other hand, a person who achieves a noteworthy name only on earth will be eternally disgraced, regardless of how flattering their headstone may be in this world.

The only question remaining is, what do I personally want written on my tombstone? Do I want empty words that are destined to be buried with me? Or do I want an everlasting inscription that reads, "I have fought the good fight, I have finished the course, I have kept the faith"?

Caves and Cave Dwellers

Mentioning the word "caveman" likely conjures up images of some hairy Neanderthal dressed in coarse, skimpy clothing, running around with a club in his hand. Well, nowhere does the Bible mention half-human prehistoric apes that grunted their way into becoming Homo sapiens and blundered their way into modern civilization. The Scriptures have a great deal to say, however, about two different kinds of cave dwellers and two different types of caves.

One sort of cave dweller goes into a cave in order to find God, while the other is the sort that enters a cave for the purpose of getting away from God. One type of cave mentioned is a literal cave, typically a horizontal tunnel hollowed out through a mountain, and often cold, damp, dark, and lonely on the inside; such a cave is a place where curious people like to explore and even, in some instances, to live. The second type of cave is a spiritual cave, one which deserves some attention.

Caves are natural hiding places and provide an environment of such quiet solitude that it can be almost deafening. However, there is nothing like the blackness and quietness of a cave to illuminate a person's spirit and enable their souls to grow like mushrooms in the dark. It was Jesus who referred to this kind of spiritual cave, saying,

> When you pray, go into your inner room, close your door and pray to your Father who is in secret, and your Father who sees what is done in secret will reward you. (Matthew 6:6)

It is in the stillness and seclusion of our "inner room" (or cave dwelling) where we can most effectively repose in the presence of God and intensely listen to His gentle whisper. It is where the mighty prophet Elijah lodged on Mount Horeb when God silently communicated with him. In Horeb's cave, the Lord's "gentle blowing" gave assurance to His discouraged prophet, and it was in this divine whisper that Elijah was given his next assignment, his marching orders to go forth and anoint his successor and to commission the king of Aram (1 Kings 19).

Almost 3,000 years have come and gone since Elijah was taken up to heaven in a fiery chariot, but God's method of maturing, deepening, enlightening, and emboldening spiritual men and women remains the same (see 2 Kings 2:11). God dwells in a cave, and if we are to draw near to Him, we must enter the inner room. The deeper we go into this cave, the closer we will come to Him. It is where we touch God and He touches us; where He consoles us, empowers us, purifies us, and lovingly connects with our spirit in an intimacy that surpasses all understanding and explanation.

In the darkness and loneliness of a cave is where King David composed Psalms 57 and 142, and it was in the obscurity of a cave that he hid from those who were determined to destroy him (see 1 Samuel 24). In First Kings, we learn that God had two groups of fifty prophets each who dwelt in caves (see 1 Kings 18:13). In the 11th chapter of Hebrews, the author mentions over a dozen great men and women of faith. Then he talks of many nameless men and women of God who were mocked, tortured, scourged, imprisoned, stoned, sawn in two, tempted, and put to death for their commitment to God—a number of whom "were wandering in deserts and mountains and caves and holes in the ground" (Hebrews 11:38).

In the darkness of a cave or "inner room," men and women grow mighty in spirit because that is where their hidden life in God resides. Like the roots of a tree, it is the life underground that is most important for the health, development, and strength of a tree. If a tree's root system (or hidden life) is shallow, the mildest storm can topple the tallest of cedars, but the tree with the deepest hidden roots can withstand the mightiest and most savage onslaughts of the weather.

Caves and holes in the ground are where God's people find God. A cave is the entrance to heaven, the door to God, and the pathway to the Almighty, and the cross of Christ marks the opening of this gateway to eternal life.

Some cave dwellers, however, do not go into the darkness to find God but to hide from Him. It is where these men do their most vile deeds, for "men loved darkness … because their deeds were evil" (John 3:19, NIV). It was in a cave that a drunken man named Lot impregnated his two daughters, and it was in a cave that five godless kings tried to escape the judgments of God—but in the end, their cave became their tomb (Genesis 19:30-38; Joshua 10:16-27).

Some salamanders, spiders, and insects that dwell in caves for hundreds of generations eventually grow completely blind and lose all pigmentation in their skin. They survive by their feelings, or their sense of touch, and hearing. Spiritually blind men run from God in the same way these creatures run from the warmth and the light of the sun; they rely only on their feelings to guide them, listening only to the voices that they want to hear.

Well, when Christ returns in great power and glory, the spiritually blind will enter the caves of the rocks and holes in the ground before the terror of the Lord and the splendor of His majesty (Isaiah 2:10, 1921). They will cry out to the mountains and to the rocks, "Fall on us and hide us from the presence of Him who sits on the throne and from the wrath of the Lamb" (Revelation 6:15-16).

The bottom line is that we didn't evolve from primitive cave dwellers, but we are all cave dwellers nonetheless. It's just that we each enter the darkness for different reasons. What is your reason? What kind of a cave dweller are you? Do you enter a cave to find God and to live in His presence or to escape from God and to rejoice in the darkness of your evil deeds?

Splitting Hairs and Slinging Hash

What would you think of a man whose house was burning down, who chose to spend the precious little time he had to escape just straightening pictures and dusting the furniture? The man would be an obvious fool, because instead of urgently rounding up his wife and children and then running from the flames, he just preoccupies himself with all of these frivolous things that are about to go up in smoke. Such a man would either be insane, or would be so oblivious to the surrounding dangers that he would have to be deaf, dumb, and blind. It would actually be hilarious to observe such bizarre behavior, if it were not so tragic to realize the awful consequences of his massively misplaced priorities.

When it comes to the fires of hell and the rewards of eternal life, though, many people appear to act in the same irrational manner as the demented simpleton inside his burning home. These types of people have been around for a long, long time, and they appear to be multiplying with each and every day. Jesus Christ Himself confronted these kinds of individuals when He said,

> Woe to you, scribes and Pharisees, hypocrites! For you tithe mint and dill and cumin, and have neglected the weightier provisions of the law: justice and mercy and faithfulness; but these are the things you should have done without neglecting the others. You blind guides, who strain out a gnat and swallow a camel! Woe to you, scribes and Pharisees, hypocrites! For you clean the outside of the cup and of the dish, but inside they are full of robbery and self-indulgence. You blind Pharisee, first clean the inside of the cup and of the dish, so that the outside of it may become clean also. (Matthew 23:23-26)

The apostle Paul had these same kinds of people in mind when he wrote to his spiritual son Timothy:

> Solemnly charge them in the presence of God not to wrangle about words, which is useless and leads to the ruin of the

hearers. Be diligent to present yourself approved to God as a workman who does not need to be ashamed, accurately handling the word of truth. But avoid worldly and empty chatter, for it will lead to further ungodliness. (2 Timothy 2:14-16)

And in a different letter, Paul again instructed Timothy, If anyone advocates a different doctrine and does not agree with sound words, those of our Lord Jesus Christ, and with the doctrine conforming to godliness, he is conceited and understands nothing; but he has a morbid interest in controversial questions and disputes about words, out of which arise envy, strife, abusive language, evil suspicions, and constant friction between men of depraved mind and deprived of the truth, who suppose that godliness is a means of gain. (1 Timothy 6:3-6)

Today, many people love to talk about God in the abstract or to discuss religious matters in ivory towers, where opinions and beliefs have little or nothing to do with the realities of salvation and the need for repentance. Even within the church, there is a growing number of preachers and teachers whose drumbeat message of "health, wealth, and prosperity" has everything to do with wishful greed and positive thinking, and little to do with spiritual commitment and obedience to God. Other churches get so hung up on their particular (often legalistic) liturgy that their days and their energies are spent just slinging hash and splitting hairs over scriptural verses, rather than preaching the powerful and eternal message of the gospel.

The gospel is the "good news," and the complete gospel—actually, the gist of the entire Bible—can be distilled down to these 25 little words:

For God so loved the world, that he gave his only begotten Son, that whosoever believeth in Him should not perish, but have everlasting life. (John 3:16, KJV)

Nowhere in all of human literature will we read of 25 more profound and moving words. The combined writings of Shakespeare, Dante, Aesop, Plato, Aristotle, Solomon, and every poet and sage in history cannot compare their expressions with those 25 little words. In just over two dozen words, God speaks volumes! They are so heavy they cannot be moved, and so weighty they cannot be lifted. They speak of God's intense love for mankind and the enormous price He paid to save men from an eternity in hell. They also speak of obedience to God's Son, grounded in repentance and the joy of everlasting fellowship with the God of the universe.

John 3:16 depicts a simplicity in our devotion to God. It is not polluted with the foolishness of legalism and the stupidity of splitting hairs and slinging hash over marginal doctrines that have no relevancy in God's economy. The devil absolutely hates it when men can see the truth of these 25 little words, so he motivates people to wrangle over lyrics and semantics, straining out gnats and swallowing camels in their religious doctrines and their philosophical persuasions.
It was Paul who said,

> I am jealous for you with a godly jealousy; for I betrothed you to one husband, so that to Christ I might present you as a pure virgin. But I am afraid that, as the serpent deceived Eve by his craftiness, your minds will be led astray from the simplicity and purity of devotion to Christ. For if one comes and preaches another Jesus whom we have not preached, or you receive a different spirit which you have not received, or a different gospel which you have not accepted, you bear this beautifully. (2 Corinthians 11:2-4)

In essence, any religious activity that draws us away from the simplicity and pure devotion to God in Christ becomes as foolish as straightening pictures in a burning house or as pointless as splitting hairs over things that have nothing to do with loving God "with all your heart and with all your soul and with all your might" (Deuteronomy 6:5).

Therefore, the Scriptures are commanding us to leave the hairsplitting to the legalists and the hash slinging to the philosophers, and let true believers cultivate the loving relationship that God made every man and woman to enjoy with Him forever!

Dumb and Dumber

It has been said that the average man speaks around 10,000 words a day, while the average woman speaks 25,000 words a day.[23] Of course this assertion has been seriously questioned, but the fact remains that the ordinary person does talk a great deal on a daily basis. Were you aware that Jesus gave us a warning about this?

> Every careless word that people speak, they shall give an accounting for it in the day of judgment. For by your words you will be justified, and by your words you will be condemned. (Matthew 12:36-37)

The truth is that some people speak all of the time but never really say anything, and without trying to sound judgmental, this can happen even in the pulpits today. If a pastor, minister, or priest does not really believe what God has said in His Word, then they really have little or nothing to say on behalf of God.

Luke tells us of such a priest when he describes how Zacharias was ministering in the temple of God and an angel of the Lord appeared to him. The messenger from heaven told Zacharias that God had heard his prayers; he and his wife, Elizabeth, were going to have a son, and they were to name him John. Well, the old preacher did not believe the words of God related to him by the angel; consequently, Zacharias was struck dumb, rendering him speechless. He was reduced to a man who could no longer communicate with words because he refused to believe in God's Word (Luke 1:5-20).

Unfortunately, a number of pastors and preachers today do not trust that the Bible is the infallible Word of God. They simply view the Scriptures as just a "literary work"; as a collection of fables; or as made-up stories (including the accounts of Adam and Eve, Jonah, Goliath, Noah, and Sodom and Gomorrah). They believe that the Bible is filled with contradictions and can be interpreted virtually any way anybody wishes. Well, like Zacharias, these religious ministers are mute; they are struck dumb and made speechless before heaven. It wasn't until Zacharias believed God and obeyed His instruction to name his son "John" that the priest's tongue was loosened and he became filled with the Holy Spirit. Then words flowed from his lips as he prophesied with great power, authority, and insight (Luke 1:57-79).

Note the following conversation when Moses felt totally inadequate to be God's spokesman:

> "Please, Lord, I have never been eloquent, neither recently nor in time past, nor since You have spoken to Your servant; for I am slow of speech and slow of tongue." The Lord said to him, "Who has made man's mouth? Or who makes him mute or deaf, or seeing or blind? Is it not I, the Lord? Now then go, and I, even I, will be with your mouth, and teach you what you are to say." (Exodus 4:1012)

Additionally, when God commissioned Ezekiel to be His mouthpiece to the rebellious house of Israel, He said,

> I will make your tongue stick to the roof of your mouth so that you will be mute and cannot be a man who rebukes them, for they are a rebellious house. But when I speak to you, I will open your mouth and you will say to them, "Thus says the Lord God." He who hears, let him hear; and he who refuses, let him refuse; for they are a rebellious house. (Ezekiel 3:26-27; see also 24:27; 33:22)

Ezekiel remained speechless until it was time for him to proclaim the Lord's words. The prophet became a sign and a warning to a stiff-necked people because he could only speak when God allowed him to; otherwise, he became a mute. God even did this with a dumb animal as He rebuked a prophet named Balaam (see Numbers 22:21-38). Peter said of Balaam,

> He received a rebuke for his own transgression, for a mute donkey, speaking with a voice of a man, restrained the madness of the prophet. (2 Peter 2:16)

Another interesting thing is how on several occasions Jesus healed a dumb person who was made mute by a demon, in much the same way Zacharias was struck dumb by an angel of the Lord. It was the prophet Samuel who said,

"Rebellion is as the sin of witchcraft, and stubbornness is as [the sin of] idolatry" (1 Samuel 15:23). So it appears these individuals became speechless through their rebellion. However, it was Jesus who healed them of their mute condition (Matthew 9:3233, 12:22; Mark 9:25; Luke 11:14).

People today can be silenced by demonic forces, even though they retain their physical ability to speak. It's just that satanic influences prevent them from speaking on Christ's behalf. The Bible truly has a great deal to say about dumb (mute) people; however, it has even more to say about dumb people whose speech is not impaired; rather, they use their voices to proclaim falsehood or to fleece others in the name of God. Isaiah says that

> [God's] watchmen are blind, all of them know nothing. All of them are mute dogs unable to bark [warn others], dreamers lying down, who love to slumber; and the dogs are greedy, they are not satisfied. And they are shepherds who have no understanding; they have all turned to their own way, each one to his unjust gain, to the last one. (Isaiah 56:10-11)

The Lord also said to Jeremiah the prophet,

> The prophets are prophesying falsehood in My name. I have neither sent them nor commanded them nor spoken to them; they are prophesying to you a false vision, divination, futility and the deception of their own minds. (Jeremiah 14:14; 29:8-9)

More than anyone else, Jesus warned of a coming deluge of false prophets in the last days (see Matthew 24:4-5). It would be far better if these false prophets were dumb and unable to speak at all, rather than speak what is false in the name of God. Lying teachers are dumber than the dumb, and they are destined to be speechless altogether when they stand before the One who made their mouths. They are going to be eternally silenced when they are rebuked by the Lord for speaking on His behalf when He did not send them with His words.

Consequently, the only ones who are truly able to speak for God are those who sincerely believe what He has said. They are the spokesmen who believe His Word, obey it, and uphold and proclaim it. All others who claim to speak for

God are, by heaven's standards, either dumb or dumber!

Steele, Jonathan. "Words Spoken." *Speechmastery*. Jonathan Steele, Apr. 2013. Web. 04 Dec. 2013.

Riddled with Riddles

Perhaps you may recall the comic-book super villain named the Riddler. He was Batman's nemesis and sworn enemy of all that is wholesome and righteous. His trademark, or signature, was always to leave some perplexing question at the scene of his crimes. He delighted in confounding his enemies with enigmas and was a master at formulating conundrums. He became such a comic-book favorite that Hollywood invested millions of dollars in order to project his character upon the big screen.

Well, it was wise old Solomon who said that one of his main purposes for writing the book of Proverbs was for people "to understand a proverb and a figure, the words of the wise and their riddles" (Proverbs 1:6).

Now here is a riddle for you: What single word does the Bible use to symbolize both Jesus Christ and the devil, as well as both the wicked and the righteous?

Give up? The word is "lion." Jesus Christ is described as "the Lion … of Judah"; Satan is portrayed as a "roaring lion"; the wicked are referred to as lions, and the righteous are depicted as being "bold as lions" (Revelation 5:5, NIV; 1 Peter 5:8; Psalm 10:9; Proverbs 28:1).

Another riddle: What shining light describes both angels and devils, the saved and the lost, and Jesus and Lucifer?

The answer is, "a star." Angels are depicted as morning stars and stars of God (Job 38:7; Isaiah 14:13). Devils are defined as stars that were thrown down from heaven by the tail of the great red dragon (Revelation 12:3-4). Lucifer is presented as "the star of the morning" (Isaiah 14:12, KJV). Christ also calls Himself the "bright morning star" (Revelation 22:16). Lastly, the saints will shine like stars and some glorious souls are brought down like stars (Daniel 12:3, 8:10).

There is only one riddle actually mentioned in the Scriptures, found in the book of Judges, chapter 14. The riddle was derived from an incident when Samson was going down to Timnah in order to become engaged to a Philistine woman. He was attacked by a lion, and with supernatural strength he ripped the lion apart. A few days later, as he and his parents were journeying to Samson's wedding feast, Samson turned aside to view the carcass of the powerful animal he killed with his bare hands just days before. To his delight, he discovered a swarm of bees had used the mouth of the lion as a cavity for a honeycomb. Samson then scooped out the honey to eat and shared some with his parents without informing them of where he found the delicious nectar. This becomes a factor in the riddle to come.

Now, during the time of judges, weddings were celebrated with a seven-day feast, complete with stand-up comedians, storytellers, and entertainers who would sing, play music, and propound riddles. Well, Samson decided to enrich himself by challenging his 30 Philistine guests with a riddle. He promised them a change of clothing each, if they could solve his puzzle within the week, and if they were unable to unravel his mystery, they, in turn, would each pay him a suit of clothing.

The Philistines enthusiastically accepted his challenge, so Samson recited, "Out of the eater came something to eat, and out of the strong came something sweet" (Judges 14:14).

Needless to say, the Philistines were stumped for almost the entire wedding feast. When they realized they had no chance of solving the mystery, they threatened to kill Samson's bride and her father if she did not pry the secret out of her groom! So she ended up breaking down the strong man with her nagging tears, and before the deadline arrived, she revealed Samson's secret to the Philistines. They said to Samson,

> "What is sweeter than honey? And what is stronger than a lion?" In response Samson said to them, "If you had not plowed with my heifer, you would not have found out my riddle." (Judges 14:18)

Samson was totally enraged with the methods that the Philistines used to solve his mystifying play on words, but he nevertheless paid his debt. Now reconsider Solomon's words:

> A wise man will hear and increase in learning, and a man of understanding will acquire wise counsel, to understand a proverb and a figure, the words of the wise and their riddles. (Proverbs 1:5-6)

In other words, it is possible to look much deeper into a riddle like Samson's and discover some profound spiritual insights. For example, the lion is "the eater." This could also apply to Satan as he "prowls around like a roaring lion, seeking someone to devour" (1 Peter 5:8). Out of the eater's mouth "came something to eat." This could also have an application to believers who resist the devil and in their victories over him, they grow spiritually (James 4:7). The second part of Samson's riddle, "out of the strong came something sweet," can apply to Jesus who said His "yoke is easy and [His] burden is light" (Matthew 11:30). Some translations even use the word "sweet" instead of "easy." Meaning, that if we humbly put our necks into His yoke, our burdens will be lighter, and keeping in step with him will be a sweet experience.

Life is riddled with riddles, and the riddles of human existence make the riddles of the Riddler seem like child's play in comparison.

"Who are we and where did we come from?"

"What is going to happen to us after we die?"

"Is there any lasting purpose to our being?"

"Are all religious beliefs essentially the same?"

"Is truth an absolute or merely relative?"

The most critical "riddle" of life is, "Who is Jesus Christ?" If we cannot correctly answer this, then we cannot correctly answer questions concerning any of life's other important riddles. All other answers to life's penetrating riddles just become wishful thinking.

After all, the answers that people come up with must be either true or false, because truth is an absolute. Two plus two is four—this is an absolute truth; it cannot be changed without becoming false. One may argue that two plus two equals thirteen, and that may be *their* truth, but is it *the* truth? Life unquestionably possesses many mysteries, yet that does not suggest every riddle can hold many different answers, and that the multitude of responses can all be *the* truth. As Shakespeare said, "Truth is truth to the end of reckoning."[24] Without a true knowledge of God and of Christ, the most important riddles in history will remain a maze of endless dead ends and a labyrinth of winding pathways going nowhere.

Are you riddled with riddles? Are you dazed with the puzzles of life and bewildered with the meaning of your existence? Only a shallow fool or an unthinking cow would not care about the important questions of life. However, a wise man will be diligent to unravel these mysteries, and only a wise man will discover that life's mysterious answers lie within "the Alpha and the Omega," "the first and the last," "the beginning and the end"—Jesus Christ Himself—who is anything but a blind speculation or an unknowable conundrum (Revelation 1:8, 17; 21:6).

Forty Thousand Quotations: Prose and Poetical, comp. by Charles Noel Douglas.

New York: Halcyon House, 1917; Bartleby.com, 2012. www.bartleby.com/348/1391.html#9. 04 Dec. 2013

Land of the Giants

Giants are fabled in fairy tales and mysteries. From *Gulliver's Travels* to *Jack and the Beanstalk*, and from the Jolly Green Giant to the one-eyed Cyclops in Homer's *Odyssey*, men of great size and terrifying countenance have stirred the imaginations of children everywhere and have been the focal point of many myths and legends.

However, the notion that real giants exist has long ago been consigned to the dustbins of fiction and to the decaying realm of make-believe. Nevertheless, the Bible speaks of a race of men whose great stature would place all of them in today's *Guinness Book of World Records*. According to Guinness, the all-time record holder for the world's tallest human being is Robert Wadlow, at 8 feet 11.1 inches in height, whereas the Biblical record appears to belong to Goliath, who stood over nine feet tall (1 Samuel 17:4).[25]

There was also a king of Bashan named Og who slept on an iron bed that measured 13½ feet in length and was 6 feet in width (Deuteronomy 3:11). Judging from the size of his bed, he too was probably between 8 and 9 feet tall. Then there was a real abnormality who appears to have been a son of Goliath—he had 6 fingers on each hand, and 6 toes on each foot. He was probably not as tall as his father but was nevertheless a man of great stature and a very menacing-looking one, to say the least (2 Samuel 21:20).

Many of our modern-day professional basketball players would be dwarfed by one or two feet in comparison to these biblical giants. These mammoth people, whose dominant genes and ideal environment enabled them to multiply in great numbers, were referred to as the "Nephilim," "mighty men who were of old," and "men of renown" (see Genesis 6:4). Their existence apparently gave rise to the tales of the Titans in Greek and Roman mythology, and even after these giants were destroyed in the Noachian flood, some of their DNA managed to be passed on in the survivors. Eventually their descendants came to be known as Anakim or the sons of Anak. In time, they settled in the ancient land of Canaan, and when their iniquity and the iniquity of the surrounding Canaanites began to overflow, God foretold to Abram (later named Abraham) that He would use Abram's descendants to destroy them (see Genesis 12:7).

Over 400 years after God made this covenant with Abram, it was time for these godless giants and the wicked Canaanites to be judged. The people of God therefore sent in 12 spies to map out the Promised Land and to evaluate the opposing forces with which they would have to contend. After 40 days of reconnaissance, the spies returned with evidence of a very fruitful and desirable country; however, 10 of the 12 spies discouraged and terrified the people of Israel with their report of giants and the mighty fortifications of the people of Canaan. Subsequently, the people of God stubbornly and foolishly wailed and cried and sniffled all night long, as they accused their Creator of wanting to kill them and their children with these giants (see Numbers 14:1-3).

Caleb and Joshua (the remaining two spies) pleaded with the people to just believe God and the Lord would give them the victory over these monstrous-looking people and their hostile neighbors. Caleb even went as far as predicting these giants would be food for them (see Numbers 14:6-9). The rebellious Israelites refused to listen to the voices of Joshua and Caleb and threatened to stone them to death instead (v. 10). So God declared in His anger that everyone in the congregation who was twenty years old and up would die out in the desert for their disobedience and disbelief (v. 29). On the other hand, we're told God rewarded Caleb's steadfast confidence in Him by keeping his forty-year-old body from aging until he turned eighty-five (see Joshua 14:711). Caleb eventually fought hand to hand with the giants, and he overran their fortified cities and won the territory of his heart's desire (v. 12). Caleb's assertions were absolutely right—the giants were food (or prey) for the people of God.

Well, thousands of years have come and gone since the extermination of these giants; however, the words of Caleb still ring true today. Giants become life-giving nourishment for our souls. They strengthen our faith in God and make us bold in Christ. Without giants we remain spiritual dwarves.

Of note is that these "Nephilim" were also called the "Rephaim;" the Moabites termed them "Emim," and the Ammonites referred to them as "Zamzummin" (Genesis 15:20; Deuteronomy 2:11, 2:20). Well, a rose by any other name is still a rose, and a giant by any other name is still a giant. In fact, we are surrounded by giants of other names today; everywhere we turn, God's people are forced to confront these intimidating, powerful, and often inescapable giants. They are the monsters of loneliness, disappointment, and despair; the giants of sickness and death; and the mammoths of economic loss and marital discord. Other giants we must face are the villains of fear and the beasts of the unknown in a world filled with painful struggles and difficulties. As we wrestle against the powerful forces of darkness, our only hope of victory is to place our faith in God and confront these powers in the name of Jesus Christ (see Ephesians 6:12).

God said the following encouraging words through His prophet Isaiah:

> Do not fear, for I have redeemed you; I have called you by name; you are Mine! When you pass through the waters, I will be with you; and through the rivers, they will not overflow you. When you walk through the fire, you will not be scorched, nor will the flame burn you. For I am the Lord your God, the Holy One of Israel, your Savior. (Isaiah 43:1-3)

Notice that God said *when* you pass through the fire and *when* you go through the waters—not *if*. God uses these giants of nature to train, deepen, and mature us into images of His Son Jesus Christ.

King David was history's best-known giant slayer. While the entire army of God's people cowered in fear and ran in terror from the sight of Goliath and his intimidating voice, David assaulted him with these words:

> You come to me with a sword, a spear, and a javelin, but I come to you in the name of the Lord of hosts, the God of the armies of Israel, whom you have taunted. This day the Lord will deliver you up into my hands, and I will strike you down and remove your head from you. (1 Samuel 17:45-46)

David's great faith and confidence in God not only produced a tremendous victory, but his triumph struck fear in the hearts of the rest of God's enemies and inspired the armies of God to rout the massive forces of the Philistines.

The people of Caleb's day wailed all night long at the thought of dueling with giants to gain the Promised Land. Undoubtedly, they were hoping if they just protested loudly enough and threw a big enough tantrum, God would be pressured into saying, "All right, everybody wait here while I destroy all the people in Canaan with just a glance, and dispose of them so that you can simply waltz right in without having to lift a finger."

But God was not manipulated with their tears or fooled by their schemes.

His attitude was, "It's My way or the highway!" So in His anger, He commanded them to do an about-face and marched them right back into the desert. There, they simply marched in circles until every last person older than 20 died in the wilderness (with the exception of Joshua and Caleb). Spiritually, the Promised Land points to heaven, and no amount of whining will change the fact that the only way to enter heaven is God's way: through faith in and obedience to His Son, Jesus Christ.

On the verge of entering the Promised Land, God's people proved to be immature and ungrateful children who needed to grow up. Without conflict, they were destined to remain little more than spiritual pygmies whose feeble souls would atrophy without struggles and without the discipline that only facing giants can produce. Let us keep in mind, therefore, whenever we confront giants in our own Christian march, we truly need to stand our ground in the name of Jesus and believe in our heart of hearts that God is too good to be unkind and too wise to make mistakes. He wants us to trust Him as He delivers us *through* our trials—not *from* them.

What God said to Joshua as he was about to meet the giants of Canaan face to face, He says to us today:

> No man will be able to stand before you all the days of your life. Just as I have been with Moses, I will be with you; I will not fail you or forsake you. Be strong and courageous, for you shall give this people possession of the land which I swore to their fathers to give them. ... Have I not commanded you? Be strong and courageous! Do not tremble or be dismayed, for the Lord your God is with you wherever you go. (Joshua 1:5-9)

Are we going to believe and obey God when confronted by our modern-day giants, or will we choose to think the worst of God in the midst of our conflicts?

"Size Matters." *Guinness World Records 2014*. Ed. Craig Glenday. London: Guinness World Records, 2013. 48-50. Print.

The Magical Mud Hole

Some would claim biblical creationists must be utter fools because they actually believe what Moses wrote—that God created our world and the universe in six days and on the seventh day, He rested (see Exodus 20:11). These gullible creationists actually suppose that God instantly fashioned Adam from the dust of the ground, not from the saliva of a gorilla or from the mucus of an ape (see Genesis 2:7). How preposterous! How intellectually unsophisticated can these people be?

After all, science boastfully and boldly insists that the systematic speculations and theories of Darwinism are beyond question, and that anyone who disagrees with Darwin's "intelligent" conjectures is as ignorant as the superstitious simpletons who once believed that the earth was flat or that it was at the center of the universe. Don't these uncultured and religious fanatics know that since two Nobel Prize winners discovered the DNA molecule, we can easily explain so much in regards to the *slow evolution* of all life?

It is really very, very simple, but since it's so very "scientific," we need to use some complex terminology to explain it (lest we appear unsophisticated). Back in 1953, the scientists' discovery of deoxyribonucleic acid (DNA), which is the nucleic acid containing all the genetic instructions used in the development and functioning of every living organism, was published. We now know DNA is a person's blueprint/recipe/code made up of nucleotides consisting of four chemicals (adenine, thymine, guanine and cytosine), labeled as the letters A, T, G and C. These (four little letters) are arranged in billions of sequences along a double-helix type of ladder structure that can be very lengthy. In fact, if all the DNA molecules in an adult were put end to end, they would reach from the earth to the sun and back over 600 times.[26] But like I said, it is all very, very simple because within a very, very, very tiny space (in each and every tiny cell in our bodies), this code, known as the human genome, is *only* three billion "letters" long. It would take someone typing 60 words per minute for 8 hours a day around 50 years to type the entire sequence of letters on the length of a person's DNA.

Furthermore, if all the information recorded in the DNA molecule's chemical structure were to be written down, the largest library in the world would have a difficult time containing the volumes required to store this vast amount of information. But like I said, it's all very, very simple, and only a fool would believe that an incredible, super-intelligent being could have created such a *simple* molecule.

In light of all this *simplicity*, the entire concept of "intelligent design" is just a superstitious and religious belief that has no place in the world of science or in the classrooms of academia. Therefore, any grade-school teacher, college professor, or scientific professional who even remotely suggests that the instructional script of three billion sequenced letters in each cell of the human body is "intelligently designed" is considered a radical nonconformist whose heretical belief in a creative designer either gets him or her fired or forces a resignation in disgrace. At the very least, he or she is ostracized or ridiculed for not blindly clinging to the ever-changing hypothesis of Darwinism.

To evolutionists, it is much more intelligent to suggest that all of life just randomly (or as theistic evolutionists would say, "divinely") arose out of some magical mud hole. It is so much more intellectual to believe that "time" is the creator of all things, not a super-intelligent and all-powerful God. It is just so brilliant to declare that "given enough time, anything can happen"—including the formation of a person's eye out of a bubbling soup of amino acids, just swirling around in a muddy hole.

I mean, what is more logical than believing in magical mud holes? After all, anyone who believes that a super-intelligent and all-powerful God created everything in short order and in methodical detail is as foolhardy as a child believing in Santa Claus, or as silly as Chicken Little screaming that the sky is falling. In spite of everything, if the idea that all of life crawled out of a mud hole is actually false, then how could this intelligent notion possibly be required learning from grade schools to grad schools? If belief in a magical puddle is a lie, then why is the science of intelligent design prohibited from being taught as a possible alternative to the miraculous marvels of a polluted pond?

The apostle Paul had to be one of these fanatical ignoramuses who didn't believe in magical mud holes. Rather, believing in God as our Creator, he wrote,

> The wrath of God is revealed from heaven against all ungodliness and unrighteousness of men who suppress the truth in unrighteousness because that which is known about

God is evident within them; for God made it evident to them. For since the creation of the world His invisible attributes, [that is,] His eternal power and divine nature, have been clearly seen, being understood through what has been made, so that they are without excuse. For even though they knew God, they did not honor Him as God or give thanks, but they became futile in their speculations, and their foolish heart was darkened. Professing to be wise, they became fools, and exchanged the glory of the incorruptible God for an image in the form of corruptible man and of birds and four-footed animals and crawling creatures. (Romans 1:18-23)

Boy, was Paul stupid, or what? How could such an intelligent man not believe in enchanted dirt puddles—those wondrous holes of pitch, bubbling with the DNA recipe of all of life? Talk about unsophisticated, uncouth, and uneducated! Today's brilliant intellectuals would insist that the next time you accidentally step into a puddle of sewage, you not curse your bad luck; just recall that without the wonder of magical mud holes, none of us would even exist.

I, however, must shamefully resign myself to the fact that I am a genuine ignoramus who just can't bring himself to believe in magical mud holes, in spite of all the "intelligent" people who say otherwise. It is truly embarrassing to admit that I am not even a theistic evolutionist, and I cower in fear of being labeled fanatical or foolish for not at least believing in "divinely orchestrated" magical mud holes. My stupidity is truly mortifying in the presence of this great Wizard of Oz called "Darwinism." The Great Oz has spoken, and only the most ignorant of ignoramuses dare challenge this great and mighty Oz that is thundering out of the smoke and fire of evolution.

Nevertheless, I am declaring that magical holes are as realistic as fairy tales and are as plausible as tooth fairies. In the face of enormous ridicule and contempt from the believers of magical mud holes, I dare to pull back this "scientific" curtain and expose this mud hole for what it truly is—an enormous, muddy lie! Darwinism is a lie, propped up and sanitized by the well-bred elite who are hell-bent on believing in anything (regardless of how laughable or absurd), as long as it isn't a God to whom they must render an account.

"Genome Facts." *NOVA Online*. Public Broadcasting Service (PBS), n.d. Web. 04 Dec. 2013.

Rolling Thunder

God tells us to "be still, and know that I am God" (Psalm 46:10, NIV). In other words, to truly get to know God, we must get alone and listen intently in prayer in order to hear and understand what God is saying.

We will never really get to know anyone, especially God, if our relationship is always filled with distractions and constantly preoccupied with dozens of other things. If our focus is on a television program, the voice of another is unconsciously tuned out. If our eyes are glued to a computer monitor we will be oblivious to the words of someone speaking in our ear. If we are chattering on a cell phone with a friend, what other people are saying does not register.

This is why we must "be still" in order to hear God's quiet voice and to listen to His gentle whispers. Even Christians, like Martha in the gospel of Luke, can be so absorbed in "doing things" for God that they fail to see the tremendous importance of sitting at Jesus' feet. However, Martha's sister, Mary, understood the value of gazing into Christ's eyes and drinking in every gracious word that flowed from His lips (Luke 10:38-42). Mary was so enraptured with Christ that her soul likely became transfixed in His company—the company of her God.

Meanwhile, Martha was overwhelmed with responsibilities to the point that she even became bitter towards her sister. She was angry and frustrated because Mary wasn't busy "doing things for Jesus" like she was. Subsequently, Christ made it abundantly clear to Martha that "only one thing [in life] is necessary": stillness with God. It is in peaceful seclusion that He can best be heard, and it is in reposing in His presence where He can best be understood (see Luke 10:38-42).

Commotion, clamor, and clatter resound in an unending symphony of racket and pandemonium in our world today. The devil is captivated with all the hubbub and bedlam. He ceaselessly orchestrates noise, and the higher the decibels, the better to zombify anyone within his range. The devil's incessant din drowns out the still, small voice of God.

Imagine being in the midst of a crowd at a screaming rock concert, a cheer-enveloped football stadium, or a blaring carnival, and consider the yelling floor traders at the world's stock exchanges. What would it take to suddenly get everyone's immediate and undivided attention? Perhaps a devastating earthquake or an explosive thunderstorm with cracks of lightning filling the sky would grab their attention, causing many to freeze with alarm and become motionless with concentration.

When men ignore the quiet utterances of God long enough, they will someday discover that He is also a God whose autograph is lightning and whose voice is rolling thunder. The Bible says, "God thunders with His voice wondrously, doing great things which we cannot comprehend" (Job 37:5). When God appeared to Job in a whirlwind, He asked him if anyone could "thunder with a voice like His" (40:9).

Any rebellious child who has a loving parent quickly discovers that his gentle mother and soft-spoken father can have a very frightening side to them when dealing with his misconduct. Similarly, God the Father has a frightening countenance at times, like when Moses and the Israelites stood at the foot of Mount Sinai:

> Now Mount Sinai was all in smoke because the Lord descended upon it in fire; and its smoke ascended like the smoke of a [great] furnace, and the whole mountain quaked violently. When the sound of the trumpet grew louder and louder, Moses spoke and God answered him with thunder. (Exodus 19:18-19)

In the midst of this experience,

> All the people perceived the thunder and the lightning flashes and the sound of the trumpet and the mountain smoking; and when the people saw it, they trembled and stood at a distance. Then they said to Moses, "Speak to us yourself and we will listen; but let not God speak to us, or we will die." (Exodus 20:18-19)

Since most people will not listen to and obey the quiet voice of God, He then tries to get men's attention with loud thunder: the thunder of natural disasters, economic collapses, contagious diseases, constant warfare, political incompetence, and unsolvable problems. Unfortunately, so many men are spiritually deaf and cannot hear these rumbling peals of God's warnings.

Did you know it had never rained on earth before the Noachian flood? Prior to this global judgment, the earth was watered with a mist that arose from the ground, not from rain falling from clouds (see Genesis 2:5-6). Do you suppose Noah and his family were thus subjected to ridicule during the decades it took to build an ark to God's specifications? I'm confident not one of the observers heeded God's many warnings spoken through Noah, and because people would not listen to God's still, small voice or to the mute testimony of pairs of countless animals unnaturally entering the ark, God's thunder followed lightning, and the flood got their attention. So, in the 600th year of Noah's life,

> All the fountains of the great deep burst open, and the floodgates of the sky were opened. The rain fell upon the earth for forty days and forty nights. (Genesis 7:11-12)

"If men learn nothing from history, it's that men learn nothing from history." God is once again going to destroy the world due to all of mankind's wickedness; only this time the earth will be destroyed by fire, not by a flood (2 Peter 3:10-12). The prophet John tells us that during the last seven years of our world's existence, flashes of lightning and peals of thunder will constantly erupt from the very throne of God (Revelation 4:5). There are actually seven consecutive voices of thunder that John is prohibited from recording, suggesting some judgments that men can't even begin to imagine will come upon the world in rapid succession (Revelation 10:1-4).

Yes, rolling thunder is God's megaphone—His last resort to get men's attention before it is too late because, unfortunately, the dead cannot hear the crack of roaring thunder nor see the flashing lightning, and those who are already spiritually dead are not easily awakened, even with the rolling thunder of God's wrath.

Do you hear the voice of God in this resounding noise, or are you so focused on the things of this world that not even rolling thunder can distract you from Satan's noisy diversions?

The Blazing Throne

Two of the most awesome and astonishing events in all of cosmic history are recorded in the Bible. The first has already occurred and is found in the very first verse of the first chapter of the first book in the Bible: "In the beginning God created the heavens and the earth" (Genesis 1:1). The other event will happen when the Creator fashions a *new* heaven and a *new* earth, as documented in the last book of the Bible: "Behold, I am making all things new. ... It is done. I am the Alpha and the Omega, the beginning and the end" (Revelation 21:5-6).

A third—and no doubt the most stunning incident of all—took place in between these two colossal episodes. It is recounted in John 3:16:

> For God so loved the world, that He gave His only begotten
> Son, that whoever believes in Him shall not perish but have
> eternal life.

God concealing all His glory within a human body, being born in humble circumstances and then willingly dying horrifically on a cross to atone for man's sins—stunning!

However, there is coming another truly spellbinding incident so momentous and dreadful that it defies all imagination and surpasses all comprehension. It is an event that very few men even consider, let alone take time to seriously meditate upon; an occasion that I personally refer to as the most awesome day in the universe, or the most terrible day in all of human history. Jesus referred to it as "the day of judgment" (Matthew 5:21, NIV; 10:15; 12:36, 41-42; Luke 10:14; 11:3132; John 5:22-24). This coming day is described by the prophet Daniel and the apostle John in very broad strokes, but in just enough detail to strike apprehension and dismay into anyone who has the good grace and intellectual honesty to envision it. Daniel writes,

> I kept looking until thrones were set up, and the Ancient of
> Days took His seat; His vesture was like white snow and the
> hair of His head like pure wool. His throne was ablaze with
> flames, its wheels were a burning fire. A river of fire was

flowing and coming out from before Him; thousands upon thousands were attending Him, and myriads upon myriads were standing before Him; the court sat [in judgment], and the books were opened. (Daniel 7:9-10)

John further describes this throne and terrible day of judgment:

I saw a great white throne and Him who sat upon it, from whose presence earth and heaven fled away, and no place was found for them. And I saw the dead [spiritually lost], the great and the small, standing before the throne, and books were opened; and another book was opened, which is the book of life; and the dead were judged from the things which were written in the books, according to their deeds. And the sea gave up the dead which were in it, and death and Hades [hell] gave up the dead which were in them; and they were judged, every one of them, according to their deeds. Then death and Hades were thrown into the lake of fire. This is the second death, the lake of fire. And if anyone's name was not found written in the book of life, he was thrown into the lake of fire. (Revelation 20:11-15)

None who are saved are among this massive sea of humanity. The unsaved souls come out of hell and their bodies are resurrected from the graves and the seas of the world. They then stand before this blazing white throne, which has wheels, denoting full access to every event in history. These resurrected human beings are referred to as the "dead," which means the spiritually dead, or to put it more graphically, the damned. They are the eternally cursed, and their final destiny and tragic fate is one of utter hopelessness and despair.

This "day" of judgment will most likely be just one day, as Almighty God is able to judge each and every damned soul separately, yet simultaneously. In this way, every spiritually "dead" person being judged will be fully aware of everyone else's judgment. This day of judgment is absolutely essential in order to demonstrate the wisdom, the righteousness, and the holiness of God. This day will show conclusively that God is truly just. Both the saved and the lost will be eternally convinced of God's moral perfection, His blamelessness, and His flawless justice.

Take, for example, Solomon. He was both a judge and a king who prefigured the coming King of kings and Judge of judges. During Solomon's reign, two prostitutes came before him with a bitter dispute. These two harlots lived alone in the same house and they each gave birth to baby boys around the same time. However, one of them fell asleep on her child during the night and suffocated him. When she awoke and realized what had happened, she quickly arose and exchanged her dead baby in the place of the other woman's living infant son.

When the mother of the living boy awoke to feed her newborn, she knew immediately that the dead child was not hers, and this incident ignited a firestorm of controversy that eventually brought their dispute before King Solomon—the wisest of wise men. This argument became so heated that no one in the courtroom could discern which woman was telling the truth, but the penetrating mind of Solomon saw through the entire thing, and he asked for a sword:

> The king said, "Divide the living child in two, and give half to the one and half to the other." Then the woman whose child was the living one spoke to the king, for she was deeply stirred over her son, and said, "Oh, my lord, give her the living child, and by no means kill him." But the other said, "He shall be neither mine nor yours; divide him!" Then the king said, "Give the first woman the living child, and by no means kill him. She is his mother." When all Israel heard of the judgment which the king had handed down, they feared the king, for they saw that the wisdom of God was in him to administer justice. (1 Kings 3:24-28)

Flavius Josephus, the first century Jewish historian, gave us a little more detail in regards to this famous episode in the life of Solomon. Josephus tells us that both the live child and the dead child were brought before the king, and Solomon said to cut both children in half and give half of each child to each mother. Because of Solomon's bizarre command, Josephus records that the entire court of witnesses began to snicker and to muffle their laughter as they secretly thought that his order to kill the living child was utterly ridiculous. They felt Solomon's decision was so foolish and immature that he had no business acting as judge. However, his tactic elicited the truth, knowing the mother of the living child would rather keep him alive, even if it meant he'd be raised by someone else. The renowned historian tells us that Solomon received tremendous glory and honor for his deep insight. Josephus also informs us that Solomon severely rebuked the lying mother for her wickedness and vileness in wanting to murder an innocent baby in order to prevent the real mother from experiencing the joys of motherhood.

Solomon had absolutely nothing to do with this woman's wickedness, but look how this woman's evil deeds and depraved heart ended up giving such glory and honor to this legendary judge and famous king! In the same manner, God will be glorified as He sits in judgment on this "great white throne" that is entirely engulfed in flames. Believe it or not, God is going to be glorified and praised for His righteousness and His wisdom, even when people are condemned to be tormented forever and ever in the lake of fire.

The natural mind cannot comprehend the things of the Spirit of God, such as the reality of this coming day of judgment and the eternal consequences of the lake of fire (1 Corinthians 2:14). Many have argued that it would be impossible for anyone to be happy in heaven if they knew that their loved one was being tormented forever in the outer darkness; however, the truth is that on this day of judgment, everyone will vividly see the wisdom and the righteousness of God's eternal justice. They will understand fully that the unrepentant sins committed against an eternal and holy God deserve everlasting retribution. Consequently, even if our child, parent, spouse, or other loved one is eternally lost, our spirits will be in full agreement with God's righteous and unbiased verdicts. Rather than God being condemned for His judgments, He will be praised (even by those who become forever separated from their loved ones).

Personally, I do not want to see anyone eternally punished—I don't care how wicked they have been in this life. Even if some murderous brute tortured my own children to death, I could not bring myself to desire that he be eternally tormented for his vicious crimes. However, I do look forward to this day of reckoning for one reason, and for one reason only: I want Christ to be vindicated! I want God's people to be vindicated and for the truth to come out about everything. I want all of history's false religions, false prophets, cults, and atheistic beliefs and philosophies to be exposed for the demonic influences they truly are. I especially want macroevolution and theories of Darwinism to be unmasked for the "intellectual" poppycock they truly are.

People are going to see, crystal clear, that God is a God of His Word—that

He means what He says, and says what He means. People mock and jeer at the Bible and its account of creation, at Christ, and at sin in general; but on this day of judgment, and before this blazing throne, no one is going to be laughing, and no one will be blaspheming God to His face—absolutely no one!

This day will be the most awesome, the most spellbinding day in all of cosmic history. This infinitely vast universe will vanish before the terrifying face of Almighty God as He sits on His blazing throne—His blinding white throne, from which fires flow like rivers of hot lava and waterfalls of inflammable gas.

Sometime when you find yourself transfixed before the crackling flames of a fireplace, think about how God is an all-consuming fire of holiness and how His righteous throne is engulfed in flames, reminding the wicked day and night for eternity that God is just and His judgments are totally valid. Realize that God is not sadistic; rather, morally perfect, and no one He sentences to the lake of fire will ever say that God is not righteous because the flames surrounding them will forever remind them that He is.

It is an everlasting destiny that no one wants to think about, much less talk about. This horrifying fate is exactly what the Son of Almighty God came to save men from. He was tortured to death in order to pay both the infernal price and the eternal cost necessary to rescue anyone and everyone who would just believe in Him.

Blood Sport

Let's face it, today's media and many of today's current politicians no longer engage in fair play when it comes to debating the issues and reporting the facts. Instead, the realm of political rivalry and biased newscasts has devolved into a blood sport of personal destruction and character assassination. The current mainstream media outlets may halfheartedly attempt to project themselves as balanced news reporters; however, most of them seethe with contempt and ridicule for anyone running for political office who is committed to Christ or who upholds God's moral laws.

This contemptuous bloodletting can also be seen coming mainly from the camps of the leftists and the liberals who cannot stomach the moral demands of God or tolerate what the Bible says on a multitude of issues, ranging from divine judgment to creationism, and from fornication to homosexuality. In short, differing opinions and ideas can no longer be seriously and civilly discussed in the court of public discourse; rather, the Stalinoid methods of harassment, intimidation, and ridicule are employed against anyone viewed as being enemies of the state, otherwise known as the "politically incorrect."

However, this blood sport is nothing new; it has simply been redressed in modern garb and repackaged in current mass media. The old adage that says, "The more things change, the more they remain the same" is especially true when it comes to the elites of almost every generation. These are the self-righteous intellectuals and modern celebrities who regard themselves as being morally superior to the common man, and who are highly distinguished from everyone who dares to disagree with them.

Their numbers particularly abound in the world of entertainment and in the classrooms of academia. They also exist in large numbers as progressive judges, attorneys, politicians, and religious reformists who encourage unrestricted personal freedoms or who demand strict adherence to their elitist way of thinking. Jesus Christ Himself was forced to deal with the elitism of His day. His political opponents were called the Herodians, and His religious enemies were referred to as the scribes, the Pharisees, the Sadducees, and the chief priests. The Herodians despised the religious leaders who, in turn, held the political powers in utter contempt. However, they all found common ground when it came to opposing Jesus Christ and resisting His followers.

They were the cultural elite who could not successfully contend with Christ in the arena of religious and political debate, so they constantly attacked His character and vilified Him with accusations. They epitomized what it means to assassinate a person's character when he cannot be debated intellectually; they had the blood sport of verbal attack down to an accomplished skill and honed to a vicious art.

The Pharisees and the cultural elite of Christ's day underhandedly called Him a drunkard and a glutton and implied that His association with prostitutes and tax collectors meant He was as immoral and dishonest as the low class of people with whom He associated (see Luke 7:34). They also accused Him of being in league with the devil and being demon possessed because He delivered people from the possession of demonic forces (see Matthew 12:24-28; Mark 3:22).

They twisted His words and distorted their intended meaning (see Mark 14:56-59; Matthew 26:60-61; 27:40). They also suggested He was a liar for claiming to be older than Abraham, and they labeled Him a blasphemer for making Himself equal with God (see John 8:56-59, 5:18; Matthew 26:62-66; Luke 22:70-71). The politics of personal destruction knew no bounds when it came to the slanderous enemies of Jesus Christ. The elitists hated Him with a passion because He repeatedly exposed their hypocrisy and always opposed their godless values.

Well, it was the Son of God who said that since the world hated and persecuted Him, it would hate and persecute His followers also (see John 15:18). He additionally warned,

> A student is not above his teacher, nor a servant above his master. ... If they have called the head of the house Beelzebul [Satan], how much more will they malign the members of his household! (Matthew 10:24-25)

Yes, thousands of years later, the only difference between the talking heads of our day and those in Jesus' day is that the flowing robes of the religious hypocrites and corrupt politicians have been exchanged for empty suits and air-filled skirts. However, the bloody pastime of demolishing the character of one's political adversaries or religious rivals remains the same. The only other thing that has changed is the volume of contempt and the amount of scorn, due to the megaphone of mass media.

With the advent of modern communication and the art of distorted sound bites, it is no wonder that fewer and fewer God-fearing people get involved in politics. The cost of the destruction of one's personal reputation and the demeaning of their families is a premium that is just too painful to pay. Therefore, as the number of champions from the liberal media's and elitists' agenda increases, the less tolerable it will become for those who obey Christ and His Word. The latter group will eventually be silenced or ruined by their opponents' "hate crime legislation" and "fairness doctrines," as well as have to endure accusations of being racist, intolerant, homophobic, hateful, ignorant, and above all, dangerous.

In short, the elimination of Christ's followers is one of the driving ambitions of the politically correct "thought police." Eventually, people like me will be sent to "re-education camps," or fined, or imprisoned, or financially devastated, or even tortured and murdered for our beliefs. It has happened under almost every dictator for the past 2,000 years and will continue to transpire until Jesus returns.

Of course, to the elitists and the uninformed, this all sounds very melodramatic and grossly exaggerated, but this truth has not been magnified beyond the facts. Looking back over the past 100 years of church history, we see that more people have been persecuted, imprisoned, and murdered for Christ's name's sake than in the previous 2,000 years combined—and the real carnage hasn't even started yet![27]

The Bible predicts that when the elitists and the liberal media finally get their beloved world leader, they will be electrified with joy (see Revelation 13:4). They will be positively elated because their man of the hour will toss the Bible over his shoulder and promise everyone heaven without hell, Christ without the cross, humanism in place of religion, and a utopia without God. He will eliminate almost all moral restraints, promising people freedom from religion while attacking Christianity as the scapegoat for all the world's ills.

Remember the atheistic communists? They, too, promised a worker's paradise without God, but instead managed to murder over 100 million people and enslave millions more with their gulags and their thought control. But like I said, we haven't seen anything yet, because as Jesus foretold,

They will deliver you to tribulation, and will kill you, and you will be hated by all nations because of My name. At that time many will fall away and will betray one another and hate one another. (Matthew 24:9-10)

Additionally, the apostle John says,

I saw underneath the altar the souls of those who had been slain because of the word of God, and because of the testimony which they had maintained. (Revelation 6:9)

He later states,

And I saw the souls of those who had been beheaded because of their testimony of Jesus and because of the word of God, and those who had not worshipped the beast or his image, and had not received the mark on their forehead and on their hand. (Revelation 20:4)

It is just a matter of time before the world witnesses such a frenzied hatred of the followers of Jesus Christ that the blood sport of character assassination will truly seem tame in comparison. As noted above, John predicted that in the last days, multitudes of Christians are going to be decapitated for their obedience to the Son of God. Perhaps it is no coincidence that fanatical Muslims have chosen the method of beheading as an effective form of retribution and intimidation.

Consequently, the world is truly being conditioned for this coming bloodbath, and in the end, it will discover too late that their blood sport of personal destruction is about to take on a life of its own. Many of the elitists in the Communist party also became victims during the Stalinist purges and Mao's Cultural Revolution, and like Nazi Germany's "ministry of propaganda" and the Soviet newspaper "Pravda," the God-hating media will realize too late that they will no longer be free to report anything but the dictates of the party line.

Decent followers of Christ have been and will be persecuted for their political incorrectness, so be forewarned by what the psalmist said:

Why are the nations in an uproar and the peoples devising a vain thing? The kings of the earth take their stand and the rulers take counsel together against the Lord and against His Anointed, saying, "Let us tear their fetters apart and cast away their cords from us!" He who sits in the heavens laughs, the Lord scoffs at them. Then He will speak to them in His anger and terrify them in His fury, saying, "But as for me, I have installed My King upon Zion, My holy mountain." ... "You shall break them with a rod of iron, you shall shatter them like earthenware." Now therefore, O kings, show discernment; take warning, O judges of the earth. Worship the Lord with reverence and rejoice with trembling. Do homage to the Son, that He not become angry, and you perish in the way, for His wrath may soon be kindled. How blessed are all who take refuge in Him! (Psalm 2:1-6, 9-12)

Amen.

"Worldwide Persecution of Christians." *The Prayer Foundation*. S.G. Preston Ministries, n.d. Web. 04 Dec. 2013.

The Unlucky Number 13

Have you ever wondered why the number 13 has been associated with some kind of ominous power? Where did this excessive fear of a simple prime number originate? It is truly amazing how even in our scientific age, our enlightened society can be so superstitious when it comes to the 13th number.

You don't think so? Well, have you ever noticed in virtually every high-rise and skyscraper in America, there is no 13th floor? How is it that Friday the 13th has become a day to be concerned about because of its irrational potential for evil or bad luck? Why do so few professional athletes dare to don a uniform with the number 13 inscribed on it? Finally, why does the number 13 in the cultic practice of tarot card reading represent the death card?

Myths and legends abound when it comes to the dreaded number

13. Here are some of the more outrageous ones that I've heard:

"A child born on Friday the 13th will be unlucky for life."

"If you cut your hair on the 13th of the month, someone in your family will die."

"If a funeral procession passes you on the 13th day of any calendar month, you are likely to die the following day."

On the other hand, some pagan and cultic circles believe the number 13 has wonderful magical powers with miraculous influences.

There is even some speculation as to why every U.S. dollar bill is designed with 13 levels in a pyramid, 13 stars, 13 arrows, 13 stripes, 13 leaves, and 13 olives. Maybe this coincidence has something to do with the 13 original colonies, or perhaps it was associated with the all-seeing eye that appears at the apex of the pyramid, symbolizing unearthly beliefs and cultic persuasions.

Some people suggest the dread attached to this cryptic number is due to there being 13 men at the Last Supper, one of whom was crucified, one who committed suicide, and the other eleven who fled in fear. Others suppose the number 13 has been given a bad rap because the Israelites murmured against God 13 times in the book of Exodus and incurred God's wrath because of it. Still others insist this phenomenon was given birth as far back as eighteen centuries before Christ, because it was once thought that Babylon's Hammurabi Code of Laws omits the 13th law in its many commands (though this theory has since been debunked, due to the discovery of a translation error).

However, I personally believe that the excessive fear of this number originated in the biblical account recorded in the book of Esther. This scriptural narration takes place more than five centuries before the birth of God's Son, and it reveals how a beautiful Jewish girl became wedded to the powerful Persian king named Ahasuerus (otherwise known as Xerxes I). This mighty king had a high-ranking counselor named Haman, who hated and despised all Jews (especially a man named Mordecai, who happened to be Queen Esther's cousin). Not knowing that Esther was also of Jewish descent, Haman schemed and concocted a systematic plan to exterminate all of the Jews in the Persian Empire. Either Haman's servants or sorcerers cast lots in order to arrive at the optimum day to slaughter every existing Jew. The lot fell on the dreaded date of the 13th day of Adar (February) in the Jewish calendar (see Esther 3:7, 13).

Through the intercession of Esther, however, Haman's evil purpose completely backfired, and on the 13th day, originally chosen to exterminate the Jewish race, the Jews themselves were given the king's authority to massacre all of their known enemies. Haman himself was hanged on the very gallows he had erected for the murder of Mordecai, and Haman's ten sons were also executed on the same crossbeam on which their father perished (Esther 9:13-14). The next day was set as a feast of celebration in honor of the liberation of Abraham's descendants and the annihilation of those who sought to destroy them. To this day, on the 14th day of Adar, the Jews commemorate Purim. This name "Purim" or "the feast of Purim" was derived from the word "Pur" meaning "the casting of the lot" (vv. 20-22, 27-28).

The lot determined that the 13th day was to be the unlucky day for God's chosen people; instead, it became a very unfortunate day for God's enemies. This historical incident is, in my opinion, most likely the origin of the apprehension associated with the 13th number. This day of Purim is what seems to have spawned countless superstitions dealing with bad luck, or in some instances (like the rescued Jews), representing good fortune or supernatural deliverance.

The point to all of this discussion over a simple number is really to talk about the reality of modern-day superstitions and the existence of genuine fears concerning mystical secrets. The Bible has a great deal to say about superstitions and the fascination with celestial bodies, sorcerers, witchcraft, divination, black magic, mediums, soothsayers, prognosticators, charms, and demon worship. When God pronounced judgment upon ancient Babylon for their many sorceries and wickedness, He said their punishment would come upon them

> in full measure in spite of [their] many sorceries, in spite of the great power of [their] spells. ... You felt secure in your wickedness and said, "No one sees me," your wisdom and your knowledge, they have deluded you. ... But evil will come on you which you will not know how to charm away. ... Stand fast now in your spells and in your many sorceries with which you have labored from your youth; perhaps you will be able to profit, perhaps you may cause trembling. You are wearied with your many counsels; let now the astrologers, those who prophesy by the stars, those who predict by the new moons, stand up and save you from what will come upon you. (Isaiah 47:913)

Like the superstitious Babylonians, Haman was a fool. His confidence was placed in a number that was selected through occult procedures, and in the end, that number proved to be his undoing. God strictly condemns the practices of sorcery, spiritism, casting spells, and foretelling the future (see Exodus 22:18; Leviticus 19:21, 31; 20:27; Deuteronomy 18:10-11; 2 Kings 21:6; Revelation 9:21; 18:23; 22:15). Not surprisingly, sacrificing children to false gods is forbidden (Deuteronomy 18:10; Leviticus 18:21; 20:2-5). So is believing in astrology and putting one's trust in anyone or anything but Him (Isaiah 47:13, Deuteronomy 8:19).

In spite of all God's warnings to fear only Him, people everywhere are ruled by superstitions. They cannot leave the house without first consulting their horoscope, and before making any major decisions, like changing jobs, choosing a career, or getting married, they must visit a palm reader or chant some mantra for good luck. What happens, though, when someone's astrological predictions contradict their fortune cookies, or their rabbit's foot accidentally breaks a mirror, or a black cat startles them into unwittingly walking under a ladder, or they win the lottery on Friday the 13th?

I suppose that such worries could truly clutter up a person's mind to the point where they wouldn't know what to think or do. The truth is that pagan beliefs are not only filled with ambiguities and foolish superstitions, but they are actually satanically inspired and demonically driven. God is the One to be consulted and revered—not numbers, spells, charms, pagan ceremonies, or voodoo rituals. These dangerous practices enslave men and cloud their spiritual understanding, shifting a person's focus away from God and blinding them to His truth.

In the book of Acts we read about seven superstitious brothers who tried to expel evil spirits out of a possessed man. Because they did not have a personal relationship with Christ, they only used His name as though they were casting a spell. Therefore, the demon overpowered the brothers, wounded them, stripped them of their clothing, and drove them away (19:13-16).

> When this episode became known to the Jews and Greeks in Ephesus, fear fell upon them all and the name of the Lord Jesus was being magnified. Many also of those who had believed kept coming, confessing and disclosing their practices. And many of those who practiced magic brought their books together and began burning them in the sight of everyone; and they counted up the price of them and found it fifty thousand pieces of silver. So the word of the Lord was growing mightily and prevailing. (Acts 19:17-20)

God does not want people to be enslaved with superstitions and directed by the powers of darkness; rather, He wants to set them free in the name of His Son Jesus, liberated by Christ's power. We need to put our confidence in Him, not our lucky stars. It is God whom we need to fear, not some unlucky number.

Fruitless Fruit Trees

Imagine a world without fruit. Personally, it wouldn't make much difference at all to me because I rarely eat fruits (or vegetables, for that matter). I suppose the only thing that keeps my veins from turning to sludge and my arteries from oozing with cholesterol is the fact that I get plenty of aerobic exercise on a daily basis. I suppose, too, that I have been blessed with some very hearty genes that keep my heart from gagging on all the meat and potatoes I consume. However, for many people, a world without fruit would be intolerable. It would be totally foreign for anyone who likes a variety in their diet and who desires to enjoy a long and healthy life.

The fact is that fruit is life sustaining with vitamins necessary for people's well being. The Bible has a great deal to say about fruit and the need to be fruitful. As a matter of fact, the very first thing God commanded of this planet's life forms was to "be fruitful and increase in number and fill the water in the seas, and let the birds increase on the earth" (Genesis 1:22, NIV). Apart from forbidding Adam and Eve from eating from the tree of the knowledge of good and evil, God commanded them to "be fruitful and multiply, and fill the earth, and subdue it" (v. 28).

God tells men to be fruitful before He tells them to multiply. Even after God destroyed the world with a flood, the very first command the Lord gave to Noah and his family was to "be fruitful and multiply, and fill the earth" (Genesis 9:1). God even repeats this commission to Noah in order to emphasize the importance of fruitfulness (v. 7). Christ Himself placed such an enormous premium upon fruit and fruitfulness that He made it the criterion for distinguishing who belongs to Him and who doesn't:

> You will know them by their fruits. Grapes are not gathered from thorn bushes nor figs from thistles, are they? So every good tree bears good fruit, but the bad tree bears bad fruit. A good tree cannot produce bad fruit, nor can a bad tree produce good fruit. Every tree that does not bear good fruit is cut down and thrown into the fire. So then, you will know

them by their fruits. Not everyone who says to me, "Lord, Lord," will enter the kingdom of heaven, but he who does the will of My Father who is in heaven will enter. (Matthew 7:16-21)

Just what exactly *is* fruit and what does God mean when he commands us to be fruitful? Is He merely speaking of procreation and producing as many offspring as possible, or could He primarily be speaking about cultivating fruitful lives that glorify Him and that impart spiritual life to as many others as possible?

Fruit is really just the unconscious byproduct of a healthy tree that receives the proper amount of nutrients and sunlight. In light of this, note Jesus' narrative:

I am the true vine, and My Father is the vinedresser. Every branch in Me that does not bear fruit, He takes away; and every branch that bears fruit, He prunes it so that it may bear more fruit. ... Abide in Me, and I in you. As the branch cannot bear fruit of itself unless it abides in the vine, so neither can you unless you abide in Me. I am the vine, you are the branches; he who abides in Me and I in him, he bears much fruit, for apart from Me you can do nothing. If anyone does not abide in Me, he is thrown away as a branch and dries up; and they gather them, and cast them into the fire and they are burned. (John 15:1-6)

Along these same lines, John the Baptist severely rebuked some of the "very religious" people of his day by saying,

You brood of vipers, who warned you to flee from the wrath to come? Therefore bear fruit in keeping with repentance; and do not suppose that you can say to yourselves, "We have Abraham for our father"; for I say to you that from these stones God is able to raise up children to Abraham. The axe is already laid at the root of the trees; therefore every tree that does not bear good fruit is cut down and thrown into the fire. (Matthew 3:7-10)

Also, Jesus gave a parable about a fig tree planted in a man's vineyard where, for three long years, the tree failed to produce any fruit. In exasperation and disappointment, the owner of the fig tree commanded the vinedresser to cut it down because it was taking up valuable space (see Luke 13:6-7). At another time, Christ went to the extreme of cursing (and thus withering) a fig tree that was full of leaves but was void of any fruit. Interestingly, a fig tree bears fruit *before* its leaves appear, so one would expect to see figs on a tree already covered with leaves. His cursing of this fruitless fruit tree was meant as a solemn warning to people who appear very "religious" or "spiritual" but whose lives are fruitless in regards to exemplifying the Lord.

God made each of us to cultivate lives that are rich in good works and productive for His honor and glory. Even when we grow old in our service for God, the Bible says,

> The righteous man will flourish like the palm tree, he will grow like a cedar in Lebanon. Planted in the house of the Lord, they will flourish in the courts of our God. They will still yield fruit in old age; they shall be full of sap and very green, to declare that the Lord is upright; He is my rock, and there is no unrighteousness in Him. (Psalm 92:12-15)

It is the ultimate tragedy to live one's life for decades on end and yet be fruitless toward God. To die fruitless before the Lord is to have lived without true meaning and to have existed without genuine purpose. Apart from God, there is no ultimate significance. All the accumulation of fame and fortune is meaningless; it amounts to a fig tree covered with branches and leaves, but void of anything truly enriching or lasting.

When it comes to bearing fruit and being fruitful for God, we are never to ask, "How come I haven't been given more to work with?" or, "Why do others have greater advantages than I have when it comes to serving God and bearing fruit for His name's sake?"

The question we need to ask is, "What do I have that can be used for the glory of my Creator?" Or stated another way, "What is in my hand?" This is actually the very first question God ever asked Moses. When Moses felt utterly inadequate for the job God was calling him to do, because he believed he was too inept and unworthy to be used by God, he pleaded with the Lord to find someone else to accomplish His purpose. Moses insisted he wasn't an eloquent speaker and was terrified that people would not believe him, so he asked God and God responded to him.

> "What if they will not believe me or listen to what I say? For they may say, 'The Lord has not appeared to you.'" And God replied to Moses, "What is that in your hand?" And he said, "A staff." (Exodus 4:1-2)

Moses turned out to be one of the most spiritually fruitful men in all recorded history, and the only thing God asked him was, "What is that in your hand?" And what was in Moses' hand, but a simple staff. It wasn't money, power, or talent, but an ugly, dead stick of wood. It was virtually worthless in terms of earthly value, but God used that shriveled tree branch to confront the powerful magicians in Pharaoh's court and to turn the Nile into blood (see Exodus 7:8-13, 19-20). He used it to produce billions of frogs, to rain down hail mixed with fire, and to bring tons of swarming locusts over the land of Egypt (8:5, 9:23, 10:13). Each time Moses extended his staff when God told him to stretch out his hand, a plague would follow. Likewise, God used the staff to send three days of darkness upon Egypt before bringing about the final plague (10:21-22). With that worthless piece of firewood, God told Moses to split the Red Sea and lead His people to the Promised Land, and later bring forth water from a bone-dry rock (see Exodus 14:16; 17:5-6; Numbers 20:11).

In the book of Judges, we read of a deliverer by the name of Shamgar who struck down 600 Philistines with an oxgoad because it was what he had in his hand (see Judges 3:31). In the book of Acts a woman by the name of Tabitha was constantly "abounding with deeds of kindness and charity," and the only thing she had in her hand was a needle and thread. In the name of Jesus, she sewed tunics and garments for the needy, widows, and orphans. When she died, people were so distraught, they sent for Peter to pray over her (see Acts 9:3642). When he interceded on her behalf, God honored her such that she is the only grown woman recorded in the Bible to have been raised from the dead. God glorified her because she glorified Him with what little she had in her hand.

To be fruitful for God does not require great resources—only a willingness to use what He has placed in our hand, regardless of how insignificant it may appear. When Christ fed the multitude with five loaves of bread and two fish, He first asked, in essence, "What do you have on hand?" (see Mark 6:38). God only wants to know what we have available to dedicate to Him in order for Him to multiply it for His glory, making our lives fruitful for His kingdom. With that, He will begin by asking us, "What is that in your hand?" Realize, too, that He is the vine, we are the branches, and that apart from Him, we can do nothing—but in Him we can bear much fruit.

The Power of One Word

What was the first word the "Father of Lies" spoke to mankind (not the first question he asked, but the very first word used when he posed the question)? The pristine word the deceiver of the human race used when speaking to man was, *indeed*. "*Indeed*, has God said, 'You shall not eat from any tree of the garden'?" (Genesis 3:1).

What an incredible word; there is no word like it! It is the devil's favorite word, and he uses it often. Beginning with that one little word he brought low our first parents, ruined a perfect world, and damned countless millions of souls to hell.

We have all heard the expression, "He is a man of few words." Well, Satan is truly a demonic being with even fewer words. His words to men are few, but they are truly weighty, and there is no word that carries more weight in his vocabulary than "indeed." The dictionary defines the word "indeed" as an exclamation denoting surprise, skepticism, and doubt. The word conveys an attitude of suspicion, distrust, and uncertainty. It makes one feel unsettled and subtly disturbs a person's assurance and peace in regards to their opinions or beliefs. Although the word "indeed" can also mean "truly" or "undeniably," the context in which the devil uses it always leaves a trace of doubt, manifesting hints of ridicule and disbelief.

Satan's every question to man begins with the sarcastic remark, "Indeed!" The sarcasm that simple word conveys often prompts men to conclude on their own that the words of God cannot be trusted; the devil doesn't have to come right out and call God a liar. He cleverly uses a word that ridicules what God has clearly said, and as a result, the word "indeed" motivates man himself to call God a liar. Ingenious, isn't it? What a word! It throws the very words of a truthful God into ambiguity and confusion.

> Indeed—did God say that He created the world in six days?
> Indeed, He did! (see Exodus 20:9-11)
>
> Indeed—did God say fornication, lying, adultery, stealing

and homosexuality are sins? Indeed! (see 1 Corinthians 6:910; 1 Timothy 1:8-10)

Indeed—did God say there is an eternal hell where unrepentant sinners go? Yes, indeed! (see Matthew 5:29-30)

Indeed—did God say Jesus Christ is the only way to heaven? Indeed, it's true! (see John 14:6)

Indeed—did God say Jonah was swallowed by a great fish? Indeed! (see Jonah 1:17; Matthew 12:40)

Indeed—did God say He destroyed the entire world with a flood because of man's wickedness? Yes, indeed! (see Genesis 6:5; 7)

Indeed—did God say, "It is appointed unto men once to die, but after this the judgment"? Indeed! (see Hebrews 9:27)

What an incredibly powerful word! No other single word has inspired more people to disbelieve and thus disobey God than that simple little utterance. The devil is truly a master of languages who has seduced myriads of gullible souls to damnation just by listening to one tiny word—*indeed*!

However, God also has *His* Word. The apostle John tells us,

> In the beginning was the Word, and the Word was with God, and the Word was God. He was in the beginning with God. All things came into being through Him, and apart from Him nothing came into being that has come into being. In Him was life, and the life was the Light of men. ... He was in the world, and the world was made through Him, and the world did not know Him. ... But as many as received Him, to them He gave the right to become children of God. ... And the Word became flesh, and dwelt among us, and we saw His glory, glory as of the only begotten from the Father, full of grace and truth. (John 1:1-4, 10, 12-14)

Jesus is God's Word to fallen man, and Christ is God's answer to Satan's favorite word, "indeed." The God of all mankind told Moses there would come a time in human history when his Word would come:

> I will raise up a prophet from among [the Jews], and I will put My words in his mouth, and he shall speak to them all that I command him. It [will] come about that whoever will not listen to My words which he shall speak in My name, I Myself will require it of him. (Deuteronomy 18:18-19)

And at the very end of the world when Christ returns in great power and tremendous glory, the apostle John says,

> I saw heaven opened, and behold, a white horse, and He who sat on it is called Faithful and True, and in righteousness He judges and wages war. His eyes are a flame of fire, and on His head are many diadems, and He has a name written on Him which no one knows except Himself. He is clothed with a robe dipped in blood, and His name is called The Word of God. (Revelation 19:11-13)

The "Word of God" then slays the wicked with His Word, or as John says, with the sharp two-edged sword that came forth from His mouth (see Revelation 1:16, Amp). Jesus is God's first Word in salvation and He is God's last Word in judgment. No one in heaven or hell can match the power of this Word, and no authority on earth can oppose this Word. There is no appeal after this Word, either—absolutely none.

Since Jesus Christ is synonymous with God's Word, the Bible gives men everywhere a very sobering warning when Paul writes,

> Remind them of these things, and solemnly charge them in the presence of God not to wrangle about words, which is useless and leads to the ruin of the hearers. Be diligent to present yourself approved to God as a workman who does not need to be ashamed, accurately handling the word of truth. But avoid worldly and empty chatter, for it will lead to further ungodliness, and their talk will spread like gangrene. (2 Timothy 2:14-17)

It was the Word of God who warned, "Every careless word that people speak, they shall give an accounting for it in the day of judgment. For by your words you will be justified, and by your words you will be condemned" (Matthew 12:36-37). It was the Word of God who also declared, "Man [does] not live on bread alone, but on every word that proceeds out of the mouth of God," and "Heaven and earth will pass away, but My words will not pass away" (Matthew 4:4, 24:35).

Be sure to remember how incredibly powerful words can be and how with just one word, the devil has damned myriads and how also with just one word —*Jesus*—God has saved multitudes. It is truly astonishing how much influence just one word can wield.

Good News, Bad News

Has anyone ever said to you, "I have some good news and some bad news to tell you"? If so, which do you want to know first and foremost? I would want to be told the bad news first because regardless of how agreeable the good news may be, the bad news is what concerns me most.

So at the risk of sounding extremely pessimistic, I'll give you the bad news first, if you don't already know it: America is a sinking ship. Today our nation is choking under the selfish ambitions and spiritual blindness of its leaders. Our country is suffocating from the moral rot of its people, and our light is going out as we are dying—dying economically, politically, educationally, militarily, and spiritually.

We are perishing in our courts, decaying in our homes, languishing in our streets and playgrounds, declining in our industries, and withering in many of our churches. Our death rattle is being heard throughout the world; our hope is dried up and our judgment is certain, because we have forsaken God. In other words, our nation is not heeding the Lord's admonition to King Asa, which still applies to us today:

> The Lord is with you when you are with Him. And if you
> seek Him, He will let you find Him; but if you forsake Him,
> He will forsake you. (2 Chronicles 15:2)

The truth is, America was once as majestic as the Titanic but now is destined to lie down beside her in a watery grave, frozen in darkness. How is that for bad news? It is hard to get much more pessimistic than this. Unquestionably, the extreme optimist would strongly disagree with my assessment of our nation, but the sad truth remains that because God has been so marginalized throughout our country, we have forsaken Him, and He has forsaken us.

God has left us to our own devices. Our captain is asleep at the stern and our ship's leaders are playing musical chairs on the deck. Most of our vessel's crew is intoxicated with unimportant matters, while the remaining crew members are preoccupied with position and fame. Only those with spiritual eyes can see what is happening, and only those with spiritual ears can understand what is going on.

Having heard the bad news, the good news is that God has lovingly provided a means of escape through His Son Jesus Christ, our only lifeboat aboard this doomed craft (see Luke 21:36). But our faith in Him is meaningless if we are not sold out to Him in obedience. To merely give God head acknowledgment is as foolish as mentally believing a lifeboat can save us but not bothering to get into it while the ship is quickly sinking into an icy grave. Time is of the essence and a sense of urgency is paramount; this is no situation to be a coward and no place to act the fool.

Abandoning ship is not an option without first saving everyone we can. We need to stay to the bitter end and remain to the last minute in our efforts to lead people to the good news—the good news of salvation in Jesus Christ. We are to

> have mercy on some, who are doubting; save others, snatching them out of the fire; and on some have mercy with fear. (Jude 22-23)

And as James tells us,

> If any among you strays from the truth and one turns him back, let him know that [whoever brings back] a sinner from the error of his way will save his soul from death and will cover a multitude of sins. (James 5:19-20)

Like the passengers of the Titanic, our world is filled with souls who fail to see the danger of their situation. They need to be awakened with the bad news and aroused with the good news before it is too late, and no news could possibly be worse to someone than finding out that they are spiritually lost and on their way to an eternal hell. Yet there is no greater news than to hear that your sins have been forgiven by the blood of Jesus Christ, and that your commitment to Him guarantees you an eternity with God in heaven.

Life—The Ultimate Super Bowl

Super Bowl Sunday has become an American tradition rivaling almost every major holiday on our calendar. Advertisers pay millions of dollars for just a 30-second window to sell their products during Super Bowl commercials. Half-time entertainment itself has become a spectacular sideshow that manages to electrify the crowds and energize the masses.

If ever the words "Super Bowl" could be replaced, it would have to be with the words "Super Hype." The Super Bowl has unquestionably become a phenomenon of extravagant and excessive promotions. With this in mind, however, I have a couple of questions concerning this sensational event—do you remember who won last year's game? How about the Super Bowl contest five years ago; do you recall who the victors in that match were? Unless you are an avid trivia buff or sports enthusiast, chances are you don't remember. You probably have difficulty recalling exactly which teams even played in the bruising skirmish, let alone who won.

Nevertheless, in the eyes of God, there is one arena where no one is a spectator. This all-consuming event is called "life." Although multitudes of people may unconsciously choose to sit on the sidelines of this earthly existence, they are in this event whether they decide to be engaged or not. The Bible uses the term "overcome" (or its derivative) almost thirty times. In the book of Revelation alone, it is used nearly a dozen times. Jesus promised several things to the ones who overcome:

> To him who overcomes, I will grant to eat of the tree of life which is in the Paradise of God. (Revelation 2:7)

> He who overcomes will not be hurt by the second death. (v. 11)

> To him who overcomes, to him I will give some of the hidden manna, and I will give him a white stone, and a new name written on the stone which no one knows but he who receives it. (v. 17)

He who overcomes, and he who keeps My deeds until the end, to him I will give authority over the nations; and he shall rule them with a rod of iron, as the vessels of the potter are broken to pieces, as I also have received authority from My Father; and I will give him the morning star. (v. 26-28)

He who overcomes will thus be clothed in white garments; and I will not erase his name from the book of life, and I will confess his name before My Father and before His angels. (3:5)

He who overcomes, I will make him a pillar in the temple of My God, and he will not go out from it anymore; and I will write on him the name of My God, and the name of the city of My God, the new Jerusalem, which comes down out of heaven from My God, and My new name. (v. 12)

He who overcomes, I will grant to him to sit down with Me on My throne, as I also overcame and sat down with My Father on His throne. (v. 21)

There is no question as to what the word "overcome" implies; it means to prevail over a difficulty after a strenuous or hard struggle. No one overcomes a good night's sleep or a sumptuous meal; rather, one overcomes a hard-fought battle.

In heaven's economy, that's what life is—a battle. It is the ultimate Super Bowl, where the stakes are eternal and the rewards and losses are everlasting. It is an intense struggle "against the powers, against the world forces of this darkness, against the spiritual forces of wickedness in the heavenly places" (Ephesians 6:12). It is a contest where "we have so great a cloud of witnesses surrounding us," where we need to "run with endurance the race that is set before us, fixing our eyes on Jesus, the author and perfecter of our faith, who for the joy set before Him endured the cross, despising the shame, and has sat down at the right hand of the throne of God" (Hebrews 12:1-2).

It is a conflict where God wants everyone to be engaged to the fullest on the playing field of life, never to give half measures or to delegate our assignments to others. When we are knocked down, get up; when discouraged, don't quit;

when bloodied, shake it off. We are to be team players and keep our eyes on Christ. If we score a goal, we need to become fans who rejoice in what God has done, never seeking glory for ourselves. Celebrating in what God Himself accomplishes, we can delight exceedingly in the privilege of playing in the "game of games" for the Lord of lords, the King of kings, the God of gods.

Keep in mind, victory and overcoming cannot be achieved apart from Christ. As the apostle John put it,

> They overcame [Satan] because of the blood of the Lamb and because of the word of their testimony, and they did not love their life even when faced with death. (Revelation 12:11)

Go ahead and watch a Super Bowl or participate in a competitive sport, but after you do, try to recall what the ultimate struggle in life truly is, and remember the following words of the Lord Jesus:

> He who overcomes will inherit these things [eternal rewards], and I will be His God and he will be My son. (Revelation 21:7)

By the way, my curiosity remains—who did win last year's Super Bowl? For that matter, who was the most recent gold medalist in women's figure skating? Who was the latest victor in the Indianapolis 500, and what team came out on top in last year's World Series? Let's face it, the greatest victories on earth are destined for the dustbins of historical trivia, while a cup of cold water given to another in Jesus' name will be remembered and will not lose its reward (see Matthew 10:42).

The Final Fork in the Road

Terror breeds terror, hatred spawns hatred, lust begets lust, and greed compounds greed. Only the power of God can draw this sickness—this poison—out of a man's heart, and only Christ replaces man's vileness with virtue, supplying both genuine love and sincere forgiveness through the Holy Spirit. Only in Jesus can men find the authentic purpose in life and discover the power of mercy, the joy of peace, and the courage to confront the hopelessness so many people sense today.

Apart from the Almighty, humanity is destined to vaporize in the nuclear fires that man's black heart will inevitably ignite. The choice lies deep within each person to select which path to take. Joshua said to the "religious" people of his day,

> Now, therefore, fear the Lord and serve Him in sincerity and truth; and put away the gods which your fathers served beyond the River and in Egypt, and serve the Lord. If it is disagreeable in your sight to serve the Lord, choose for yourselves today whom you will serve: whether the gods which your fathers served which were beyond the River, or the gods of the Amorites in whose land you are living; but as for me and my house, we will serve the Lord. (Joshua 24:14-15)

The world has come to a fork in the road, as has every individual who has reached the age of reason. God does not force Himself upon anyone, nor does He predestine anyone to an earthly fate or to a fixed eternity. A man's will is sovereign; God will not transgress upon man's freedom to choose. To do so would negate the very essence of love and the very meaning of free will. We cannot escape the consequences of our choices, but we must choose. Failure to choose is itself a choice, and that choice will have definite results. Concerning this fork in the road, God says,

> "See, I am setting before you today a blessing and a curse—

the blessing if you obey the commands of the Lord your God that I am giving you today; the curse if you disobey the commands of the Lord your God and turn from the way that I command you today. (Deuteronomy 11:26-28, NIV)

He later says,

See, I have set before you today life and prosperity, and death and adversity. ... I call heaven and earth to witness against you today, that I have set before you life and death, the blessing and the curse. So choose life in order that you may live, you and your descendants, by loving the Lord your God, by obeying His voice, and by holding fast to Him; for this is your life and the length of your days. (Deuteronomy 30:15, 19-20)

In the first chapter of Proverbs, the wisest of wise men tells us that wisdom shouts in the street and pleads with the naïve—who seem to like being simpleminded—to listen to the voice of God. He warns that, because people hate knowledge and do not choose the fear of the Lord, their waywardness will kill them, and their complacency will destroy them.

Lastly, it was the Son of God Himself who urged men,

Enter through the narrow gate; for the gate is wide and the way is broad that leads to destruction, and there are many who enter through it. For the gate is small and the way is narrow that leads to life, and there are few who find it. (Matthew 7:13-14)

The fork in the road cannot be avoided or altered because it is on life's highway. We had no choice when it came to our own existence; we didn't ask to be given life, but now we must choose which life we will live. Our decision will determine where we will live forevermore. Let us choose wisely.

References

Misery Has Two Daughters

1. "Global Hunger." *Bread for the World*. Bread for the World, n.d. Web. 3 Dec. 2013.

Plucking Chickens and Strumming Guitars

2.. "Love That Purifies and Transforms." *Reflections* (Nov. 2009): n. pag. *C.S. Lewis Institute*. C.S. Lewis Institute, Nov. 2009. Web. 3 Dec. 2013.

Sex—The Mystery of all Mysteries

3.. D'Ambrosio, Marcellino. "Our Heart Is Restless." *The Crossroads Initiative*. Crossroads Productions, Inc., n.d. Web. 04 Dec. 2013.

The Naked Evolutionist

4.. See *Darwin's Black Box: The Biochemical Challenge to Evolution* by Michael Behe (The Free Press, 1996).

Other books on this subject I would also recommend are *The Human Difference* by John Allan (Lion Publishing Corporation, 1989), *When Science Fails* by John Hudson Tiner (Baker Book House Company, 1974), *Creation or Evolution?* by the staff at Plain Truth Ministries (Plain Truth Ministries—Worldwide, 1996)

It's Not That Complicated

5.. Khurana, Simran. "Religion Quotes by Mark Twain." *About.com Quotations*. About.com, n.d. Web. 03 Dec. 2013.

Old School

6.. Dawkins, Richard. *The God Delusion*. Boston: Houghton Mifflin, 2006. Print.

God Is Blind

7.. King, Martin L., Jr. "I Have a Dream." Speech. Lincoln Memorial, Washington, DC. 28 Aug. 1963. *American Rhetoric*. American Rhetoric. Web. 03 Dec. 2013.

The Foolish Wise Man

8.. Josephus, Flavius. "Book VIII, Chapter 7, Paragraph 5." *The Antiquities of the Jews*. Trans.

William Whiston. Blacksburg, VA: Unabridged, 2011. N. pag. Print.

Shining Pews and Roasting Marshmallows

9.. Bonner, Bill. "Sitting on Bayonets." *LewRockwell.com*. LewRockwell.com, 1 June 2004. Web. 03 Dec. 2013.

The Spiritual Invasion

10.. *Illegal Immigration: Border Crossing Deaths Have Doubled Since 1995; Border Patrol's Efforts to Prevent Deaths Have Not Been Fully Evaluated*. Rep. no. GAO06-770. Washington, DC: United States Government Accountability Office, 2006. Print.

11.. "Canada-United States Border." *Wikipedia*. Wikimedia Foundation, 28 Nov. 2013. Web. 03 Dec. 2013.

12.. Elbel, Fred. "How Many Illegal Aliens Are in the U.S.?" *The American Resistance*. The American Resistance Foundation, 2005. Web. 03 Dec. 2013.

The End of Cockroaches

13.. Kunkel, Joseph G. "Are Cockroaches Resistant to Radiation?" *The Cockroach FAQ*. U. Massachusetts Amherst, 9 Mar. 2012. Web. 04 Dec. 2013.

14.. Ramanujan, Krishna. "Research Reveals Key to World's Toughest Organism." *Phys.org*. Phys.org, 19 Oct. 2009. Web. 04 Dec. 2013.

Heart of Stone

15.. "The Same Sun Which Melts Wax Hardens Clay." Web log post. *Puritan Quotes (Wordpress)*. The Puritan Quoter, 12 Nov. 2010. Web. 04 Dec. 2013.

What's My Excuse?

16.. "New Statistics on Church Attendance and Avoidance." *Barna Group*. The Barna Group, Ltd., 3 Mar. 2008. Web. 04 Dec. 2013.

The $19,000 Lunch

17.. Calder, Rich. "Nets Buyer & Pals Hoop It Up." *New York Post Online Edition*. NYP Holdings, Inc., 23 Oct. 2009. Web. 04 Dec. 2013.

Hazardous Area—Hard Hats Required

18.. D'Ambrosio, Marcellino. "Ignorance of Scripture Is Ignorance of Christ." *The Crossroads Initiative*. Crossroads Productions, Inc., n.d. Web. 04 Dec. 2013.

Smoking Section

19.. "Global AIDS Overview." *AIDS.gov*. U.S. Department of Health & Human Services, 2 Dec. 2013. Web. 04 Dec. 2013.

20.. Falco, Miriam. "Secondhand Smoke Kills 600,000 Worldwide Annually." Web log post. *CNN Health - The Chart*. Cable News Network, 26 Nov. 2010. Web. 01 Dec. 2013.

The Color of Cowards

21. Olson, David T. *The American Church in Crisis: Groundbreaking Research Based on a National Database of Over 200,000 Churches*. Grand Rapids, MI: Zondervan, 2008. Print.

22. Rainer, Thom S. *The Unchurched Next Door: Understanding Faith Stages as Keys to Sharing Your Faith*. Grand Rapids, MI: Zondervan, 2003. Print.

Dumb and Dumber

23. Steele, Jonathan. "Words Spoken." *Speechmastery*. Jonathan Steele, Apr. 2013. Web. 04 Dec. 2013.

Riddled with Riddles

24 *Forty Thousand Quotations: Prose and Poetical,* comp. by Charles Noel Douglas. New York: Halcyon House, 1917; Bartleby.com, 2012. www.bartleby.com/348/1391.html#9. 04 Dec. 2013

Land of the Giants

25. "Size Matters." *Guinness World Records 2014*. Ed. Craig Glenday. London: Guinness World Records, 2013. 48-50. Print.

The Magical Mud Hole

26. "Genome Facts." *NOVA Online*. Public Broadcasting Service (PBS), n.d. Web. 04 Dec. 2013.

Blood Sport

27. "Worldwide Persecution of Christians." *The Prayer Foundation*. S.G. Preston Ministries, n.d. Web. 04 Dec. 2013.

Made in the USA
Las Vegas, NV
27 June 2021